Kevin Brabazon, MPA
Robert Disch, MA
Editors

Intergenerational Approaches in Aging: Implications for Education, Policy and Practice

Intergenerational Approaches in Aging: Implications for Education, Policy and Practice has been co-published simultaneously as *Journal of Gerontological Social Work*, Volume 28, Numbers 1/2 and 3 1997.

Pre-publication
REVIEWS,
COMMENTARIES,
EVALUATIONS . . .

"**B**rabazon and Disch are keen observers of the times, selecting a variety of hot topics for this new publication. . . . I am delighted with their emphasis on volunteerism and service–timely topics central to intergenerational discussion."

Jane Angelis, PhD
Director
Illinois Intergenerational Initiative
Southern Illinois University
and Commissioner
Illinois Commission for Community Service

More pre-publication
REVIEWS, COMMENTARIES, EVALUATIONS . . .

"**P**rovides a wealth of concrete examples of areas in which intergenerational perspectives and knowledge are needed. It challenges our conventional conceptions of what gerontology is or could be if it included not only a lifecourse paradigm but an intergenerational one as well."

Robert C. Atchley, PhD
Director
Scripps Gerontology Center
Miami University

* * *

"**P**articularly useful in Brabazon and Disch's survey of this cross-disciplinary field–in its formative stage of development–is the attention given to ways to evaluating networks in diverse settings as well as policy relevant research and program development."

W. Andrew Achenbaum, PhD
Deputy Director
Institute of Gerontology
and Professor of History
University of Michigan, Ann Arbor

"**A** milestone in the development of intergenerational studies. . . . A powerful plea for an integrated approach across the full range of relevant topics. The editors' approach has an international relevance that will stimulate work, arising from the different aspects of intergenerational activity represented in the book, in other countries."

Gordon Lishman, OBE
Operations Director
Ageconcern (National Council of Ageing-UK)

The Haworth Press, Inc.

Intergenerational Approaches in Aging: Implications for Education, Policy and Practice

Intergenerational Approaches in Aging: Implications for Education, Policy and Practice has been co-published simultaneously as *Journal of Gerontological Social Work*, Volume 28, Numbers 1/2 and 3 1997.

These books were published simultaneously as special thematic issues of the
Journal of Gerontological Social Work and are available bound separately. For
further information, call 1-800-HAWORTH (outside US/Canada: 607-722-5857),
Fax 1-800-895-0582 (outside US/Canada: 607-771-0012) or e-mail getinfo@
haworth.com

Intergenerational Approaches in Aging: Implications for Education, Policy and Practice

Kevin Brabazon, MPA
Robert Disch, MA
Editors

Intergenerational Approaches in Aging: Implications for Education, Policy and Practice has been co-published simultaneously as *Journal of Gerontological Social Work*, Volume 28, Numbers 1/2 and 3 1997.

The Haworth Press, Inc.
New York • London

Intergenerational Approaches in Aging: Implications for Education, Policy and Practice has been co-published simultaneously as *Journal of Gerontological Social Work*, Volume 28, Numbers 1/2 and 3 1997.

The Haworth Press, Inc., 10 Alice Street, Binghamton, NY 13904-1580 USA

Cover design by Thomas J. Mayshock Jr.

Library of Congress Cataloging-in-Publication Data

Intergenerational approaches in aging : implications for education, policy and practice / Kevin Brabazon, Robert Disch, editors.
     p. cm.
Includes bibliographical references and index.
ISBN 0-7890-0356-2 (alk. paper)
    1. Gerontology–Study and teaching (Higher)–United States. 2. Geriatrics–Study and teaching (Higher)–United States. 3. Aged–Services for–Government policy–United States. I. Brabazon, Kevin. II. Disch, Robert.
HQ1064.U5I578 1997
305.26′071′173–dc21
                                                        97-39668
                                                             CIP

INDEXING & ABSTRACTING

Contributions to this publication are selectively indexed or abstracted in print, electronic, online, or CD-ROM version(s) of the reference tools and information services listed below. This list is current as of the copyright date of this publication. See the end of this section for additional notes.

- *Abstracts in Social Gerontology: Current Literature on Aging*, National Council on the Aging, Library, 409 Third Street SW, 2nd Floor, Washington, DC 20024

- *Academic Abstracts/CD-ROM*, EBSCO Publishing Editorial Department, P.O. Box 590, Ipswich, MA 01938-0590

- *Academic Search: data base of 2,000 selected academic serials, updated monthly*, EBSCO Publishing, 83 Pine Street, Peabody, MA 01960

- *AgeInfo CD-Rom*, Centre for Policy on Ageing, 25-31 Ironmonger Row, London EC1V 4QP, England

- *AgeLine Database*, American Association of Retired Persons, 601 E Street, NW, Washington, DC 20049

- *Alzheimer's Disease Education & Referral Center (ADEAR)*, Combined Health Information Database (CHID), P.O. Box 8250, Silver Spring, MD 20907-8250

- *Applied Social Sciences Index & Abstracts (ASSIA) (Online: ASSI via Data-Star) (CDRom: ASSIA Plus)*, Bowker-Saur Limited, Maypole House, Maypole Road, East Grinstead, West Sussex RH19 1HH, England

- *Behavioral Medicine Abstracts*, University of Washington Department of Social Work & Speech and Hearing Sciences, Box 354900, Seattle, WA 98195

- *Biosciences Information Service of Biological Abstracts (BIOSIS)*, Biosciences Information Service, 2100 Arch Street, Philadelphia, PA 19103-1399

(continued)

- *Brown University Geriatric Research Application Digest "Abstracts Section,"* Brown University, Center for Gerontology & Health Care Research, c/o Box G-B 235, Providence, RI 02912

- *caredata CD: the social and community care database*, National Institute for Social Work, 5 Tavistock Place, London WC1H 9SS, England

- *CINAHL (Cumulative Index to Nursing & Allied Health Literature), in print, also on CD-ROM from CD PLUS, EBSCO, and SilverPlatter, and online from CDP Online (formerly BRS), Data-Star, and PaperChase. (Support materials include Subject Heading List, Database Search Guide, and instructional video.)*, CINAHL Information Systems, P.O. Box 871/1509 Wilson Terrace, Glendale, CA 91209-0871

- *CNPIEC Reference Guide: Chinese National Directory of Foreign Periodicals*, P.O. Box 88, Beijing, People's Republic of China

- *Criminal Justice Abstracts*, Willow Tree Press, 15 Washington Street, 4th Floor, Newark, NJ 07102

- *Current Contents. . . . see: Institute for Scientific Information*

- *Expanded Academic Index*, Information Access Company, 362 Lakeside Drive, Forest City, CA 94404

- *Family Studies Database (online and CD/ROM)*, National Information Services Corporation, 306 East Baltimore Pike, 2nd Floor, Media, PA 19063

- *Family Violence & Sexual Assault Bulletin*, Family Violence & Sexual Assault Institute, 1121 E South East Loop #323, Suite 130, Tyler, TX 75701

- *Gay & Lesbian Abstracts*, National Information Services Corporation, 306 East Baltimore Pike, Second Floor, Media, PA 19063

- *Human Resources Abstracts (HRA)*, Sage Publications, Inc., 2455 Teller Road, Newbury Park, CA 91320

(continued)

- *IBZ International Bibliography of Periodical Literature*, Zeller Verlag GmbH & Co., P.O.B. 1949, D-49009 Osnabruck, Germany

- *Index to Periodical Articles Related to Law*, University of Texas, 727 East 26th Street, Austin, TX 78705

- *Institute for Scientific Information*, 3501 Market Street, Philadelphia, PA 19104-3302 (USA). Coverage in:
  a) Research Alert (current awareness service)
  b) Social SciSearch (magnetic tape)
  c) Current Contents/Social & Behavioral Sciences (weekly current awareness service)

- *MasterFILE: updated database from EBSCO Publishing*, EBSCO Publishing, 83 Pine Street, Peabody, MA 01960

- *National Clearinghouse for Primary Care Information (NCPCI)*, 2070 Chain Bridge Road, Suite 450, Vienna, VA 22182-2536

- *New Literature on Old Age*, Centre for Policy on Ageing, 25-31 Ironmonger Row, London EC1V 3QP, England

- *Periodical Abstracts, Research I (general & basic reference indexing & abstracting data-base from University Microfilms International (UMI), 300 North Zeeb Road, P.O. Box 1346, Ann Arbor, MI 48106-1346)*, UMI Data Courier, P.O. Box 32770, Louisville, KY 40232-2770

- *Periodical Abstracts, Research II (broad coverage indexing & abstracting data-base from University Microfilms International (UMI), 300 North Zeeb Road, P.O. Box 1346, Ann Arbor, MI 48106-1346)*, UMI Data Courier, P.O. Box 32770, Louisville, KY 40232-2770

- *Psychological Abstracts (PsycINFO)*, American Psychological Association, P.O. Box 91600, Washington, DC 20090-1600

- *Social Planning/Policy & Development Abstracts (SOPODA)*, Sociological Abstracts, Inc., P.O. Box 22206, San Diego, CA 92192-0206

- *Social Science Citation Index. . . . see: Institute for Scientific Information*

(continued)

- *Social Science Source: coverage of 400 journals in the social sciences area; updated monthly,* EBSCO Publishing, P.O. Box 2250, Peabody, MA 01960-7250

- *Social Sciences Index (from Volume 1 & continuing),* The H.W. Wilson Company, 950 University Avenue, Bronx, NY 10452

- *Social Work Abstracts,* National Association of Social Workers, 750 First Street NW, 8th Floor, Washington, DC 20002

- *Sociological Abstracts (SA),* Sociological Abstracts, Inc., P.O. Box 22206, San Diego, CA 92192-0206

SPECIAL BIBLIOGRAPHIC NOTES

*related to special journal issues (separates)
and indexing/abstracting*

☐ indexing/abstracting services in this list will also cover material in any "separate" that is co-published simultaneously with Haworth's special thematic journal issue or DocuSerial. Indexing/abstracting usually covers material at the article/chapter level.

☐ monographic co-editions are intended for either non-subscribers or libraries which intend to purchase a second copy for their circulating collections.

☐ monographic co-editions are reported to all jobbers/wholesalers/approval plans. The source journal is listed as the "series" to assist the prevention of duplicate purchasing in the same manner utilized for books-in-series.

☐ to facilitate user/access services all indexing/abstracting services are encouraged to utilize the co-indexing entry note indicated at the bottom of the first page of each article/chapter/contribution.

☐ this is intended to assist a library user of any reference tool (whether print, electronic, online, or CD-ROM) to locate the monographic version if the library has purchased this version but not a subscription to the source journal.

☐ individual articles/chapters in any Haworth publication are also available through the Haworth Document Delivery Service (HDDS).

Intergenerational Approaches in Aging: Implications for Education, Policy and Practice

CONTENTS

SECTION VII: THE ROAD AHEAD

ABOUT THE EDITORS

Kevin Brabazon, MPA, is President of the New York State Intergenerational Network, which provides support for program development and advocates intergenerational public policies. As Consultant to The Brookdale Foundation's "Relatives as Parents Program," he develops services for grandparents who are raising grandchildren because the biological parents are unable or unwilling to do so. Also an Adjunct Lecturer in the Robert Wagner Graduate School of Public Administration at New York University, he has published several essays on intergenerational policies and practices. His most recent article appeared in the *Southwest Journal on Aging*.

Robert Disch, MA, is Director of Intergenerational Programs and Administrator of the Post Master's Program on Aging at the Brookdale Center on Aging at Hunter College, City University of New York. In these capacities, he has directed intergenerational oral history projects linking high school students with Homebound, with veterans of World War II, and with community elders. At present, he is directing a three-generation educational program in which retired reading teachers mentor undergraduates as tutors for at-risk children. His publications include books and articles in the fields of literature, ecology, and race relations. In 1988, he edited *Twenty-Five Years of the Life Review: Theoretical and Practical Considerations* (The Haworth Press, Inc.), which includes his essay "The Young, the Old and the Life Review" on intergenerational life-history projects. Mr. Disch is a Lecturer for the New York Council for the Humanities and has won two study grants from the National Endowment for the Humanities.

Preface

This volume, devoted to the topic of intergenerational perspectives as they inform education, policy issues and analysis, and the nature of practice, will, I think, prove a welcome addition to the libraries of social workers, and also to other professionals in the field of gerontology and geriatrics. Kevin Brabazon and Robert Disch selected a stunning array of authors, all of whom are experts in the field, each writing about consequential matters.

There are interesting areas of disagreement among the authors; for example, between co-authors Elizabeth Larkin and Sally Newman, and Ed Rosenberg, Lois Layne, and Maureen Power. The reader will find, I believe, the argument about what *intergenerational studies* are an interesting one, and one worth our consideration.

A number of the articles report on exciting models of service and of education, and given the present emphasis by the White House on volunteerism and volunteer service, reports like that of Anita Rogers and Andrea Taylor on an intergenerational mentoring program or Matt Kaplan's article about "Intergenerational Community Service Projects" may prove to be particularly useful.

All of the articles meet that test of usefulness, and Marc Freedman's paper "Towards Civic Renewal" merits, I think, particularly close attention for what it says about our society and about the contributions older people can make to its survival as a civil community. I commend all of the articles in this issue to you.

Rose Dobrof, DSW

[Haworth co-indexing entry note]: "Preface." Dobrof, Rose. Co-published simultaneously in the *Journal of Gerontological Social Work* (The Haworth Press, Inc.) Vol. 28, No. 1/2, 1997, p. xv; and: *Intergenerational Approaches in Aging: Implications for Education, Policy and Practice* (ed: Kevin Brabazon, and Robert Disch) The Haworth Press, Inc., 1997, p. xv. Single or multiple copies of this article are available for a fee from The Haworth Document Delivery Service [1-800-342-9678, 9:00 a.m. - 5:00 p.m. (EST). E-mail address: getinfo@haworth.com].

Introduction

Kevin Brabazon, MPA
Robert Disch, MA

This Intergenerational Volume has its origins in a dialogue between staff people from the Brookdale Center on Aging and the New York State Intergenerational Network. The collection is an attempt to take a broad view of the emerging intergenerational field.

At this point in its development, the field is conveniently divided by theoreticians and practitioners into three major areas of interest: Intergenerational Issues, Intergenerational Programming, and Intergenerational Education.

Intergenerational issues are those that create social stress from one or more of the following challenges: age isolation caused by demographic change and geographic mobility; "NORCS" and self-segregation of elders in "Sun Cities"; and out migration of younger elements of a population. Other stress factors include competition for needed resources or catastrophic interventions like drugs or AIDS that can remove a generation from a functional role in a family or community. Intergenerational issues also arise when a community with a high percentage of elders fails to pass a school bond issue or from entitlement programs that rely on cross generational transfers of resources when demographic changes challenge the stability of such programs.

Kevin Brabazon is President of the New York State Intergenerational Network and Adjunct Lecturer in public and non-profit management at the Robert Wagner School of Public Service, New York University. Robert Disch is Director of Intergenerational Programs for the Brookdale Center on Aging of Hunter College and a member of the Executive Committee, New York State Intergenerational Network. He has published a collection of essays on the Life Review and is editing an anthology of intergenerational short stories.

[Haworth co-indexing entry note]: "Introduction." Brabazon, Kevin, and Robert Disch. Co-published simultaneously in the *Journal of Gerontological Social Work* (The Haworth Press, Inc.) Vol. 28, No. 1/2, 1997, pp. 1-2; and: *Intergenerational Approaches in Aging: Implications for Education, Policy and Practice* (ed: Kevin Brabazon, and Robert Disch) The Haworth Press, Inc., 1997, pp. 1-2. Single or multiple copies of this article are available for a fee from The Haworth Document Delivery Service [1-800-342-9678, 9:00 a.m. - 5:00 p.m. (EST). E-mail address: getinfo@haworth.com].

As intergenerational issues became more clearly defined during the 1960s and 1970s, some appeared to be resolvable through intergenerational programming. In 1963 the Foster Grandparent Program recruited elders to help solve the problem of caring for orphaned babies. While originally intended to provide productive roles and financial support for low income elders, the success of Foster Grandparents alerted policy makers and program strategists to the potential that planned intergenerational linkages might possess as a means for resolving other intergenerational issues.

The forms that intergenerational programming took fell into five major categories which, at their best, benefit the young, the old, and the community alike. These include youth or children serving elders; elders serving children, youth or families; young and old jointly providing community service, services to one another, or sharing a program experience; arts programming; and oral history projects. Intergenerational programming, the heart of the intergenerational "movement," is then the provision of services to different age groups while drawing on the strengths or valuable attributes of each age cohort.

While intergenerational learning can take place in any intergenerational setting, the formalization into specific educational processes or strategies developed as educators felt a need to provide children with a "life-cycle" view of the world. These educators developed and attempted to implement aging and intergenerational curricula into formal educational settings from kindergarten to graduate school. On the other hand, the formation of university-based intergenerational education centers was, at least to some extent, motivated by a desire to improve the design and quality of programming, to sharpen methods of research and evaluation, and to develop competency training and professional standards.

It was with these ideas in mind that we selected papers and organized this collection. In the process we greatly benefited from the editorial advice of Ms. Dorothy Fabian, the members of the NYSIgN Board of Directors, the membership of the Special Advisory Committee for this issue, and from the insights of many workers in the intergenerational vineyard, both in the United States and abroad.

SECTION I:
DEFINING
THE INTERGENERATIONAL FIELD

Since the beginning of the decade there has been extensive discussion on whether individuals and organizations involved with intergenerational programming, education, and issues constitute a "movement," a "field," a "trend," or simply a disparate collection of ideas and activities. The two papers included in Section I present contrasting views by established scholars in the intergenerational area. The first (Larkin and Newman) argues that intergenerational studies should be treated as an academic discipline with appropriate competencies established and the awarding of academic degrees. The second (Rosenberg, Layne & Power) avers that intergenerational studies be regarded as part of a multi-disciplinary field, that their strength lies in their ability to access resources from, and be included in, a variety of academic disciplines.

This is an important debate. If the intergenerational field is an academic discipline, there are imperatives to develop competencies and establish professional standards, such as exist for counseling, social work, education, etc. If, on the other hand, it is a multi-disciplinary field, it will share generic training with other areas of human services and draw on or "borrow" trained professionals from more specialized but related fields, such as gerontology, psychology, and early childhood education.

The inclusion of both papers in this edition reflects the general lack of consensus in the intergenerational field as well as the editors' desire to make at least two of the prevailing viewpoints available to readers.

Intergenerational Studies:
A Multi-Disciplinary Field

Elizabeth Larkin, EdD
Sally Newman, PhD

INTRODUCTION

Intergenerational Studies as a new multi-disciplinary field is emerging from a growing body of intergenerational research and program evaluation that is now available to professionals and academics in the fields of child and adult development, psychology, education and gerontology. Research and practice in these fields recognize that there are common needs and issues affecting the young and old, that a similar knowledge base and professional skills are shared by those who serve these populations, and that mutual benefits accrue when these generations form relationships with one another.

In this paper, we argue that the time has come to examine the emerging intergenerational human service field as an academic discipline that draws from a number of different areas of expertise to inform the work of intergenerational specialists. We present elements of a common knowledge-base that grow out of the goals and outcomes of intergenerational programs and the intergenerational field, and suggest how Intergenerational Studies might be integrated into the system of higher education.

The development of many types of intergenerational programs and the

Elizabeth Larkin is Associate Professor, Wheelock College. Sally Newman is a member of the University of Pittsburgh's School of Education faculty and is Founder and Executive Director of *Generations Together: An Intergenerational Studies Program* of the University of Pittsburgh.

[Haworth co-indexing entry note]: "Intergenerational Studies: A Multi-Disciplinary Field." Larkin, Elizabeth, and Sally Newman. Co-published simultaneously in the *Journal of Gerontological Social Work* (The Haworth Press, Inc.) Vol. 28, No. 1/2, 1997, pp. 5-16; and: *Intergenerational Approaches in Aging: Implications for Education, Policy and Practice* (ed: Kevin Brabazon, and Robert Disch) The Haworth Press, Inc., 1997, pp. 5-16. Single or multiple copies of this article are available for a fee from The Haworth Document Delivery Service [1-800-342-9678, 9:00 a.m. - 5:00 p.m. (EST). E-mail address: getinfo@haworth.com].

involvement of diverse human service and educational institutions in these programs has led to the need for a fuller understanding of the nature and the importance of a broader field of study and raises questions about the professional preparation of practitioners in this field. Human service professionals are becoming more aware that it is necessary to enlarge their knowledge base related to intergenerational and interprofessional issues. Educators, too, are aware of the need to train students to become proficient intergenerational professionals who can successfully bridge different service delivery systems and work collaboratively with others trained in a variety of disciplines. Politicians recognize the demand to consider policies that better reflect the changes taking place in society to secure the well being of the future for all generations. As James Gambone suggests:

> If intergenerational studies was an accepted academic discipline, with a strong multi-disciplinary approach and if it were implemented in colleges and universities across the country, within ten years everyone would know about the power to the intergenerational perspective and its relationship to positive social change. (Cliff, 1994)

Advocates for an intergenerational perspective are lobbying local and federal governments in many areas of the USA for policies that bring new visions for social change. The segregated services and funding streams of the past are being challenged by these innovative ideas and new social agendas. Intergenerational programs that are based on solid theoretical frameworks, continued research, and high quality professional preparation and practice are those which are likely to strengthen the fabric of society as a whole. These programs must be carefully planned to occur over time, and involve the interaction of diverse populations of older adults and younger people in relationship building exchanges that are designed to benefit both populations. Typically these programs involve the collaboration of multiple systems in the community, but they should not depend on the efforts of a few visionary individuals for their success.

They should be grounded in serious and thoughtful study as a multi-disciplinary field that reviews their developmental and social history, prepares professionals for work and continued study, expands research across several related disciplines and examines the social and political implications for the future.

A BRIEF HISTORY OF THE INTERGENERATIONAL FIELD

Intergenerational programs have their roots in the Foster Grandparent Program which was created in 1963 as a source of meaningful work for low income older adults in service to at-risk children and youth. This first intergenerational program model provided opportunities for interactions that benefited both populations. It was the first of many programs in which systematically planned ongoing and mutually satisfying interactions between younger and older generations were inherent in the design. The concept of intergenerational exchange has gained recognition during the last two decades as educators, service providers, policy makers and funders became convinced of the intrinsic value of bringing older and younger age groups together. Furthermore, the importance of the intergenerational exchange is being reaffirmed with a growing body of research literature that reports on the positive outcomes of collaborative programming for the young and the old.

Intergenerational programming has expanded in response to a rapidly changing society in which extended families have been geographically separated, and age-segregation within communities in terms of residential planning, recreational facilities and educational institutions has tended to separate generational cohorts. It has been suggested that the segregation of groups of people by age has resulted in a serious breakdown of interaction and communication among the generations. The long term consequences of this issue are considered to be crucial to social function and organization in our society (Cliff, 1994).

In response to this issue, intergenerational programs have been developed as a vehicle to effectively connect older and younger generations by providing them with opportunities to develop meaningful and productive relationships. Additionally, they enable communities to promote civic responsibility, as an alternative to self interest. Intergenerational programs that have emerged during the past two decades are changing the way education is provided to children and youth, and how services are provided to older adults and others in our communities. In child care, Head Start and K-12 schools, trained older adults have become part of the learning environment as caregivers, mentors, resource persons, or content specialists. In higher education, retired professionals have been able to support undergraduate and graduate students in course work, research assignments and integration into university life. In systems that serve the elderly, children and youth have become friendly visitors, advocates and liaisons for the dependent older adults in the community.

Though the focus of intergenerational programs in the 1960s and 1970s was primarily to address a geographic separation and the perceived psychological gap between the old and the young, currently its broader purpose is to address a range of social issues that have an impact on both these generations. Issues such as drugs, homelessness, illiteracy, school drop out, teen pregnancy, and the need for child care have become the catalyst for the development of intergenerational programs. This expanded focus has reinforced the involvement in intergenerational initiatives by professionals from various human service fields. This involvement underscores the importance of examining the need for a field of studies that addresses program development preparation of professionals, research and public policy through an intergenerational lens.

DEFINING INTERGENERATIONAL STUDIES AS A NEW ACADEMIC FIELD

The Intergenerational Studies field is grounded in approximately 25 years of intergenerational program development that has sought to address the needs of our country's children, youth and older adults. As a multi-disciplinary field, it researches fundamental social issues affecting children, youth and older adults, examines the intergenerational programs designed to address these issues, prepares practitioners with skills needed to work in the intergenerational arena, and promotes public policy initiatives that support intergenerational programmatic and academic efforts.

Throughout the short history of intergenerational programs, successful development has represented collaboration among professionals in multiple fields whose combined efforts contributed to the design and implementation of models that meet the needs of both the young and the old. While collaboration of professionals from diverse disciplines continues to be necessary, it is now evident that there is also a shared body of knowledge needed by all qualified professionals entering the intergenerational field that may be unique to this field. Learning to think intergenerationally rather than from the perspective of one particular group's needs shifts the service provider's approach to activity planning that fosters interpersonal relationships across these ages. Learning to work across systems that serve children, youth or older adults requires professionals to understand how to integrate systems that typically are disparate.

The intergenerational field requires an understanding of how age affects learning and social interactions and of how various academic disciplines contribute to policies and programs that will effectively address pressing social issues that affect the old and the young. Service providers require a theoretical context, a cognitive framework and interpersonal skills for working with all ages to be prepared for work in the intergenerational field. It is a field that encompasses a body of knowledge drawn from many academic disciplines including child development, education, gerontology, social work, psychology, sociology, family studies and social policy.

Integenerational Studies will integrate the language, content and relevant research of these fields, crossing traditional academic boundaries and creating a new, comprehensive multi-disciplinary area of professionalism and research.

As education and human service fields add more and diverse intergenerational programs, the body of knowledge about the field's development and outcomes is increasing. Beneficial outcomes of these programs are expected in several areas: diminished ageist behaviors and attitudes among participants; increased positive exchange among generations, improved services to children, youth and older adults; and wider recognition of the value of interprofessional collaboration. The delivery of successful intergenerational programs depends upon a sound theoretical framework, continuing reflection of professional practices, and an evolving dialogue about intergenerational issues.

CONNECTIONS TO OTHER DISCIPLINES

In this article we cannot provide a comprehensive look at the full scope of what Intergenerational Studies might include, but we offer an outline of some possible content. Research that focuses on a narrow age range can be pertinent and take on other shades of meaning when viewed through the intergenerational lens or combined with studies about other ages. Intergenerational Studies therefore contributes to these established fields as well as drawing from them.

An intergenerational model of service and education advocates for both young and old, which implies that all staff members need to have sufficient knowledge of child and adult development framing the program's content in order to generate mutually beneficial outcomes. By linking child development, education and gerontology, practitioners are prepared with skills to implement intergenerational programs from an informed perspective that reflects an understanding of the generations at both ends of the life course. Developmentally appropriate practices with interage groups grow from a foundation of knowledge about the intellectual, physical, psychosocial and emotional needs and capabilities of all participants.

The field of child psychology has been transformed in recent years by such noted researchers as Vygotsky, who looked at development as embedded within a social context rather than studying the child in isolation under the premise of objective science (Tudge & Rogoff, 1989). Multicultural concerns have promoted increased attention to developmental differences across socioeconomic, gender, racial and ethnic groups (Greenfield & Cocking, 1994). The notion that children ideally should be raised at home by their mothers has also been called into question in modern day American culture (Kessen, 1979). These perspectives on child development are not only relevant, but critically important to understanding the dynamics of relationships among young children growing up in today's world and elders who have years of life experiences that shape complex personal histories in completely different contexts.

An understanding of the implications of previous historical eras for adults' opportunities to work, become educated, or care for families comes from the field of sociology. Major events such as wars, the Great Depression, waves of immigration, for example affect the country's economy, cultural norms, family values, and so forth. Then, each member of a family must be understood within the larger context as well as within the family as a system. This background establishes a context for facilitating positive relationships across generational cohorts.

Gerontologists contribute to the multi-disciplinary knowledge base with research on aging and the development of social policies for a growing population of citizens over the age of 65. For example, studies have broadened the practitioners understanding of the importance of friendships among the elderly, especially women who tend to live longer and in greater poverty (Grambs, 1989; Lewittes, 1989). In addition, there is a growing body of literature on issues related to death and dying, loss, and grief in old age (Conway, 1988), which can be combined with similar studies of other age groups. Issues of self esteem, dependence, autonomy, industry and gratification are relevant in the development of persons across the life course (Erikson, 1950).

Teacher training programs rely not only on the field of human development of curriculum design and evaluation and analysis of systems that promote human growth and development. Working with both children and elders for their mutual growth entails understanding how to construct experiences that are engaging, intellectually stimulating and that promote the growth of the participant. Effective integrational curriculum is a process that unfolds over time, that promotes understanding, enhances knowledge and contributes to positive relationship building. It is responsible to the individuals and must adapt to meet the needs of different groups of persons involved in these programs.

Understanding the diverse systems representing children, youth and older adults involved in the intergenerational programs is essential in developing agency Partnerships that coordinate these programs. Intergenerational professionals need an understanding of developmental and learning needs of the participants, of programs that address these needs and of the complexity of systems involved in intergenerational programs.

The growing impetus for intergenerational programming comes from several main directions: advocates from the field of gerontology who hope to reduce ageism and to improve the quality of service of isolated and institutionalized older adults (Newman, Vander Ven & Ward, 1992; Moody, 1988); the children's care movement that recognizes the need for intergenerational settings for young children in child care outside the home (Smith & Newman, 1993); the family literacy movement that is working to break the cycle of poverty (Kerka, 1991; Sticht, Beeler, & McDonald, 1992); the rights and roles of grandparents who are becoming primary caregivers in increasing numbers (Cherlin, 1986; Kornhaber, 1985); the need in many school systems to provide special academic, social, and emotional support for students (Freedman, 1993; Newman & Larimer, 1995); the trend toward community building and strengthening families in our diverse society (Newman & Brummer, 1989; Kingson, Hirshorn, & Corman, 1986; Seedfeldt, Jantz, Serock, & Bredekamp, 1990; Dellmann-Jenkins, Lambert, & Fruit, 1991; Dychtwald, 1989) and most recently the results of the 1995 White House Conference on Aging with recommendations that call for integration of older adults into activities that affect America's children and youth.

Intergenerational Studies includes critical commentary and research from all of these perspectives, as well as from age-specific literature on human development and family systems (Brody, 1990; Erikson, 1950, Gardner, 1990; Kagan, Klugman & Zigler, 1983; Kuehne, 1990). Students in Intergenerational Studies will integrate information from different disciplines and become familiar with the literature specifically focused on the relative value and effects of intergenerational programming on the participants, systems and communities they affect (Dellmann-Jenkins, Lambert, & Fruit, 1991; Kuehne, 1988; Miller & Blalock, 1984; Kaplan, 1993; Newman, 1994; Kordesh, 1995).

Intergenerational Studies will prepare professionals working with older and younger persons to design, implement and assess the programs that create valuable cross generational connections. Intergenerational specialists will encourage and engage in research that contributes to the understanding and expansion of intergenerational initiatives. Students entering the field will understand the characteristics of systems involved in intergenerational programming and will be prepared with knowledge, skills and insights that enable them to successfully pursue a career or job whose focus is improving the quality of life for the community's young and old. They will become knowledgeable about and advocates for initiatives that support the expansion of local, state and public policy.

THE PLACE OF INTERGENERATIONAL STUDIES IN HIGHER EDUCATION

Currently, intergenerational specialists, though limited in number enter existing educational and human service roles where they can initiate intergenerational connections. They might work as program administrators in community centers, as teachers in schools, as intergenerational coordinators in childcare or long-term care settings or as intergenerational program developers for national organizations such as the American Association of Retired Persons (AARP), National Council on the Aging (NCOA), National Parks and Recreation, National Association of the Education of Young Children (NAEYC) or Generations United (GU). With such career goals in mind, given the current academic paths available to them, students need to enter a program that trains them for work either with young people or older adults. Only in programs with great flexibility can students combine course work that spans other ages by using credits to design their own curriculum. In this case, students still need to integrate the material independently, lacking a forum for exploring the implications of the content from an intergenerational perspective.

If Intergenerational Studies is conceived of as a unique discipline that combines and integrates research, professional practices, curriculum design and program evaluation in the context of intergenerational programs, then where does it fit in the existing system of higher education? Related disciplines, i.e., Early Childhood Education and Gerontology, focus narrowly on one end of the developmental spectrum. Family Studies is primarily concerned with the interrelationships among biologically connected generations, whereas intergenerational studies that are based on the development of intergenerational programs are designed to connect people outside their own family system. Psychology as a discipline provides a useful theoretical context for understanding human development and prepares professionals for therapeutic interventions, a strategy not directly inherent in the intergenerational studies approach to human interaction.

The broadest discipline that may be appropriate to embrace intergenerational studies may be education with course offerings in human development, curriculum design, family interactions, program evaluation, learning strategies and systems analysis. Courses in educational administration provide the information and skills needed to develop, manage, supervise and replicate intergenerational programs. Courses in adult education inform students on adult learning characteristics and teaching strategies for well high-functioning older adults and for frail, more dependent, older adults in the context of their interaction as co-learners and resource persons in intergenerational learning experiences. Courses in public policy can provide the information needed to promote and advocate for intergenerational initiatives on local, state and national levels. Specialized content courses within education can prepare students with skills for working in diverse intergenerational settings in administrative, direct service or research related positions.

Because of the growing number of issues and programs that pertain to both young and old some colleges and universities are currently offering intergenerational courses, workshops and institutes as they relate to education, social work, family and human development and early childhood education.

As the variety of intergenerational studies options increase in higher education institutions it is timely to consider strategies for formalizing these studies as a multi-disciplinary academic field. We propose consideration of a new academic field that:

- integrates a selected body of knowledge from related disciplines, i.e., education, child and adult development, early childhood, and gerontology;
- offers a variety of alternative academic learning options and outcomes;
- involves the participation of teams of faculty from several existing academic disciplines;
- involves a strong community partnership in its development and implementation.

The body of knowledge drawn from the related disciplines can be linked or presented independently in the context of the academic options being offered. The options can vary with the size, focus and location of the institution to include: a degree in Intergenerational Studies, a minor in Intergenerational Studies, independent study, elective courses in a variety of disciplines or intergenerational training workshops for professionals. Intergenerational Studies' initiatives in higher education may be directed toward providing a new cadre of professionals for the human service intergenerational field, reinforcing the professionalism of persons working in these fields, developing new academic partnerships in the process of addressing some of the social issues affecting the young and old, and expanding the community's awareness of the interdependence of the two generations at the opposite end of the human continuum. These initiatives would result in an increase in the body of knowledge that enables students, faculty and professionals to understand the myriad aspects of learning and information needed to effectively create an intergenerational perspective within our society.

AUTHOR NOTE

Elizabeth Larkin developed the Intergenerational Studies Program in the Graduate School of Wheelock College in Boston, which was the first intergenerational Master's degree program in the country. She has served as a consultant to new intergenerational initiatives and teaches curriculum design, early childhood and elementary education.

Sally Newman is an innovator in intergenerational programs and a well-known author, lecturer, and researcher on issues related to the development of outcomes of this social phenomenon. Dr. Newman has edited and co-authored the first textbook on intergenerational issues, *Intergenerational Programs: Imperatives, Strategies, Impacts, Trends* and has conducted some of the seminal research in the field. She is senior author on a new textbook, *Intergenerational Programs: Past, Present, Future* to be published in summer 1997 by Taylor & Francis.

REFERENCES

Brody, E.M. (1990). *Women in the middle: Their parent-care years.* New York: Springer.

Cherlin, A.J. (1986). *The new American grandparent: A place in the family, a life apart.* New York: Basic Books.

Cliff, M. (1994, Winter). Intergenerational studies: The field responds. *Exchange: A Newsletter of Intergenerational Issues, Programs, and Research* (Generations Together, University of Pittsburgh, Pittsburgh, PA), 9, 5.

Conway, P. (1988). Losses and grief in old age. *Social Casework: The Journal of Contemporary Social Work*, 69 (9), 541-549.

Delmann-Jenkins, M., Lambert, D., & Fruit, D. (1991). Fostering preschoolers' presocial behaviors toward the elderly: The effect of an intergenerational program. *Educational Gerontology*, 7 (1), 33-40.

Dychtwald, K & Fowler, L. (1989. *Age wave: The challenges and opportunities of an aging America.* New York: Bantam.

Erickson, E. (1950). *Childhood and society.* New York: Norton.

Freedman, M., & Jaffe, N. (1993). Elder mentors: Giving schools a hand. *NASSP Bulletin*, January, 22-28.

Garner, H. (1990). *Art education and human development.* Los Angeles: The J. Paul Getty Trust.

Grambs, J.D. (1989). Being female, ethnic and old. In M.R. Block, *Women over forty: Visions and realities.* New York: Springer.

Greenfield, P.M. & Cocking, R.R. (1994). *Cross-cultural roots of minority child development.* Hillsdales, NJ: Lawrence Erlbaum Associates.

Isaacs, L.W. & Bearison, D.J., (1986). The development of children's prejudice against the aged. *International Journal of Aging and Human Development*, 23(3), 175-194.

Kagan, S.L., Klugman, E. & Zigler, E.F. (1983). *Children, families, and govern-*

ment: Perspectives on American social policy. New York: Cambridge University Press.

Kaplan, G. (May, 1991) Suppose they gave an intergenerational conflict and nobody came. Phi Delta Kappan, Kappan Special Report.

Kaplan, M. (1993). Recruiting senior adult volunteers for intergenerational programs: Working to create a "jump on the bandwagon" effect. *The Journal of Applied Gerontology,* 12 (1), 71-82.

Kerka, S. (1991). Family and intergenerational literacy. ERIC Clearinghouse on Adult, Career, and Vocational Education, Columbus, OH. (ED 334 467).

Kessen, W. (1979). The American child and other cultural inventions. *American Psychologist,* 34 (10), 815-820.

Kingson, E. (1988). Generational equity: An unexpected opportunity to broaden the politics of aging. *The Gerontologist,* 28 (6), 765-772.

Kingson, E., Hirshorn, B., & Cornman, J. (1986). Ties that bind: The interdependence of generations. Cabin John, MD: Seven Locks Press.

Kordesh, R.S. (1995). Intergenerational policies: After the 1994 elections. *Exchange: A Newsletter of Intergenerational Issues, Programs, and Research* (Generations Together, University of Pittsburgh, Pittsburgh, PA), 10, 1-2.

Kornhaber, A. & Woodward, K. (1985). *Grandparents/grandchildren: The vital connection.* New Brunswick: Transition Books.

Kuehne, V.S. (1990). A comparative study of children's extra-familial intergenerational relations. Unpublished doctoral dissertation, Northwestern University, Evanston, IL.

Kuehne, V.S. (1988). "Younger friends/older friends": A study of intergenerational interactions. *Journal of Classroom Interaction,* 24 (1), 14-21.

Lewittes, H.J. (1989). Just being friendly means a lot–Women, friendship, and aging. In *Women in the later years.* Binghamton, NY: The Haworth Press, Inc.

Miller, S.M. & Blalock, P. (1984). Children and the aged: Attitudes, contact, and discriminative ability. *International Journal of Aging and Human Development,* 19 (1), 47-53.

Moody, H.R. (1988). *Abundance of life: Human development policies for and aging society.* New York: Columbia University Press.

Newman, S. & Larimer, B. (1995). *Senior Citizen School Volunteer Program: Report on cumulative data 1988-1995.* Pittsburgh, PA: University of Pittsburgh, Generations Together.

Newman, S. (1994). *Spanning the generations: The valuable resources of younger and older persons.* Paper presented at the National Conference on Aging. Washington, D.C.

Newman, S., Vander Ven, K. & Ward, C.R. (1992). *Practitioner's manual for the productive employment of older adults in child care.* Pittsburgh, PA: University of Pittsburgh, Generations Together.

Newman, S. & Brummel, S.W. (1989). *Intergenerational programs: Imperatives, strategies, impacts and trends.* Binghamton, NY: The Haworth Press, Inc.

Seedfeldt, C., Jantz, R.K., Serock, K., & Bredekamp, S. (1990). *Young and old together.* Washington, DC: National Association for the Education of Young Children.

Seedfeldt, C. (1984). Children's attitudes toward the elderly: A cross-cultural comparison. *Intergenerational Journal of Aging and Human Development,* 19, 4, 319-328.

Seedfeldt, C., Jantz, R.K., Serock, K., & Bredekamp, S. (1982). Elderly persons' attitude toward children. *Educational Gerontology,* 8, 493-506.

Smith, T. & Newman, S. (1993). Older adults in early childhood programs: Why and how. *Young Children,* 48 (3), 32-35.

Sticht, T.G., Beeler, M.J., & McDonald, B.A. (Eds.) (1992). The intergenerational transfer of cognitive skills. In *Programs, policy and research issues, Vol. 1.* Norwood, NJ: Ablex.

Tudge, J. & Rogoff, B. (1989). Peer influences on cognitive development: Piagetian and Vygotskian perspectives. In M.H. Bornstein & J.S. Bruner (Eds.). *Interaction in human development.* Hillsdale, NJ: Lawrence Erlbaum Associates. 17-40.

Vander Ven, K. (1988). Pathways to professional effectiveness for early childhood educators. In B. Spodek, O.N. Saracho. & D. L. Peters (Eds.), *Professionalism and the early childhood practitioner.* New York: Teacher's College Press.

Whitebrook, M., Howes, C., & Phillips, D. (Eds.). (1989). *National child care staffing study.* Oakland, CA: Child Care Employee Project.

Intergenerational Studies' Growing Pains: The Quest for Identity and Implications for Practice

Ed Rosenberg, PhD
Lois E. Layne, PhD
Maureen Power, PhD

SUMMARY. Intergenerational studies (IGS), arising from grass-roots and community activities, appears to be maturing into adolescence, a time of identity confusion and identity seeking. What range of IGS programs currently exists? What can we learn about the current status and future prospects of IGS by examining gerontology, a related field? Is IGS an academic discipline, a profession, or a multi-disciplinary field of study? What is it best for IGS to be? This paper notes the variety of IGS in education and practice settings, and compares IGS' history to the development of gerontology, yielding insights into what we might expect for IGS in the coming decade. We provide

---

Ed Rosenberg is Associate Professor, Sociology and Social Work, Graduate Gerontology Program, Appalachian State University, Boone, NC. Lois E. Layne is Professor of Psychology at Western Kentucky University and Executive Director of the WKU Adult Day Health Care Center, which serves 75 elders and their families and provides training opportunities for over 400 students a year. Maureen Power is Professor of Urban Studies at Worcester State College where she teaches in the areas of housing, health care, human services, social work and aging.

Portions of this paper were presented at the annual meetings of the Association for Gerontology in Higher Education, Fort Worth, TX, February 1995, and the American Society on Aging, Atlanta, GA, March 1995.

[Haworth co-indexing entry note]: "Intergenerational Studies' Growing Pains: The Quest for Identity and Implications for Practice." Rosenberg, Ed, Lois E. Layne, and Maureen Power. Co-published simultaneously in the *Journal of Gerontological Social Work* (The Haworth Press, Inc.) Vol. 28, No. 1/2, 1997, pp. 17-31; and: *Intergenerational Approaches in Aging: Implications for Education, Policy and Practice* (ed: Kevin Brabazon, and Robert Disch) The Haworth Press, Inc., 1997, pp. 17-31. Single or multiple copies of this article are available for a fee from The Haworth Document Delivery Service [1-800-342-9678, 9:00 a.m. - 5:00 p.m. (EST). E-mail address: getinfo@haworth.com].

17

definitional criteria for IGS, academic disciplines and professions to evaluate the claim that IGS is "an emerging academic discipline." Based on the definition of IGS, the current state of IGS and the history of gerontology, IGS is not and perhaps cannot become an academic discipline, could evolve further into a profession or subfield of one or more existing professions, and is best viewed within higher education as a multi-disciplinary field of study. *[Article copies available for a fee from The Haworth Document Delivery Service: 1-800-342-9678. E-mail address: getinfo@haworth.com]*

INTRODUCTION

A convergence of social, demographic, political and economic factors has created a climate in which the growth and development of intergenerational programs, projects and studies have flourished and one now finds content qualifying as "Intergenerational Studies" (IGS) in many educational institutions around the country. Hoping to shed the remnants of its "warm fuzzy" image, IGS is increasingly a focus of graduate and undergraduate education, research initiatives and a wide range of academically grounded pursuits in colleges and universities, human services and communities. From its unlabeled beginnings three decades ago in grass roots and community activities, IGS appears to be maturing into "adolescence," traditionally a time of identity confusion and identity seeking. Its emergence in various forms raises basic questions about what IGS is and will become. Specifically, is IGS emerging as an academic discipline, engaged in the process of becoming a profession, or settling in as a multi-disciplinary field of study? To what extent can IGS provide a new, illuminating focus on current and projected issues and policy questions? Finally, will the future see a job classification of "intergenerational specialist"? That is, what are the implications for social work and other human services practitioners?

Just as social work (e.g., Weick, 1981) has made use of Lawton and Nahemow's (1973) "person-environment fit" model, we may start by assessing the "IGS-environment fit": that is, the extent to which the IGS perspective is suited to meeting the "environmental press" of contemporary societal and academic demands for analysis and explanation. With today's economic uncertainties, changing demographics, pressures on family life, seemingly pervasive violence, confusion over what constitutes "the common good" (and whether such a concept is even relevant anymore) and the role of government, and social policies (or lack thereof) that seem to rekindle class, race and gender divisiveness, the turbulent '90s could well benefit from an approach that uses, as a core concept, the generational exchange.

In short, IGS is coming of age in a social climate conducive to a lifespan generational exchange framework. The Carnegie study plaintively reminds us of the sorry state of *Today's Children* (Hamburg, 1994), while Erikson, Erikson, and Kivnick (1986) underscore the ongoing need for *Vital Involvement in Old Age.* At the same time the plight of young dependents is dramatically worsening; terms like "rectangularization of the survival curve" and "healthspan" describe longer, healthier lives for older Americans who are retiring earlier and seeking out new, more socially engaged roles that redefine and expand the traditional "retiree" role. Predicted generational equity battles are perceived as more likely as families, communities, Congress and the President agonize over the allocation of limited resources in times of growing demand.

A growing focus on community service and service-based learning is another contextual factor demonstrating the IGS-environment fit since intergenerational programs typically use one of three approaches: elders serving youth, youth serving elders, or elders and youth together serving the community. Moody and Disch (1989) link intergenerational programs to an "ideal of citizenship"; that is, intergenerational programming is "a collaborative task within life span development" wherein "old and young are joined in a common historical task of shaping the public world and understanding themselves as participants in that world" (101-102). Such a perspective brings IGS more into focus in both societal and academic contexts.

One motivating force behind the various adaptations of institutions of higher learning over the past two decades has been a growing concern for relevance and viability. The development of institutes and, at some colleges and universities, degree programs in such fields as Urban Studies, African-American Studies, Women's Studies, and Environmental Studies illustrate a trend toward structured multidisciplinary education and the gradual erosion of boundaries between traditional disciplines. Here, too, IGS finds a good "fit."

The focus on IGS also comes at a time when colleges and universities are welcoming elders on their campuses, both integrated into the regular curriculum and in separate institutes of learning in retirement (ILRs) which have mushroomed throughout the country. Thus IGS is not only emerging as a topic in academic settings; the "graying of the classroom" (Kay, Jensen-Osinski, Beidler, & Aronson, 1983) itself testifies to the growing merit of the intergenerational perspective (e.g., Ogazalek & Power, 1992). The continued involvement of older people in education and society implies both that the body of intergenerational knowledge will continue to grow and that IGS itself will be enlivened by intergenerational exchanges in the classroom.

Just as intergenerational programming shows great diversity across the country, IGS appears in varied manifestations in academia. Current forms of IGS offerings in academic settings include credit-bearing courses and experiences, seminars, workshops and forums, research and training initiatives, and the development of technical and training materials, libraries and resource centers.

On the undergraduate level, credit and non-credit courses, concentrations and certificate programs are appearing in such areas as human development and family living, social services, urban studies, gerontology, recreational studies, child growth and development, and extension services. Examples of IGS courses include "Intergenerational Issues and Prospects for the 21st Century" (Urban Studies Institute, Worcester State College) and "Intergenerational Program Administration" (Department of Human Development, Family Living and Community Educational Services University of Wisconsin at Stout).

Coordinated IGS graduate programs are extremely rare. Only Wheelock College currently offers the Masters Degree in Intergenerational Studies. However, Masters-level courses, such as "Intergenerational Program and Curriculum Development" (Lesley College) and "Intergenerational Experiences in Society" (University of Pittsburgh School of Social Work), are found in increasing frequency in social work, gerontology and other areas. As higher education responds to changing economic, demographic and political realities, there seems enormous potential for post-graduate certificate programs in IGS for teachers, human service professionals, and others whose certification or licensure requires continued professional development activities.

The development of intergenerational programming has been a focus of study at the University of Southern Illinois (Angelis, 1992). Both Texas Tech University and the University of Wisconsin at Stout have spearheaded research initiatives developing competencies in IGS, activities consistent with the emergence of IGS as a professional field of study (Olson, personal communication, March 12, 1995). The University of Pittsburgh's Generations Together program has developed training programs at community colleges and manuals for training older people as child care providers (Newman, Vander Ven, & Ward, 1992). Temple University's Center for Intergenerational Learning, through its Linking Life Times curriculum and its focus on mentoring, has provided national leadership in intergenerational community service. Temple University and the University of Pittsburgh both have sponsored national conferences and training programs. Higher education is also the launching pad for demonstration programs and on-going intergenerational community service projects, such as the Intergenerational Urban Institute at Worcester State College. IGS bibliographies are starting to appear (e.g., Wilson, 1994).

Examples of non-credit education in retirement abound. There are over 180 Centers for Learning in Retirement across the country; The Center for Creative Retirement at the University of North Carolina at Asheville has piloted several innovative intergenerational programs. In Des Plaines, IL, Oakland Community College mixes "Emeritus" and for-credit programs in early childhood development. Elderhostel reported offering intergenerational programs at 76 of its sites in 1994. But IGS is not only reflected in the courses, research and demonstration projects around the country; empirical studies that analyze and document the breadth of this emerging field contribute to a growing literature base. The array is eclectic, exciting and perhaps somewhat disorganized, reflecting the vitality, growth spurts and inconsistent integration of an "adolescent" field.

What can be learned about IGS's current status and future prospects by examining the history of other fields of inquiry? Comparison to gerontology, a field that is also of relatively recent emergence and that is similarly multidisciplinary, might yield instructive insights.

INTERGENERATIONAL STUDIES AND GERONTOLOGY

There are interesting parallels between the fledgling field of intergenerational studies and the more established field of gerontology. Both emerged in response to social needs; both grew out of the need to provide services to vulnerable individuals in our society; advocacy groups have spurred the growth of programs in both gerontology and IGS; and in both fields community programs preceded the growth of the field in academia.

Parallels also exist in the emergence of IGS and gerontology in higher education. First, there was a recognition that services could be better provided by people who had knowledge and skills and who understood developmental processes. Higher education responded with the development of academic curricula, research and involvement in applied programs. The recognition that there were employment opportunities for graduates stimulated the development of courses and curricula to prepare graduates.

The multidisciplinary nature of both gerontology and IGS was recognized at the outset, and offerings in higher education sprang up in a variety of disciplines and departments. Thus academic offerings in both fields tend to have a multidisciplinary flavor, often housed in such departments as early childhood education, home economics, social work, sociology, gerontology and human services. The development of courses and programs in both areas was often dependent on a key, committed leader and the availability of external funding.

However, there are also contrasts in the emergence of the two fields of study, and the differences illuminate some of the obstacles and issues confronting IGS as it struggles to become established. Although future hindsight may show the development of the two fields to have followed a similar path, today IGS is a new arrival. While intergenerational education and service programs have experienced a period of tremendous growth in the last decade, gerontology can claim a 75-year history in higher education (Peterson & Bolton, 1980). Early academic gerontology programs were research-oriented, investigating the basic biological and psychological processes of aging. Programs at Stanford, Duke and the University of Chicago provided a foundation of empirical studies upon which other academic programs in gerontology were built.

A second phase in the development of gerontology was stimulated by federally funded career training grants in the 1960s which were targeted for the preparation of practitioners. Funding was expanded in a third phase of development in the 1970s and peaked with the funding of multidisciplinary centers of aging in the mid-to-late 1970s. Thus two instrumental elements in the history of gerontology's growth were the early research traditions which provided an empirical foundation for the field, and the availability of federal funds to develop research and training programs in aging.

The emergence of IGS presents a contrast to the development of gerontology described above. While many of the same conditions stimulated the growth of both fields, IGS labors under two handicaps. First, the field lacks the research foundation crucial for academic acceptance; second, the 1990s has offered scant financial support for new research and training programs. The response of academics has been to develop demonstration projects and applied programs where opportunities for funding do exist. Federal funding has not supported academic programs in IGS.

The development of academic gerontology was accompanied by a proliferation of professional organizations, journals, curriculum guides, summer workshops for faculty, standards documents and studies of competencies and skills (Peterson & Bolton, 1980). Parallel events are just beginning to occur in IGS.

What is the relationship between IGS and gerontology? Aging is an integral part of IGS. Those engaged in research, teaching, and service need a grounding in aging. But is IGS an inherent part of gerontology? This question can be approached empirically: since no IGS journal currently exists, where are scholarly articles published? At what types of conferences are IGS research papers presented? A bibliography covering 15 years of journal articles on intergenerational topics (Wilson, 1994) cites 143 articles published in gerontology journals, 82 articles published in child development or school journals, and 120 articles in other journals (e.g., social work, counseling). Clearly gerontology journals have accepted intergenerational education, research and service programs as part of their purview. Similarly, in the past two years the American Society on Aging, the Association for Gerontology in Higher Education, and the Gerontological Society have increased the number of IGS presentations and workshops at their annual meetings.

If IGS is an emerging subfield or cognate of gerontology, what is the place of the fledgling IGS knowledge base in gerontology education programs? The growing body of knowledge related to intergenerational programs could be integrated into existing courses. Intergenerational topics could be added to gerontology course as topics like demographics or death are now included. Intergenerational content could comprise a multidisciplinary course. Intergenerational studies could also be an area of emphasis or concentration within a gerontology degree program. The intergenerational area of emphasis would include a sequence of courses that could include research and evaluation issues, models and theoretical frameworks, management, program development, and social policy implications.

If IGS continues to parallel gerontology, perhaps the future and final form of IGS in academia will be the similar to gerontology. Peterson, Wendt and Douglass (1994) report that gerontology offerings in higher education institutions range from one course to doctorates, with a steady growth in the numbers of programs culminating in degrees. Still, relatively few institutions offer degrees in gerontology: 80% of the credentials are certificates, areas of concentration, or minors. It is probably most realistic to expect and encourage similar growth in IGS. As an ancillary or adjunct field, IGS complements many majors such as life span development, family studies, child development, public policy, gerontology, social work, urban studies, and recreation.

As IGS attracts more interest from academics, human service professionals and policy makers, questions of identity and place become more salient. How is IGS to be defined, and where does it belong? A discussion of IGS and the IGS-gerontology relationship (Cliff, 1994; Newman, 1994) concluded that it is important to bring together professionals working in different areas of IGS and to introduce IGS into the college curriculum.

There were different opinions on how to effectively accomplish this and there were reservations about whether a new academic discipline is indeed emerging. Do the parallels between gerontology and IGS support the conclusion that IGS is a multi-disciplinary field of study? Is IGS an academic discipline, best conceptualized as a separate and unique entity? Or is IGS best approached as a foundation for professional practice? Whatever the answers to these questions, we must then ask what are the unique aspects of IGS that justifies its distinction from those existing fields of study with which its content matter so obviously overlaps?

INTERGENERATIONAL STUDIES:
AN EMERGING ACADEMIC DISCIPLINE?

In weighing advocates' claim that IGS should be accepted as a new academic discipline (e.g., Newman, 1994), one must begin by determining the empirical traits of a discipline, i.e., the criteria by which the claim will be evaluated. It is also possible that IGS is best classified as a multi-disciplinary profession, in which case criteria can be found in other sources, such as occupational sociology. In this section we will list and describe the criteria for disciplines and professions, and will argue that disciplinary or professional status should be accorded based on congruence with these criteria. Finally, the consequences of "discipline" and "professional" status are addressed.

By asking "Is intergenerational studies a new academic discipline?" we frame the issue as a research question. Thus we can attempt to answer it via appropriate standard research methodologies. To do this we must first define the concept "academic discipline." This involves noting major dimensions of the concept and describing those dimensions in terms of empirical indicators, that is, operationalized criteria that we feel validly represent the essential elements of the concept "academic discipline."

Next we must develop a definition of the concept we call "intergenerational studies." The definition must be acceptable to the majority of the scientific community, or at least that part of it actively interested in IGS. The definition should list the overarching goal or goals of IGS. Based on the goals, the definition must then allow us to delineate limits, boundaries or parameters so we can determine what qualifies as IGS and what does not. Finally, in addition to specifying these parameters, the definition must contain the essential components, the sine qua non, of intergenerational studies.

Then, by applying the criteria for determining a discipline to the definition of IGS, it should be fairly easy to determine whether or not IGS as it exists today can be considered an academic discipline. In addition to meeting the criteria per se, we should ascertain that IGS does not unduly overlap other disciplines. Often some overlap is inevitable and even desirable–for example, the attention paid by both sociologists and psychologists to interpersonal and small-group dynamics–but a new discipline should in substantial part address turf untrammelled by its predecessors.

This determination, however, does not answer other questions which are also equally or even more salient. These are: (1) So what? What significant practical consequences hinge on whether or not IGS is an academic discipline (vs. an interdisciplinary or multi-disciplinary field of study)? (2) What is it best for IGS to be? It could well be, given the goals of the field and the defining criteria for an academic discipline, that IGS most benefits from not being labeled an "academic discipline." This may not be true, but we should not a priori rule it out of the realm of possibility; (3) What are the practice implications of various definitions (or statuses) of IGS? What can and should the contribution of IGS be to public, private non-profit and for-profit practitioners, programs and organizations?

Definitions

It is surprisingly difficult to find relevant and sufficiently detailed definitions of "academic discipline" to address the question of IGS's identity. Newer fields of inquiry, like environmental studies (e.g., Brough, 1992) and conflict resolution (e.g., Harty & Modell, 1991), have attempted to assume an identity without explicitly matching their qualifications to a predetermined set of criteria. One can find more direct definitional efforts in education encyclopedias and encyclopedic dictionaries, but these run toward the conceptual and abstract (e.g., Parsons, 1968; Kiger, 1971). While not disputing their validity, such definitions are not sufficiently empirical to help evaluate IGS's claim as a discipline.

Useful definitions of "profession" (Krause, 1971; Pavalko, 1972; Greenwood, 1957; Moore, 1970) are easier to find and, since those reviewed here chronologically precede a useful definition of "discipline," will be addressed first. Such definitions are relevant because one potential role for the IGS specialist is as a "professional." Generally accepted traits or indicators of a profession include: (1) a relatively long, specialized training period involving the acquisition and application of symbols (vs. things); (2) a body of theory; (3) public acceptance of the professional's expertise and neutrality, so that the professional's interpretations and advice are considered credible; (4) licensure or credentialing; (5) intra-profession regulation including a code of ethics, control over selection of new members, and control over training; (6) relevance to dominant social values; (7) a professional (sub)culture, including professional association/s and journal/s, and; (8) a "service" motivation (vs. purely self-interest).

Since there seems considerable overlap between disciplines and professions (a "professional" has usually received formal training in a "discipline"), it is not surprising that disciplinary criteria resemble those of professions, overlaying an academic flavor. Dressel and Mayhew (1974), for example, list the basic attributes of a discipline as: (1) a general body of knowledge (with taxonomic potential); (2) a generally accepted literature base; (3) a specialized vocabulary; (4) a generally accepted body of theory (or theories), and; (5) a generally accepted methodology, which includes provisions for replication, theory/hypothesis-testing and validation.

Lessons from Gerontology

In evaluating IGS's claim as a discipline and/or profession, let us return to the parallel with gerontology. Peterson and Bolton (1980) provided a focused examination of gerontology as an academic discipline. Fifteen years ago the debate was not so much over gerontology's disciplinary status as over the desirability of that status: "although some gerontology educators believe that if gerontology does not yet possess these [disciplinary] characteristics, it soon will, most others would agree that it does not, cannot, and should not" (1980:50). There was general agreement that in 1980 gerontology did not possess the traits of a discipline due to its relative youthfulness and the "rapidity of its expansion within higher education" (1980:50). Based on Dressel and Mayhew's (1974) criteria, Peterson and Bolton noted that gerontology had made strides toward building a literature base and taxonomy for classifying gerontological knowledge, but needed continued progress in theory building and methodological development before it could validly argue for recognition as a distinct discipline.

At about the same time, McKee (1982:299) described gerontology as a multi-disciplinary field, an assessment few would dispute. "There is no single discipline answering to the name 'gerontology,'" he wrote. "Old age is studied from the perspectives of many different disciplines, which together make up the field of gerontology in their common application to old age."

Peterson, Douglass, Bolton, Connelly, and Bergston (1987), after describing the range of organizational structures that characterize gerontology instruction in higher education, echoed McKee's evaluation. Gerontology education typically leads to a minor or certificate, they noted, not to an undergraduate or graduate degree. When added to the range of organizational structures, they concluded it was infeasible to argue that gerontology be considered an independent academic discipline. They felt gerontology is better described as a multi-disciplinary field of study.

Mangum (1990:27) also refrained from labeling gerontology a discipline, though noting that other disciplines "have developed interests" in aging. He wrote that "the term 'multidisciplinary' is usually applied to gerontology in recognition of the fact that it draws on the theoretical, empirical, and methodological content of several established but separate disciplines. . . ."

Finally, Rich, Connelly, and Douglass (1990:iv) acknowledged the continued debate over the nature and focus of gerontology, including "whether gerontology is a discipline or a profession." Other possibilities, they note, include aging studies focusing on one scientific discipline, aging studies focusing on one humanistic discipline, and integrating gerontological issues and concerns into professional education programs.

The most logical conclusion is that the pervasiveness of interest in aging found across the traditional disciplines coupled with gerontology's overarching embrace of these disciplines precludes gerontology from being per se an academic discipline.

The Case of Intergenerational Studies

Newman (1994:2) writes, "The time has come . . . to recognize intergenerational studies as a viable discipline, with a valuable body of knowledge, a solid theoretical framework, and broad research opportunities." But is IGS really all that, today? We argue it is not. There are, we grant, research opportunities galore. But IGS is still busy building the solid empirical knowledge base and literature necessary to a scientific discipline, and much of the literature is not theoretically grounded. As has occurred in other disciplines, this "first-generation" knowledge/literature base emerges from the less rigorous, less systematic, less representative, more speculative and relatively untested works indicative of a nascent field. Similarly, the methodologies and vocabulary evident in IGS literature are drawn from other disciplines and fields of study. Perhaps most importantly, attempts to build a unique theoretical framework are still in their infancy (e.g., Bengston & Roberts, 1991; Cliff, 1994; Newman, 1995; Roberts & Bengston, 1990): IGS theory needs an explicit axiomatic base, an agreed-upon set of core concepts, logical linking mechanisms (theoretical propositions) between the concepts, and the articulation of predicted outcomes. Such a theory, whether induced from extant studies or borrowed/deduced from other disciplines, obviously would guide (and thus coordinate) IGS research, which would then reflect back upon theory, supporting, amending or rejecting it. If disciplinary status is the goal, IGS has a long way to go.

But there is obvious uncertainty about the best identity and place for IGS. More recently, Newman and Larkin (personal communication, February 1, 1995) have described IGS as "a multidisciplinary human service field," claiming the field examines "generational issues and professional practice questions related to a new knowledge base." These issues and questions include "commonalities and differences across the life span, the interdependence of family members across the life course, the effect of societal change on all generations, cross-cultural generational values, the involvement of partnered systems to promote generational change, and the impact of intergenerational programs on the well-being of younger and older persons." Still, even with this as a working definition, it is clear that, like gerontology in the past, IGS cannot yet claim recognition as an academic discipline.

But whether or not such a goal is in fact attainable, we must also ask (as has gerontology) whether such a goal is desirable, is worth pursuing. A discipline is accorded departmental status in higher education and, with it, the right to award degrees. This "legitimization," as Peterson and Bolton (1980) call it, can be important, especially when politicians (and the public) are scrutinizing and holding higher education accountable in unprecedented ways, and when processes like "downsizing" or "rightsizing" are decimating higher education curricula. But, as Peterson and Bolton note, obtaining the status and prestige of a discipline for the sake of "organizational survival" is not related to whether or not the field meets disciplinary criteria.

If IGS cannot (and/or should not) qualify as a discipline, alternative identities are available. One is to argue for its establishment as a profession and to endeavor to satisfy those criteria. Meeting the criteria for a profession seems to be a goal both more readily attainable (although, again, there is a long way to go) and more consistent with current trends in IGS toward service and application. Whether IGS should or could become a distinct profession, with its own credentialing, etc., or whether it should become a sub-specialty of, say, social work, is problematic and beyond the scope of this paper. (Those concerned with these issues–and social workers should be–should closely follow the ongoing debate in gerontology over program accreditation and professional credentialing; see, e.g., Connelly, 1995; Johnson, 1995; Lubben, 1995; Peterson, 1995.) Clearly, however, such a path would prove valuable for practitioners and policy makers. While academia has a role in this identity, it would not be a dominating one.

Another, more academically-located option, is to view IGS as an adjunct to extant professions and disciplines, drawing from and contributing to them in an integrative, multidisciplinary fashion, but per se neither a full-fledged discipline nor a full-fledged profession. In this role IGS, like gerontology, would produce specialists who typically go by some other name: social worker, policy analyst, etc. This does not demean IGS; instead, it demonstrates the contributions IGS can make to a variety of professions and in a variety of arenas, ranging from higher education to practice to policy-making.

In conclusion IGS, which has pervaded existing disciplines and practices conceptually for decades, is attempting to carve out a unique identity and niche and achieve its own legitimacy. Whether compared to accepted criteria or to gerontology, a field whose development IGS seems to parallel, IGS cannot today be considered an academic discipline. But the question of whether or not IGS is or can become an academic discipline is one that perhaps need not be asked until an underlying question is answered: what is the best–not merely the currently most accurate–identity for IGS? To answer this, we must collect, evaluate and try to reach a consensus based on the needs and goals of those who practice, those who teach, those who study, and those in the political arena whose decisions affect our lives. As it exists today, the most common and perhaps most beneficial function of IGS may be its ability to enhance professional practice. If this is true, then the best role for IGS in higher education is as an interdisciplinary field. For this to become the rule rather than the exception at campuses and in professional training programs across the country, current curricula must be integrated and coordinated (rather than scattershot), and new curricula may need to be developed if the proponents of IGS sincerely want to build the field from its most common current apparition, which is multidisciplinary, to a truly interdisciplinary field of study.

AUTHOR NOTE

Ed Rosenberg's recent work has appeared in the *Encyclopedia of Aging*, *Educational Gerontology*, and the *Southwest Journal on Aging*.

Lois E. Layne developed and coordinates the Gerontology Program at WKU and has participated with the Kentucky Association for Gerontology as founder, past president, and board member.

In 1994 Maureen Power was appointed Executive Director of the Intergenerational Urban Institute, a service and education program that links the generations. In 1993 she was the recipient of the "Fran Pratt Award" for outstanding leadership from the Massachusetts Intergenerational Network.

REFERENCES

Angelis, J. (1992). The genesis of an intergenerational program. *Educational Gerontology* 18(4), 317-327.

Bengston, V., & Roberts, R. (1991). Intergenerational solidarity in aging families: An example of formal theory construction. *Journal of Marriage and the Family* 53(4), 856-870.

Brough, H. (1992, January-February). Environmental studies: Is it academic? *World Watch*, pp. 26-33.

Cliff, M.J. (1994, Winter) Intergenerational studies: The field responds. *Generations Together Exchange*, pp. 1, 5.

Connelly, J. R. (1995, Summer). The time for accreditation has come. *Generations*, p. 25-27.

Dressel, P. L., & Mayhew, L. B. (1974). *Higher education as a field of study*. San Francisco: Jossey-Bass.

Erikson, E., Erikson, J., & Kivnick, H. (1986). *Vital involvement in old age*. New York: Norton.

Greenwood, E. L. (1957). Attributes of a profession. *Social Work*, 2(3), 45-55.

Hamburg, D. (1994). *Today's children*. New York: Times Books.

Harty, M., & Modell, J. (1991). The first conflict resolution movement, 1956-1971. *Journal of Conflict Resolution*, 35, 720-758.

Johnson, H. R. (1995, Summer). The foibles and follies of gerontological imperialists. *Generations*, p. 23-24.

Kay, E., Jensen-Osinski, B., Beidler, P., & Aronson, J. (1983). The graying of the college classroom. *Gerontologist* 23(2), 196-199.

Kiger, J. C. (1971). Disciplines. In L. Deighton (Ed.), *The encyclopedia of education:* Vol. 3 (pp. 99-101). New York: Macmillan.

Krause, E. (1971). *The sociology of occupations*. Boston: Little, Brown.

Lawton, M. P., & Nahemow, L. (1973). Ecologs and the aging process. In C. Eisdorfer & M. P. Lawton (Eds.), *Psychology of adult development and aging* (619-674). Washington, DC: American Psychological Association.

Lubben, J. (1995, Summer). A reaction to the debate. *Generations*, p. 31-32.

Mangum, W. (1990). Glossary. In T. A. Rich. J. R. Connelly, & E. B. Douglass (Eds.), *Standards and guidelines for gerontology programs* (2nd ed.) (pp. 26-28). Washington, DC: Association for Gerontology in Higher Education.

McKee, P. L. (1982). *Philosophical foundations of gerontology*. New York: Human Sciences Press.

Moody, H., & Disch, R. (1989). Intergenerational programming in public policy. In S. Newman & S. Brummel (Eds.), *Intergenerational programs: Imperatives strategies impacts, trends* (pp. 101-110). New York: The Haworth Press, Inc.

Moore, W. E. (1970). *The Professions: Roles and rules*. New York: Russell Sage Foundation.

Newman, S. (1995, February). *History and current status of the intergenerational field*. Paper presented at the meeting of the Association for Gerontology in Higher Education, Fort Worth, TX.

Newman, S. (1994, Winter). Intergenerational studies: A new academic discipline. *Generations Together Exchange*, 1-2.

Newman, S., Vander Ven, K., & Ward, C. (1992). *Practitioner's guidelines for the productive employment of older adults in child care*. Pittsburgh: University of Pittsburgh, Generations Together.

Ogazalek, V., & Power, M. (1992). The Worcester State College "Elder Connection": Using multimedia and information technology to promote intergenerational education. In E. Barrett (Ed.), *Sociomedia* (pp. 533-546). Cambridge, MA: MIT Press.

Parsons, T. (1968). Professions. In D. Sills (Ed.), *International Encyclopedia of the Social Sciences:* Vol. 12 (pp. 536-547). New York: Macmillan.

Pavalko, R. (Ed.) (1972). *Sociological Perspectives on occupations.* Itasca, IL: Peacock.

Peterson, D. A. (1995, Summer). Professionals in the field of aging should be credentialed. *Generations*, p. 28-30.

Peterson, D. A., & Bolton, C. R. (1980). *Gerontology instruction in higher education.* New York: Springer.

Peterson, D. A., Douglass, E. B., Bolton, C. R., Connelly, J. R., & Bergstone, D. (1987). *Gerontology instruction in American institutions of higher education: A national survey.* Washington, DC: AGHE.

Peterson, D. A., Wendt, P. F., & Douglass, E. B. (1994). *Development of gerontology geriatrics, and aging studies Programs in institutions of higher education.* Washington, DC: Association for Gerontology in Higher Education.

Rich, T. A., Connelly, J. R., & Douglass, E. B. (1990). *Standards and guidelines for gerontology Programs* (2nd ed.). Washington, DC: Association for Gerontology in Higher Education.

Roberts, R., & Bengston, V. (1990). Is intergenerational solidarity a unidimensional construct? A second test of a formal model. *The Journals of Gerontology* 45(1), S12-S20.

Weick, A. (1981, March). Reframing the Person-in-environment perspective. *Social Work*, 140-143.

Wilson, J. (1994). *Intergenerational readings/resources 1980-1993: A bibliography of books, journal articles, manuals. Papers/reports/studies, curricula, bibliographies, directories, newsletters, data bases, and videos.* Pittsburgh: University of Pittsburgh, Generations Together.

SECTION II:
GRANDPARENT CAREGIVING

Grandparent caregiving has recently emerged as a major social issue which, by its very nature, is intergenerational. According to census data, 3.7 million children are living in households headed by grandparents and 1.4 million of these are in households with no parent present. The American Association of Retired Persons indicates that these populations are growing rapidly, expanding 27% between 1993 to 1994 alone.

The most common reasons for such family changes are: substance abuse; child abuse, neglect or abandonment; incarceration; death; divorce; parental joblessness; and HIV-AIDS infection in the biological parent. Given the rapid increase in incarceration and AIDS infection rates for women, and the intractability of social problems like substance and child abuse, the number of grandparent caregivers is likely to grow for the foreseeable future.

Because of their focus on the needs of children, the issue has been recognized in the child welfare and foster care networks for some time. Its recent adoption by the aging network suggests that it will be one of those socially challenging issues that require the active collaboration of service delivery systems. In recent years intersystem grandparent caregiving networks and task forces have appeared in Illinois, Michigan and Massachusetts.

The papers in this section engage the grandparenting issue from three major perspectives:

- There are a variety of stress factors that affect caregivers as their role changes from grandparent to parent, not least of which is the change in the role itself. A number of these factors are highlighted in the first paper (Morrow-Kondos, Weber, Cooper and Hesser).
- Grandparents are inclined to put their grandchildrens' needs before their own, especially in situations where resources are limited. There-

fore, the needs of grandparents as well as grandchildren should be considered when planning services for skipped-generation families. This issue is approached from a health care perspective in the second paper (Grant, Gordon, and Cohen).

- No matter what social class grandparent-headed families are in, they are likely to encounter problems of legal status. The legal system is not yet adequately responsive to the needs of these nontraditional families. The third paper in this section outlines legal and economic issues faced by grandparent caregivers (Flint and Perez-Porter) and suggests how the legal system could be more responsive.

Becoming Parents Again:
Grandparents Raising Grandchildren

Diane Morrow-Kondos, MS
Joseph A. Weber, PhD
Kathy Cooper, MS, RN
Jenny L. Hesser

SUMMARY. As the middle generation attempts to deal with the challenges of unemployment, increasing divorce rates and substance abuse, it is becoming increasingly common for the older generation to be called upon to raise grandchildren. The purpose of this qualitative study was to explore the complex problems grandparents have when raising their grandchildren. Grandparents reported their relationships with adult children, becoming surrogate parents and legal issues as major areas of stress. *[Article copies available for a fee from The Haworth Document Delivery Service: 1-800-342-9678. E-mail address: getinfo@haworth.com]*

Because of current demographic, social, and economic circumstances many grandparents are assisting, in varying degrees, to support and raise

Diane Morrow-Kondos is Eldercare Case Manager and Founder and Former Director, Grandparents Raising Grandchildren (support group), Tulsa, OK. Dr. Joseph A. Weber is Director, Gerontology Institute, Oklahoma State University, Stillwater, OK. Kathy Cooper is a Graduate Research Associate at Oklahoma State University and doctoral student. Jenny L. Hesser is a Graduate Research Assistant at Oklahoma State University and master's degree student.

[Haworth co-indexing entry note]: "Becoming Parents Again: Grandparents Raising Grandchildren." Morrow-Kondos, Diane et al. Co-published simultaneously in the *Journal of Gerontological Social Work* (The Haworth Press, Inc.) Vol. 28, No. 1/2, 1997, pp. 35-46; and: *Intergenerational Approaches in Aging: Implications for Education, Policy and Practice* (ed: Kevin Brabazon, and Robert Disch) The Haworth Press, Inc., 1997, pp. 35-46. Single or multiple copies of this article are available for a fee from The Haworth Document Delivery Service [1-800-342-9678, 9:00 a.m. - 5:00 p.m. (EST). E-mail address: getinfo@haworth.com].

their grandchildren. Grandparents have always been an important part of the family structure, playing a strong role in keeping the family together and acting as arbitrators between the generations (Dychtwald & Flower, 1989). Traditionally, their most important function has been very simply "being there," in a symbolic dimension which helps maintain the identity of the family and preserves a sense of continuity (Bengston & Robertson, 1985).

People today are living longer because of access to medical technology and healthier lifestyles. A longer life expectancy means more people live long enough to become grandparents (Bengston & Robertson, 1985; Brubaker, 1990; Rosenwaike & Dolinsky, 1987). The availability of the grandparent, combined with a rise in the number and severity of social problems such as unemployment, divorce, substance abuse, mental illness, and child abuse, has in some cases expanded the grandparent role. This expanded role frequently now includes parenting of grandchildren (Creighton, 1991; Kennedy & Keeney, 1988; Minkler & Roe, 1992).

Early research (Albrecht, 1954; Apple, 1956; Barranti, 1985; Cherlin & Furstenberg, 1986; Jones, 1973; Neugarten & Weinstein, 1964) suggests that the majority of grandparents envision a fun or indulgent relationship with their grandchildren. The passive and fun loving grandparent-grandchild relationship does not fit the actual role experienced by many grandparents who are raising their grandchildren. As times change, roles and responsibilities also change.

Current research suggests that there are no clear grandparenting roles for the many grandparents who assume the responsibility of raising their grandchildren (Jendrek, 1993; Purnell & Bagby, 1993; Wagner, Weber & Cooper, 1995).

This study discussed some of the complex problems and role inconsistencies grandparents encountered when they became parents to their grandchildren. The focus of the study was to examine the feelings and experiences of grandparents raising grandchildren and to share these experiences with others.

METHODOLOGY

The convenience sample consisted of volunteer respondents from a group of grandparents participating in a support group, "Grandparents Raising Grandchildren" in a metropolitan city in the Southwest. Each respondent was currently involved in raising at least one grandchild under the age of eighteen. They were included in the study because information from grandparents actually seeking support would help define the issues grandparents themselves view as critical versus what issues might be surmised to be important to them. They were given the opportunity to discuss grandparenting issues involving their relationships with their adult children and grandchildren.

Ten white middle-class grandparents, eight women and two men, ranging in age from 39 to 58 years (M = 51.4 years) comprised the sample. Half of the respondents were maternal grandparents and half were paternal grandparents. Grandparents were equally divided in regard to marital status; half were married and half were single. Seven of the participants were raising only one grandchild while the remaining grandparents had two or more grandchildren currently living with them. The grandchildren's ages ranged from one to sixteen years (M = 4.16 years). Of the sixteen grandchildren, thirteen were males and three were females. The grandchildren had been living with their grandparents from one to four years (M = 1.6 years). Because the study was exploratory and qualitative in nature, no attempt was made to mitigate any differences due to participant characteristics.

Ten open-ended questions were used in a non-structured format using standardized interviewing techniques. The interview specifically focused on issues related to grandparenting roles and grandparenting stressors. The interview questions were designed to elicit information about their new parenting experience, their relationship with their adult children, and their perception of their grandparenting role. Interviews varied in length from one to three hours. Brief notes were taken during the interviews and permission was gained from each individual respondent to allow the interview to be tape recorded.

GRANDPARENTS DISCUSS GRANDPARENTING EXPERIENCES

Grandparenting Roles

There appears be a large gap between the role that the respondents viewed as ideal and the role in which they are presently immersed. Grandparents were asked to describe the ideal grandparent-grandchild relationship. None of the grandparents felt their current situation of being a surrogate parent to their grandchildren was ideal. In discussing the grandparents' perception of the ideal grandparent-grandchild relationship, eight of the ten talked about spending time in leisure activities with their grandchildren and the word "fun" was mentioned by all.

One of the grandmothers felt that she did have the ideal grandparent-grandchild relationship with two grandchildren who do not live with her.

Describing the role of the indulgent grandparent, she stated, "I have the ideal relationship with two other grandchildren. They come to see me, I dote on them, and buy them things." Her comments reflect a desire to have the same type of passive relationship with the child she is currently parenting. Another respondent, a grandfather, described the ideal relationship with his grandchild as one voluntary in nature, with frequent visits. Envisioning the ideal relationship with his grandchild he stated, "He would come to visit, talk about problems, I would give him love and support."

Respondents were also asked to explain what they anticipated their relationship with their grandchildren would be like in five years. Half of the grandparents responded they hoped, within the next five years, adult children would have their lives in order and would resume their parenting responsibilities. This would enable them to take on the desired "passive" grandparent role.

One grandparent stated, "I hope my daughter can make positive changes in her life, take the kids back, and I can be a grandma again." Another grandparent hoped, "Ideally one of the parents will mature enough to take over the parenting responsibilities so I can be a part-time grandmother again."

The remaining half of the grandparents anticipated no significant changes in their caretaking arrangements in the next five years. These grandparents appear to have accepted that their adult children will probably never be able to successfully resume their parenting responsibilities. For example, one grandfather stated, "We'll still be raising our grandson, while our son will still be out there doing his own thing; it's a vicious circle. I just pray he (the adult child) will settle down some day."

In an effort to better understand their roles, participants were asked two specific questions. The first question considered the reasons grandparents have taken over the parental role. In response to this question all of the grandparents expressed their concerns about their grandchildren's well-being and felt it was their duty to help the children enjoy a positive childhood experience.

In conjunction with this question of roles, grandparents were also asked about the difficulties with raising their grandchildren. Many of the grandparents discussed the role in which their grandchildren viewed them and how they dealt with attempting to clarify often confusing and shifting roles. The name that grandchildren called their grandparent raised many concerns and uncertainties for grandparents.

For example, the grandmother of a two year old said that although she always tells him that she is his grandma, he still calls her "mama." When his mother visits, he also calls her "mama." The grandmother worries about the grandchild's confusion at having two mothers. Another grandmother of a four year old reported that her grandchild recently asked if he could call her "mommy" but she said, "No, I'm your Nana." She now questions whether that was the right thing to say.

One grandmother felt very strongly about the grandchildren not calling her "mom." She has told her grandchildren, "You call me grandma, I am your grandma. No matter what terrible things your mother did to you, she is still your mom." Despite her insistence the grandchildren still frequently call her "mom."

A grandmother raising two grandsons reported incongruity even among the two grandchildren. The three year old calls her "grandma" but the younger child, whom she has cared for since infancy, calls her "mama."

Sadness was felt by six grandparents at not being the type of grandparent they had always envisioned. These grandparents were disappointed in their current role. One grandmother quite eloquently summed up her feelings:

> You cannot be a grandparent and a parent too. You grieve because it hasn't turned out like you thought. You expected to rear children and then sit back and be a grandparent. Now I can't be a grandparent. I have to be a parent. . . . again.

A grandfather concurred adding:

> You can't be parents and grandparents both. You have to pick one role and stick with it. If you're going to do a good job raising these kids, unfortunately, it must be the grandparent role that goes.

Grandparenting Stressors

The most difficult stressors grandparents experienced are dealing with adult children, legal issues, and becoming a surrogate parent. Grandparents candidly discussed the strain placed on intergenerational relationships.

Grandparents' reactions to their adult children brought strong responses. Disappointment and guilt were common threads running through their responses. Some typical comments were:

- Where did we go wrong?
- How could I have raised a child that turned out so bad?
- I'm so disappointed with the person my child has become.

The feelings expressed by the grandparents were often ambivalent. Despite the negative feelings towards their adult children, many grandparents voiced feelings of hope and looked toward the future optimistically. Grandparents discussed the fact that clear boundaries must be drawn between grandparents who are raising their grandchildren and their adult children. As one grandfather said, "This can only help to protect our grandchildren and ensure that we are not taken advantage of."

Respondents were asked to describe their relationship with their adult child. Only one respondent felt that her relationship with her adult child was good. She felt the situation was out of her son's control because he was in the service and out of the country. Her motivation for taking care of the grandchildren was to help her son. This grandmother acknowledged that her former daughter-in-law was not truthful or dependable and had very possibly abused the grandchildren. Despite this, she remains sympathetic to her former daughter-in-law and continues to try to help her.

Nine of the respondents described their relationships with their adult children in negative or ambivalent terms. Many complex emotions surfaced when discussing adult children such as anger, resentment, guilt, hate, and disappointment. Four of the grandparents alluded to feelings of disappointment associated with their adult children. A grandmother who is raising three young grandchildren described her relationship with her daughter, "Our relationship is strained at best. I really don't like the person she has become, we have little in common. There are many disappointments to deal with."

Guilt was a strong emotion expressed by two of the grandparents. One grandmother stated, "It's hard for me to accept that I raised a child that is incapable of being a good parent." Another grandmother who is raising her son's child described her relationship with her son by reporting, "My son resents any advice or interference. We get along if I watch what I say."

Two of the grandparents felt resentment toward their adult child. One respondent discussed that she felt many complex emotions related to her son including pain, anger, and sadness. Also, she constantly fights off resentful feelings towards him. Another participant said that although he thought he still loved his son, he did not like him and resented him for what he had done to the family.

The stress of dealing with adult children was an ordeal for almost all the grandparents. Some of the comments made about coping with the adult children follow:

- Taking care of the baby is easy, it's dealing with my daughter that's tough!
- I have a great deal of difficulty getting along with my son. We have very different ideas about child rearing.

- I don't like my son. Sometimes I want to kill him for what he's done to all of us.

Other factors that caused stress for the grandparents were the fatigue resulting from the physical act of taking care of young children, lack of time to pursue their own interests and the effects on their own health. The need to sacrifice and to drastically alter their own lives was referred to by half of the respondents. One grandmother expressed this feeling of sacrifice as she explained:

> I gave up everything, my business, my social life. I had to give up the life I had. It was hard but it was the only way to survive. There is very little of my old life left; I miss it.

Despite the negatives, grandparents enjoyed the opportunity to know their grandchildren on a close and personal level. Showing love to their grandchildren was identified as the most positive aspect of the situation. A grandmother of a two year old summed up her feelings of love when she said, "There's nothing better than warm baby snuggles to get your day off to a good start."

Forty percent felt that the chance to raise their grandchildren in a safe, loving environment was extremely important. Transmitting good values and helping the grandchild to grow to be a productive person was viewed by these respondents as a positive consideration. A grandfather illustrated this feeling by commenting, ". . . the satisfaction, knowing we're doing the right thing, molding him, giving him good guidance."

Three of the respondents felt positive about their ability to draw on their parenting experiences. They felt more knowledgeable about children and more confident of their abilities at this point in their lives. One grandmother said, "I'm happier with myself now than I was when my own child was young." A grandfather who felt he was getting a second chance at parenting reported the most positive aspect of raising his grandchild is ". . . being a parent again with all the wisdom and knowledge I've accumulated over the years."

Grandparents were asked if they had encountered any legal problems associated with their situation. Half of the grandparents had legal custody of their grandchildren, two had legal guardianship and three had no legal standing. Of those that had legal custody, two are attempting to adopt the grandchild.

Those without any legal standing are in the most tenuous circumstances. Noncustodial grandparents must get permission from the parents to seek medical care or enroll the child in school. At the mercy of the custodial parents, they are often victims of blackmail. The adult child often threatens to remove the child from their home. All of the respondents in this category conveyed a feeling of being "in limbo." One grandfather expressed ambivalent feelings about his legal standing by suggesting, "Sometimes I think we should either make our son (who has legal custody) take responsibility for his son or that we should try to adopt him."

Those respondents with legal custody reported few legal problems. The exception was a grandparent who received custody in another state. When her daughter-in-law kidnapped the children she discovered the custody arrangement had not transferred between states. She reported that there was a great deal of time and money involved in clarifying her legal standing.

One set of respondents (a married couple) who have legal custody of their grandchild are currently in the process of adopting her. They have had legal custody since the child was six weeks old, a period of two and a half years. Their daughter, who has had very little contact with her child, is now seeking to terminate all of the grandparents' legal rights to her and to reinstate herself as the legal parent.

Grandparents' Perceived Needs

Almost all of the respondents felt that financial assistance was a critical need. One grandfather said the reason he and his wife had not tried to adopt their grandchild was because they would lose all financial assistance from the state.

Ninety percent of the respondents had at least one extremely supportive family member. Actively involved family members included other adult children, sisters, former in-laws, and the parents themselves. One of the respondents stated that her own mother was very understanding of what she is doing because she raised a grandchild herself for a period of five years.

Other responses identified the need for informal support and understanding from friends, family members and co-workers. Other concerns expressed included the need for time away from the grandchildren. The physical exhaustion associated with raising young children led to the desire for an occasional respite from responsibility and uninterrupted time with their spouse.

Only three people mentioned friends as a positive source of support. Two of the three were the youngest respondents in the study, aged 39 and 42, and reported that most of their friends still had young children so their social activities naturally included children. One respondent felt her friends had been a source of stress rather than support. She remarked,

"Our friends complain that we can't go out anymore. They don't understand why we're doing what we're doing. None of them offer to help, to give us a break."

SUMMARY

Grandparenting Grandchildren

Respondents that had been taking care of their grandchildren for a relatively short period of time (a year and a half or less) expressed the hope that they would eventually return to a desired level of passive involvement. Those that had been involved in parenting their grandchildren for a longer period of time (a year and a half or more) seemed to have accepted the fact that they would be permanent caregivers to their grandchildren. The longer grandparents remain in the role of surrogate parent, the more likely the role of parenting the grandchild becomes a reality.

Role transitions and anticipatory socialization help explain the process of learning a role (e.g., grandparenting) before being in an actual situation where it is appropriate (Burr, 1972; Burr, Leigh, Day & Constantine, 1979; Cottrell, 1942; Merton, 1968; Sarbin & Allen, 1968). As a person looks ahead to becoming a grandparent, they usually have adequate time to understand the appropriate norms surrounding the transition into the role. When a person is suddenly expected to raise a grandchild, they do not have adequate opportunity to prepare for this event and may experience difficulty in accepting their new surrogate parenting role.

As Cottrell (1942) suggests, the adjustment to a role transition ". . . varies directly with the degree of importance attached to the definiteness of the transitional procedure used by the society in designating the change in the role" (p. 619). For example, if a person moves into the role of raising grandchildren and society labels this as normal, the transition is likely to be smooth and easy. However, if the new role is considered unusual or unexpected by family and friends, the transition will be obscure and the person may experience difficulty.

Family Support

Family members provided a strong sense of emotional and physical support for most of the respondents. Grandparents talked about how essential a support network is in maintaining sanity. Friends were seen as a support for only three respondents. Because the median age of respondents was 51.4 years, it was assumed that most of their peers no longer have children in the home and adapting activities to include them was not desirable to the friends. One grandmother reported being too exhausted to go out, after the time arrangements are made for someone to watch the child. Several other respondents said they did not ever leave their grandchildren with baby-sitters due to a fear of kidnapping by the adult child.

Grandparents Supporting Grandparents

The role of grandparenting grandchildren is not only ambiguous, but the stress of dealing with an accumulation of legal, physical, financial and emotional factors is prevalent. The interactive nature of these stressors has a negative effect on grandparents and grandchildren. The surrogate parenting role has multiple stressors, at home, at work, and in the community, which may interact to have a more negative effect on outcomes (Pearlin, 1983). For example, the negative effects of returning to work after retirement to make ends meet, going to court to obtain custody of a grandchild, helping a grandchild with homework, and emotionally accepting the surrogate parenting role may be even stronger when a grandparent deals with the sum of these events versus dealing with only one or two at a time.

In order to help grandparents cope with the interactive effect of multiple stressors, support groups such as "Grandparents Raising Grandchildren" are being organized across the country. These groups allow grandparents an opportunity to discuss immediate concerns and involve community professionals in the problem solving process. Many community professionals volunteer to share their expertise on legal matters, child raising practices, health issues and decision making techniques.

Possibly the most important aspect of grandparenting support groups is the encouragement and camaraderie among participants. Members often develop strong emotional bonds as they share their joys and sorrows with one another. As one grandmother said, "Not only have I learned a great deal about my grandchild and myself but I finally realize I'm going to make it."

CONCLUSIONS

This study points to the need for an increase in awareness among professionals about the unique problems that grandparents encounter when raising their grandchildren. The scope and complexities involved are unfamiliar to most, yet touch professionals in many areas including the schools, health care and legal systems, and social service agencies. Awareness and education about the needs and rights of grandparents raising their grandchildren is imperative for professionals in these fields.

Education for the grandparents themselves is also essential. Grandparent support groups are a needed educational resource for grandparents raising their grandchildren. These support groups assist grandparents in coping with the bureaucracies and provide emotional support of others in similar situations.

Further qualitative research focusing on grandparenting role transitions and stressors is needed to understand the current trend of parents who are becoming parents to their grandchildren. Future research studying grandparents who are raising their grandchildren should consider investigating ethnic and cultural diversity, and any coping mechanisms employed to reduce stress.

REFERENCES

Abrecht, R. (1954). The parental responsibilities of grandparents. *Marriage and Family Living, 16,* 201-204.

Apple, D. (1956). The social structure of grandparenthood. *American Anthropologist, 58,* 656-663.

Barranti, C. R. (1985). The grandparent/grandchild relationship: Family resource in an era of voluntary bonds. *Family Relations. 34,* 343-351.

Bengston, V. & Robertson, J. (1985). *Grandparenthood.* Beverly Hills, California: Sage Publications.

Brubaker, T. H. (1990). Families in later life: A burgeoning research area. *Journal of Marriage and the Family, 52,* 959-981.

Burr, W. R. (1972). Role transitions: A reformulation of theory. *Journal of Marriage and the Family, 34,* 407-416.

Burr, W. R., Leigh, G. K., Day, R., & Constantine, J. (1979). Symbolic interaction and the family. In W. Burr, R. Hill, F. Nye, & I. Reiss (Eds.). *Contemporary theories about the family* (pp. 42-111). New York: Free Press.

Cherlin, A. & Furstenberg, F. (1986). *The new American grandparent.* NY: Basic Books, Inc.

Cottrell, L. S. (1942). The adjustment of the individual to his age and sex roles. *American Sociological Review, 7,* 617-620.

Creighton, L. (1991, December). Silent saviors. *U.S. News and World Report,* pp. 80-89.

Dychtwald, K. & Flower, I. (1989). *Age wave.* Los Angeles, CA: Jeremy P. Tarcher, Inc.

Jendrick, M. (1993). Grandparents who parent their grandchildren: Effects of lifestyle. *Journal of Marriage and the Family, 55*(3), 609-621.

Jones, F. C. (1973). The lofty role of the Black grandmother. *Crises, 80,* 19-21.

Kennedy, J. F. & Keeney, V. T. (1988). The extended family revisited: Grandparents rearing grandchildren. *Child Psychiatry and Human Development, 19,* 26-34.

Merton, R. K. (1968). *Spiritual theory and social structure.* New York: Free Press.

Minkler, M. & Roe, K. (1993). *Grandmothers as caregivers.* Newbury Park CA: Sage.

Neugarten, B. & Weinstein, K. (1964). The changing American grandparent. *Journal of Marriage and the Family, 26*(2), 119-204.

Pearlin, L. (1983). Role strains and personal stress. In H. B. Kaplan (Ed.). *Psychosocial stress: Trends in theory and research* (pp. 3-32). New York: Academic Press.

Purnell, M. & Bagby, B. (1993). Grandparent rights: Implications for family specialists. *Family Relations, 42*(2), 173-178.

Rosenwaike, I. & Dolinsky, A. (1987). The changing demographic determinants of the growth of the extreme aged. *The Gerontologist, 27* (3), 275-280.

Sarbin, T. & Allen, V. (1968). Role theory. In G. Lindzey & E. Aronson (Eds.). *The handbook of social psychology: Vol. I* (pp. 488-567). Reading, MA: Addison-Wesley.

Wagner, E., Weber, J. & Cooper, K. (1995). Grandparents' visitation rights: Who decides? *Family Perspective, 29* (2), 153-162.

An Innovative
School-Based Intergenerational Model
to Serve Grandparent Caregivers

Roy Grant
S. Gail Gordon, MSE, CSW
Sue T. Cohen, MS

SUMMARY. There has been an enormous increase in foster care placements, especially with grandparents and other extended family members, since 1985. This is primarily attributable to problems associated with parental drug use, principally of crack cocaine. Drug related problems that lead to kinship foster placement include prenatal drug exposure, child maltreatment, incarceration, and early death by violence or AIDS or other illness. Grandparents caring for their children's children have a variety of social, mental health, and medical needs because of this stressful role. Following a literature review, a comprehensive social service and medical program developed through the partnership of a large urban teaching hospital, a foundation involved in funding programs for older adults, and an inner city school district is described. *[Article copies available for a fee from The Haworth Document Delivery Service: 1-800-342-9678. E-mail address: getinfo@haworth.com]*

Roy Grant is Associate Director of School and Community Programs for the Department of Pediatrics, Mount Sinai Medical Center in New York City. S. Gail Gordon is Director of Early Childhood Services at Little Sisters of the Assumption Family Health Services, where she works with high risk families and their children. Sue T. Cohen is Program Coordinator for the Department of Community Relations at Mount Sinai Medical Center.

[Haworth co-indexing entry note]: "An Innovative School-Based Intergenerational Model to Serve Grandparent Caregivers." Grant, Roy, S. Gail Gordon, and Sue T. Cohen. Co-published simultaneously in the *Journal of Gerontological Social Work* (The Haworth Press, Inc.) Vol. 28, No. 1/2, 1997, pp. 47-61; and: *Intergenerational Approaches in Aging: Implications for Education, Policy and Practice* (ed: Kevin Brabazon, and Robert Disch) The Haworth Press, Inc., 1997, pp. 47-61. Single or multiple copies of this article are available for a fee from The Haworth Document Delivery Service [1-800-342-9678, 9:00 a.m. - 5:00 p.m. (EST). E-mail address: getinfo@haworth.com].

47

BACKGROUND

There has been an enormous increase in the number of children placed in foster care since 1985. According to the 1990 census, there are more than 400,000 children living in foster homes. This was expected to increase to 500,000 by 1995. New York City is home to about 3% of the nation's children but accounts for more than 10% of children in foster care. Between 1987 and 1991, foster care placements in New York City nearly doubled, from 25,700 to just under 51,000 (Citizens' Committee for Children, 1993).

There has been an even greater increase in kinship foster placement, typically in households headed by the maternal grandmother. In April 1985, 151 children were placed through the City's Child Welfare Administration (CWA) in kinship homes. In 1988 there were 3,400 children. By June 1989 the number had grown to 14,000. In October 1989 *The New York Times* reported that there were 19,000 children formally placed in kinship foster care by CWA, a number greater than the entire 1987 New York City foster care population. The most recent figure available is for 1992, 22,000 children in kinship foster care (Citizens' Committee for Children, 1993; Thornton, 1991).

The full magnitude of the phenomenon of grandparents caring for their children's children is clarified when a distinction is made between formal and informal placement. While the 1990 census revealed fewer than a half million children in any kind of foster care, the Census Bureau reported that in 1991 3.3 million children were living in households headed by grandparents. In half of these homes, the biological mother was present, in 17% of homes both parents were present, in 5% only the father was present, and in 28% (924,000) of homes the grandparent(s) cared for the child in the absence of any biological parent (Jendrek, 1994).

There is general agreement that a principal reason for the growth of foster care since 1985 is the increased use of the street drug crack cocaine. Many of the other factors considered are also related at least in part to parental substance abuse. These include teen parenting, divorce, economic pressures, child maltreatment, parental illness and death (Strom and Strom, 1993), AIDS (Minkler, Driver, Roe, & Bedeian, 1993), poverty, and homelessness (Kelley, 1993). Many children come into the care of their grandparents because of the increasing number of women/mothers who are incarcerated, now estimated at 90,000. Two-thirds have children under 18 years of age, more than half of whom (approximately 53%) stay with their grandparents (Dressel and Barnhill, 1994).

There are several reasons why kinship foster placement has been so heavily used to meet the increasing demand for foster homes. There are policy requirements in many municipalities to place children entering foster care with blood relatives if possible (Kelley, 1993). Placement with relatives is often considered to be less disruptive or traumatic to the child, and ties with the biological parents are maintained (Dubowitz and Sawyer, 1994). A systematic Baltimore study of the incidence of maltreatment of children in foster care (N = 296) revealed that the risk is lowest in kinship households (Zuravin, Benedict, & Somerfield, 1993). A 1991 study of permanency planning for children in foster care revealed that adoption is least likely in kinship homes, because there already is a familial relationship. This makes kinship placement least desirable if the long-term goal is adoption. If, however, placement is short-term with the goal of reuniting child and biological mother, kinship households are most appropriate (Thornton, 1991).

Kinship care may be financially advantageous to the municipality. In New York City, until a lawsuit forced equality in the stipend for kinship and non-related foster parents, placements with relatives were often kept informal. Informal placements did not entitle the kinship caregiver to the foster care stipend, only to the much lower monthly Public Assistance grant in the child's name. When the lawsuit reduced municipal financial incentives, it may also have provided an additional incentive for relatives to care for children in their extended family (Thornton, 1991).

Demographically, the statistics reveal a trend towards kinship care occurring primarily in the African-American community. According to 1990 census data, more than 12% of African-American children live with grandparents, compared with 5.86 among Hispanic and 3.6% among white children. This has been related to the traditional role of extended family members in African-American culture (Minkler, Roe, & Robertson-Beckley, 1994); however, another factor may be relevant.

A major reason for the rate of increase in foster placement since 1985 is identified prenatal drug exposure. In New York City and elsewhere, babies born with positive drug toxicology were automatically discharged from the hospital to a foster preferably kinship home. (This City policy was changed subsequently, and a full CWA investigation indicating child maltreatment is now required before the baby may be removed from the custody of the biological mother.) An objective review of incidence and reporting trends revealed that while crack use during pregnancy was essentially similar for low-income African American women using public sector medical services and middle-income white women using private medical care, low-income African American women were ten times more likely to be identified and have their babies tested for drug exposure (Chasnoff, Landress, & Barrett, 1990). With increased identification of prenatal drug exposure comes increased out of home placement, including kinship households.

STRESSORS AFFECTING GRANDPARENT CAREGIVERS

The caregiving role of grandparents has been discussed along a continuum from "day care grandparents" who care for children while biological parents work (a role which is far more involved than being a "babysitter") to "custodial grandparents" who have a legal relationship as caregiver. An intermediate role is the "living with grandparent" who may or may not have a biological parent present in the household.[1] In a study of 114 grandparent caregivers, parental substance abuse and/or emotional problems were the most frequent factors associated with the grandparent assuming a custodial relationship to the child. More than half of the custodial grandparents assumed the role in part to keep the child out of a foster boarding home, or to protect the child's physical safety. The caregiving role is therefore assumed under duress, which is almost inevitably a source of stress. Some grandparents minimized their own health problems to appear more ready to assume care of the child.

The intermediate role of informal but primary caregiver may be more stressful for the grandparent, because of a limited ability to make essential decisions and because there are no legal safeguards to the relationship if the biological parent returns (Jendrek, 1994).

A 1993 study (N = 41) of stressors affecting grandparent caregivers found a higher level of financial strain than they anticipated. Social isolation because of their age relative to parents of same aged children (and the impact of child rearing on relationships with their peers) was also very stressful. The caregiving responsibilities negatively affected relationships with their own children, the grandchildren's biological parents. The grandparents often feel resentment and anger. A major stressor is anxiety about the child's future if the grandparent dies. Because of the prior life experiences of the grandchildren, grandparents are frequently very concerned about the children's psychological well being (Kelley, 1993).

Two studies done between 1988 and 1990 of African-American grandparent caregivers found significant stressors include fears of physical safety because of neighborhood drug activity, economic problems caused by their drug addicted child (biological parent to the grandchild), and the need to compromise personal goals (e.g., leaving a job, no time for recreation) to meet child care responsibilities. Again, an additional source of stress was special care needs of the grandchild (Burton, 1992). This is an especially significant factor, because many of the specific reasons for kinship placement are likely to negatively impact upon the emotional and developmental status of the child. Except if the child has been raised by the grandparent from infancy (most likely if the placement was made because of positive drug toxicology), the child has experienced early instability of care including loss (by death or abandonment), abuse and neglect, inconsistent caregiving and physical environment (substance abusing parent, homelessness), and other possible consequences associated with poverty (poor nutrition, no primary pediatric care). Sometimes the impact of child care responsibilities on the grandparent includes compromised physical and/or mental health. In one study 86% of grandparents reported increased anxiety and depression, 61% increased use of tobacco, 36% increased use of alcohol, 35% increased health problems including exacerbation of arthritis and diabetes, 8% reported a recent slight stroke, and 5% a recent mild heart attack (Burton, 1992).

DEVELOPING AND IMPLEMENTING A COMPREHENSIVE SERVICE PROGRAM

These studies, corroborated by our field experience, reveal that the large and growing population of grandparents caring for their children's children have a wide range of service needs. These include social service and mental health interventions for isolation, anxiety, and depression, and to help with intrafamilial conflict; concrete assistance to alleviate financial problems and clarify legal status; special developmental and mental health services for the children; and assistance meeting the parenting and special needs of the children. The value of social support networks has been emphasized. For example, their benefits for grandparents raising grandchildren who were prenatally drug exposed have been described (Minkler, Roe, & Robertson, 1994). While the need is documented in the literature, there are no reports of programs to meet the health needs of grandparent caregivers. The primary service population described is African-American families; little has been written about Hispanic grandparent caregivers.

In response to these issues, in 1993 a partnership among a large urban teaching hospital (The Mount Sinai Medical Center in New York City), a foundation involved in innovative programs for older adults including grandparent caregivers (the Brookdale Foundation), and a school district serving a predominantly Hispanic inner city population (Manhattan Community School District Four–East Harlem), joined together to plan and implement a model program for grandparents caring for their children's children.

The Mount Sinai Medical Center operates a School Health Program which includes four licensed pediatric clinics located within East Harlem elementary schools. Each school has a poverty index (families with income at or below poverty) between 93% and 100%. Medical care includes comprehensive physical examinations, acute care and follow-up, immunizations, and walk-in triage and care. Children served are primarily between the ages of four and twelve years. Intensive social services for families are included, as are mental health and child development services. More than 2,000 children and families receive care each year. During the 1994-95 school year, 10,500 walk-in visits were seen at the four sites.

The mental health and social service component of the program consistently receives referrals based on serious school problems evidenced by hyperactivity, inattention, behavioral problems, depression, and academic failure. Through our work with these children, we found that more than three-fourths experience significant social and family problems. An initial review of 64 referrals received during the 1992-93 school year revealed that 29% of referred children were not living with a biological parent. Of these children, 80% were living with grandparents or other extended family members (the others in foster boarding homes). During the 1993-94 school year, with a more formal review procedure, we found that 32% of 128 referred children were living in households without a biological parent. Again, four out of five were in kinship households. More than one of five children referred for school problems had experienced the death of a parent and/or sibling within the past twelve months.

These field experiences are consistent with the results of the first systematic study (N = 275) of the school problems of children in kinship care. Based on teacher ratings, nearly half (47%) had poor attention and concentration, and more than half (53%) had poor work study habits. Behavior problems including hyperactivity, demand for attention, and over-aggressiveness were prominent. Children whose kin caregiver was relatively young (<35 years) did better in school than those with older caregivers (Dubowitz and Sawyer, 1994).

Based on experience delivering school-based medical services, the Mount Sinai Pediatric School Health Program was ready to begin a program for kinship families, with a potential initial service population already identified. Staffing was enhanced with a full-time social worker/ health educator to work with the grandparent caregivers in a variety of roles, a half-time bilingual medical assistant, and later a part-time mid-level medical provider for these adults. Program start-up could have been immediate upon receipt of funding. However, gradual, phased-in program development was done to fully engage the grandparents in the program and include them as decision makers. The subsequent strong commitment to and utilization of the program, with minimal resistance and noncompliance, is attributed to this start-up strategy.

The program began in May 1994 with an intensive recruitment phase. Invitations were sent to about 100 kinship and foster parents. No one was turned away. All interested grandparents were visited in their homes during the summer of 1994 except those who specifically requested otherwise. Working grandparents were visited during lunch hours near their place of employment.

Each grandparent was asked about most pressing service needs and priorities. Virtually all initially requested assistance for the grandchild or grandchildren for whom they are caring. For example, when asked about medical needs, they frequently raised concern about limited access to pediatric care for the child because of problems affecting Medicaid receipt. This was as true of grandparents whom we later learned had very significant personal unmet health needs as it was of grandparents in good health.

School problems–understanding developmental needs, special education recommendations and referrals, and receiving support in dealing with teacher complaints–were an additional priority. In working with the grandparents to meet the children's needs, a bond was developed between grandparents and social worker. The social worker was able to demonstrate ability and value without intruding into the grandparents' personal affairs. This process of building trust, and of demonstrating program value, is frequently overlooked in developing a new program. Because inner city families are often involved with many different agencies and programs of varying quality, the importance of earning rather than expecting or demanding trust cannot be overemphasized.

Health and formal social services began with weekly group meetings in October 1994. By this time a core group of about two dozen grandmothers (and one grandfather) had been developed. Fifteen additional grandparents too ill to come to the program site received regular home visits.

Each weekly group initially had a health education focus to minimize resistance that a more formal counseling or therapy approach might engender. Topics were selected by the grandparents themselves. Because of the resources of the Medical Center, an expert in each field was enlisted (at no cost to the program) to lead presentations and answer questions. Topics included asthma, breast health, diabetes, stress management, high blood pressure, memory loss and the aging process, discipline, how to talk to your child about sex, female sexuality, diet and cholesterol, hypertension and stress, elder abuse, domestic violence, exercise and physical fitness adapted for age (including participation in a walking program), risk factors for child cardiac problems, first aid, and conflict resolution. Through these general presentations, the grandparents raised personal health concerns related to the topic. Out of these discussions came their request for assistance in meeting their own health care needs.

At this point a mid-level medical practitioner (a physician's assistant with clinical oversight provided through the Medical Center) was added to the program. One weekly medical session was initially provided, and home-based medical screenings were offered to grandparents unable to come to the school site. Had medical services been introduced earlier, they almost certainly would not have been well utilized. This gradual program development strategy increases utilization and compliance while reducing costs.

Following each session the social worker remained with interested grandparents for a more personal discussion. This generated a smaller core group of grandparents (eight) interested in weekly counseling sessions. Several grandparents unable to attend sessions drop off food for the group before traveling to work. A walk-in policy applied to the health education and counseling groups. At the request of the latter, an enrollment limited therapy group was started. This met a major program goal, providing regular weekly group therapy, through the grandparents' direct participation in planning.

DESCRIPTION OF FAMILIES SERVED

Based on an analysis of 23 grandparent headed households using school-based program services, the following profile applies: The age range of the grandparents is from 42 to 72, with the mean being 58 years. Thirteen (57%) of the grandparents are Hispanic, ten (43%) are African-American. This is roughly the same as the ethnic distribution of the school served.

Maternal drug use contributed to the change in custody to the grandparents in the majority of cases. For *six* families (26%), maternal drug use led to neglect and eventually abandonment of the child. In *three* families (13%), custody changed when the mother was incarcerated on drug-related charges. In *one* family (4%) custody changed when the mother entered a drug rehabilitation program. Custody changed in *one* family (4%) when CWA removed two children because the newborn tested positive for pre-natal cocaine exposure. (The older child had also been prenatally drug exposed.) In *seven* families (30%), the mother abandoned the child for other reasons: one was left in Puerto Rico with the maternal grandmother after a visit; one child was abandoned by the father when he met another woman; one family split up when the mother became homeless and left the children with the grandmother rather than bring them into the shelter system. In *three* families (13%), the mother died of AIDS. One mother was an intravenous drug abuser, the other two contracted AIDS through heterosexual contact with an intravenous drug abuser.

Two (9%) are extended families. In one, the maternal grandmother is caring for the child by day while the mother works. In the other, the grandmother is the primary caregiver because circumstances including military service have led the parents to temporarily relocate out of state.

A total of *three* (13%) of the mothers were young teenagers when their first child was born. *Two* of the grandmothers (9%) are caring for children born to two of their own daughters.

HEALTH CARE NEEDS OF THE GRANDPARENT CAREGIVERS

A comprehensive review of the health care needs of the grandparents using the program is ongoing. The following is based on a preliminary analysis of questionnaires completed by 23 grandmothers regularly using school-based program services:

SOURCE OF HEALTH INSURANCE:[2]

Medicare and/or Medicaid	19 (83%)
Private	4 (17%)

SOURCE OF PRIMARY MEDICAL CARE:

Hospital	10 (43%)
Private	5 (22%)
Community clinic	1 (04%)
None	7 (30%)

DATES OF LAST MEDICAL CONTACT (INCLUDES EMERGENCY CARE):

Within past six months	8 (35%)
Six months to one year ago	6 (26%)
One to two years ago	4 (17%)
Three to five years ago	1 (04%)
More than five years ago	4 (17%)

CHRONIC MEDICAL PROBLEMS:

Vision problems	15 (65%)
Heart problems/chest pains	11 (48%)
Arthritis	10 (43%)
Severe/recurrent pains	10 (43%)
Asthma	8 (35%)

High blood pressure	8 (35%)
Dental problems	7 (30%)
Diabetes	5 (22%)
Digestive problems	5 (22%)
Urinary infections	5 (22%)
Gynecological problems	5 (22%)
Thyroid problems	4 (17%)
Ulcers	3 (13%)
Anemia	3 (13%)
Cancer	1 (04%)

UTILIZATION OF MEDICAL SERVICES

Our review of these questionnaires indicates no relationship among health status, insurance status, and utilization of medical services. For example, one grandmother with Empire Blue Cross/Blue Shield insurance was not engaged in medical care and does not have a primary physician. Another grandmother, age 42, has eight grandchildren, two daughters, and one step-daughter in her household. She has a diagnosed cardiac condition, asthma, and arthritis, reports a medical visit for a "heart problem" within the past six months, but does not have a primary physician.

Several discussions were held to learn from the grandparents why their utilization of community-based medical care is so low, in many cases despite diagnosed chronic medical conditions of considerable severity including diabetes, high blood pressure requiring medication (which long since lapsed), and asthma.[3] There was unanimous agreement among the grandparents that the primary reason for non-utilization is the feeling that medical providers do not respect them. This involves long waits to be seen after being on time for appointments, lengthy delays scheduling follow-up appointments, the feeling that doctors do not listen to them or try to make themselves understood, and that doctors seem in too much of a rush to be thorough. The scenario presented repeatedly was waiting months for an appointment, being on time, being kept waiting several hours, seeing the doctor for less than fifteen minutes, not feeling that the medical problems were taken care of, and not feeling that there was an avenue to complain or otherwise improve the medical relationship. This impression was presented for hospital-based clinics as well as physicians in private practice.

Even when a primary physician was named by the grandparent, there often was no ongoing preventive care or medical management. Some of the grandparents had previously received prescriptions for high blood pressure, asthma, and diabetes but no longer kept medical appointments or took the prescribed medications. One diabetic grandmother had not been to the doctor for a decade. She was in crisis when we screened her medically, and our intervention was potentially life saving.

The unresponsiveness of the medical care system to the needs of these older women is consistent with the conclusions of a recent round table discussion including several gerontologists and representatives of the Commonwealth Fund and the National Institutes of Health (Butler, Collins, Meier, Muller & Pinn, 1995). A gender gap in medical care was discussed in terms of lack of respect for the older female patient, greater out of pocket expenses for chronic conditions affecting women more than men (e.g., osteoporosis compared to prostate problems), gender bias in medical education, delayed diagnosis and referral of women with cardiovascular disease compared to men, and inadequate preventive care. Many of these problems are related to the functioning of the Medicare system and therefore have public policy implications.

THE IMPACT OF PROVIDING
SCHOOL-BASED MEDICAL CARE

Beginning February 1995 (seven months after program start-up), one three-hour session per week was provided by a physician's assistant at the elementary school clinic site. Services include physical examinations, including pelvic examinations, screening, prevention and medical management, acute care, and prescriptions. Patient education is provided to encourage better utilization of available community health resources and better understanding of medications and other interventions. When a primary physician is involved, the physician's assistant exchanges information with consent to ensure continuity of care. There was an initial sense of amazement that the school-based physician's assistant saw the grandparents promptly (less than one week between scheduling and appointment; virtually no waiting time the day of the appointment). The most frequent comment in response to program physician's assistant has been, "He really listens to me" and "He really is interested in helping me."

During these first six months of availability of school-based medical care, this service has emerged as a bridge back to medical services in the community, not a substitute for them. Many grandparents became reengaged with their former primary doctor because of a renewed trust in the medical service system generalized from their positive experiences in this school-based program. Use of hospital emergency rooms for acute care has diminished.

After a year of program operation, the knowledge that someone is available on a walk-in basis to help with social and medical problems has proven extremely important to many grandparents. This helps reduce stress and the feeling of isolation which exacerbates medical problems and may precipitate crises.

Most recently medical care has been extended, at the request of several grandparents, to medically unserved adult children of the grandparents (typically the child's aunts and uncles). The first adult screened by the physician's assistant was referred to Mount Sinai Hospital after a school-based screening, where she was diagnosed with Graves disease.

ADDITIONAL PROGRAM SERVICES

There are a variety of programs serving grandparent caregivers in Upper Manhattan. Each has a somewhat different focus and program capabilities. We have developed a network of these program providers, designed for sharing of information of common interest and of program resources. School-based medical care to grandparents who are primarily served in these other programs will be extended beginning the fall of 1995. A new pro bono legal services program for grandparents was presented. Within two months, seven grandparents in our program alone each had a lawyer working on guardianship issues and wills.

The scarcity of community-based mental health services for children led to short-term therapy being provided at the school site either by the school-based pediatric clinic social worker or the Grandparent Caregivers Program social worker, with formal clinical supervision. Pediatric neuro-developmental assessments are arranged through the Medical Center to help clarify children's special needs when school recommendations are in question. These services to the children are essential in building trust and reducing stress for the grandparents.

CASE VIGNETTES

Case One: E. Q. is a 43-year-old Hispanic woman. Her daughter, now 25, became a crack cocaine addict. Ms. Q. assumed care of her four grandchildren, now aged 6, 5, 4, and 3 years to keep them out of the foster care system. Each child was prenatally exposed to cocaine. Ms. Q. works full-time. Because the children are placed with Ms. Q. through Family Court, money is available for babysitting while she works.

The oldest child received preschool mental health services, was retained in kindergarten, and is now recommended for special education. He is immature, easily frustrated with delayed language, and physically very small for his age. The second oldest child has cerebral palsy, the third may have an attention deficit disorder, and the youngest has frequent temper tantrums. The program social worker helped get the younger children into day care, clarified and arranged special education services for the older children, advocated with the foster care agency, and regularly visits Ms. Q. near her job on her lunch hour for supportive counseling.

Case Two: L. C. is a 50-year-old Hispanic paternal grandmother caring for three grandchildren ages 7, 5, and 3. The children's parents never maintained independent housing. When they were evicted from the mother's apartment, Ms. C. took in the family. The 7 year old has muscular dystrophy as does his father. Ms. C. had been informally responsible for the children since infancy because of their biological mother's immaturity and unavailability to care for them, having been a victim of severe physical and sexual abuse when she was a child.

Ms. C. did not have legal standing as caregiver to the children, who were still in their mother's custody. Ms. C. could not make decisions for their medical care, and many important medical appointments were missed. Educational planning for the oldest child was disrupted because Ms. C. could not sign consent and the biological mother did not keep any appointments.

With intensive counseling and outreach to both mother and grandmother, the social worker was able to facilitate transfer of custody to the grandmother through Family Court. This required walking the family through the process and staying in court with them several full days until the matter was resolved. Through advocacy, the oldest child is now receiving special education services in a barrier free school. Ms. C. has requested and receives counseling for herself on a weekly basis, advocacy with Public Assistance, and interventions for her adult sons.

Ms. C. has not been to a doctor in ten years. Only after the needs of the children were met did she focus on her own health care. Ms. C. is a carrier for muscular dystrophy and has neuromuscular problems which make it difficult for her to walk. She has serious asthma which has been without adequate medical management or monitoring.

Case Three: E. J. is a 67-year-old African-American woman whose husband died more than 20 years ago. She has lived in East Harlem her whole life and raised five daughters, each of whom has had steady employment and several of whom graduated college. During the 1980s one daughter with two children became addicted to crack cocaine. Ms. J. assumed responsibility for the youngest child while the paternal grandmother cares for the older child. This daughter of Ms. J's died recently of an AIDS related cancer. Ms. J. is obese and gets virtually no exercise. She has arthritis, an untreated thyroid condition, glaucoma, and is easily fatigued. Ms. J. reports that caring for her grandson is extremely tiring. Primary medical care is provided by a private doctor in the community. She has requested and receives bereavement counseling for her grandson, who is in special education for learning disability, and for herself.

Ms. J. makes excellent use of medical services provided in this program. Following a workshop on breast health, Ms. J. received through the program her first mammogram in many years.

AUTHOR NOTE

Roy Grant recently organized and leads a network of school health providers developing a multi-site outcome strategy focusing on children with asthma. His study of the impact of Medicaid managed care on school health financing will soon appear in Volume 14 of *Research in the Sociology of Health Care.*

NOTES

1. In our field experience, the "custodial" role is that of a formal kinship foster parent. The "living with" role is that of an informal kinship parent who is primary caregiver. Consistent with Jendrek, we find that most grandparents who take legal action for custody do so after several years as informal primary caregiver.

2. Uninsured grandparents were assisted, receiving Medicaid enrollment in the program–so by the time the questionnaires were completed all had some form of insurance.

3. There is a literature discussing problems of access to medical care for low-income individuals which emphasizes geographic, economic, and cultural/language barriers. In East Harlem, medical care is available at a choice of hospitals, community clinics, and private practitioners within five blocks or less from the home of each participating grandparent. As noted, all had insurance or were eligible for Medicaid. Each facility has Spanish language capability at least by translation. Therefore other factors account for the limited utilization of available medical services. Unfortunately there is virtually no literature exploring utilization from the standpoint of patient behavior and perceptions of the medical care system.

REFERENCES

Burton, Linda M. (1992). Black grandparents rearing children of drug-addicted parents: Stressors, outcomes, and social service needs. *Gerontologist*, 32(6), 744-751.

Butler, R.N., Collins, K.S., Meier, D.E., Muller, C.F., & Pinn, V.W. (1995). Older women's health: 'taking the pulse' reveals gender gap in medical care, part one. *Geriatrics*, 50(5), 39-40, 43-46, 49.

Chasnoff, Ira, Landress, Harvey J., & Barrett, Mark E. (1990). The prevalence of illicit drug or alcohol use during pregnancy and discrepancies in mandatory reporting in Pinellas County, Florida. *The New England Journal of Medicine*, 332(17), 1202-1206.

Citizens' Committee for Children (1993). *Keeping Track of New York's Children: A Citizen's Committee for Children Status Report*. New York, New York.

Dressel, Paula L., & Barnhill, Sandra K. (1994). Reframing gerontological thought and practice: The case of grandmothers with daughters in prison. *Gerontologist*, 34(5) 685-691.

Dubowitz, Howard, & Sawyer, Richard J. (1994). School behavior of children in kinship care. *Child Abuse & Neglect*, 18(11), 899-911.

Jendrek, Magaret Platt (1994). Grandparents who parent their grandchildren: Circumstances and decisions. *Gerontologist*, 34(2), 206-216.

Kelly, Susan J. (1993). Caregiver stress in grandparents raising grandchildren. *IMAGE–Journal of Nursing Scholarship*, 25(4), 33-337.

Minkler, Meredith, Roe, Kathleen M., & Robertson-Beckley, Relda J. (1994). Raising grandchildren from crack-cocaine households: Effects on family and friendship ties of African-American women. *American Journal of Orthopsychiatry*, 64(1), 20-29.

Strom, Robert D., & Strom, Shirley K. (1993). Grandparents raising grandchildren: Goals and support groups. *Educational Gerontology*, 19(8), 705-715.

Thornton, Jesse L. (1991). Permanency planning for children in kinship foster homes. *Child Welfare*, 70(5), 593-601.

Zuranvin, Susan J., Benedict, Mary, & Somerfield, Mark. (1993). Child maltreatment in family foster care. *American Journal of Orthopsychiatry*, 63(4), 589-596.

Grandparent Caregivers:
Legal and Economic Issues

Margaret M. Flint, JD
Melinda Perez-Porter, JD

In 1995, there were 2.5 million grandparents caring for their grandchildren; 911,000 of those grandparents were the primary caregivers of their grandchildren. These numbers have and will continue to rise due to deaths from AIDS,[1] alcohol and substance abuse,[2] divorce, imprisonment, teenage pregnancies, abuse and neglect, unemployment and poverty. Grandparents must worry about the financial burdens of caring for their grandchildren at a time when they also have the physical and mental burdens associated with growing older.[3] As the number of grandparents caring for grandchildren continues to rise, grandparents will need to understand the financial and legal issues they inadvertently undertake when they assume the care of their grandchildren. Similarly, in order to be responsive to the needs of grandparent caregivers, it is imperative that those who work with them have an understanding of the myriad of issues grandparents confront when, out of love for their grandchildren, grandparents become their primary caregivers.

This article highlights the legal and financial issues confronted by grandparent caregivers. The authors are most familiar with the laws of New York State where they practice. Laws of other states are mentioned

---

Margaret M. Flint is Director of the Elderly Project, Volunteers of Legal Service, Inc., New York City. Melinda Perez-Porter is Director, Grandparent Caregiver Law Center, Brookdale Center on Aging of Hunter College.

[Haworth co-indexing entry note]: "Grandparent Caregivers: Legal and Economic Issues." Flint, Margaret M., and Melinda Perez-Porter. Co-published simultaneously in the *Journal of Gerontological Social Work* (The Haworth Press, Inc.) Vol. 28, No. 1/2, 1997, pp. 63-76; and: *Intergenerational Approaches in Aging: Implications for Education, Policy and Practice* (ed: Kevin Brabazon, and Robert Disch) The Haworth Press, Inc., 1997, pp. 63-76. Single or multiple copies of this article are available for a fee from The Haworth Document Delivery Service [1-800-342-9678, 9:00 a.m. - 5:00 p.m. (EST). E-mail address: getinfo@haworth.com].

for illustrative purposes. You should consult the laws of your state before advising clients.

TYPES OF CAREGIVING RELATIONSHIPS

Grandparents can assume the care of their grandchildren informally, as when the child is left in the grandparent's care for an indefinite period; or formally, through legal custody, guardianship, adoption or by becoming a foster parent. When assisting a grandparent caregiver, it is important to determine what, if any, authority the grandparent has obtained.

Informal Arrangements

A child may be living with a grandparent because she has been abandoned by her parents, or because the parent has entrusted the child to the grandparent. When neither parent is able or willing to care for a child, legal custody and/or guardianship may be obtained by another person or the State official charged with the protection of children. In the absence of a legal proceeding transferring legal custody or guardianship, the parents retain all parental rights. If one or both parents are not available to make decisions for the child, legally, there is a vacuum of authority.

Grandparents who are not guardians may experience problems obtaining medical care for their grandchildren. For example, New York State law specifically allows parents and children under 18 who are married to consent to their necessary medical care.[4] Other minors, however, need the specific consent of their parents or guardians.[5] In an emergency, hospitals will usually provide treatment to the child without the parents' consent. If informal arrangements for medical treatment cannot be made by the grandparent with the child's doctor, it will be necessary for the grandparent to obtain legal guardianship or custody.

Grandparent caregivers may have difficulty enrolling their grandchildren in school or accessing school records. The Education Laws of New York State permit anyone who is the "custodian" of a child to enroll the child in school.[6] Custodians include persons other than parents who are caring for a child whose parents are dead, ill or incarcerated or whose whereabouts are unknown.[7] Grandparents should contact their Board of Education to find out what documentation they need to enroll a child in school and participate in decisions about the child's education.

In some states, a parent may delegate certain responsibilities–such as the authority to consent to medical care, or to enroll a child in school–to another person, by signing a form detailing the responsibilities so delegated. In California, a parent may authorize a grandparent or other caregiver to enroll a child in school and authorize school-related medical care.[8] In Washington, D.C., a parent or legal guardian may authorize another person to consent to medical, surgical, dental, developmental screening, and/or mental health examinations or treatment.[9] In states where this practice is not authorized by statute (such as New York), a written statement from a parent giving a third person the power to take certain action on behalf of the child will often be effective. Even in the absence of a written document, a non-parent caregiver will often be able to obtain needed medical care or enroll the child in school by explaining the situation and documenting their relationship with the child.

Custody

An order of custody gives a person the legal right to physical possession of a child. Parents have a presumptive right to custody.[10] If parents cannot agree about custody, in most states, the court will award custody to one parent based on the child's best interests.[11] If a non-parent files for custody of a child and one of the child's parents objects, the non-parent will have to prove that the parent is unfit, not merely that it is in the child's best interest to live with the non-parent.[12]

A non-parent who obtains legal custody may make most day-to-day decisions about the care of the child but does not have control over a child's property and does not assume financial responsibility for the child.[13]

Guardianship

A court order of guardianship may be obtained if the child's parents are deceased, consent to the guardianship, or are not suitable guardians for the child.[14] A guardianship may be of the person of the child, the property of the child or both.[15] Thus, if a child owns property–because of a personal injury award or an inheritance, for example–only a guardian of the property of a child will have access to the child's funds.

Although a guardian may make all decisions concerning the child, including where the child will live, educational and medical decisions and religious upbringing, the parents' rights are not terminated.[16] The parents may be entitled to visitation and continue to be financially responsible for the support of the child.[17]

A guardian does not assume financial responsibility for the child. A grandparent who has been appointed the legal guardian of a grandchild may be able to have the grandchild's medical care covered by the grandparent's health insurance policy. It is important to check the policy. Not all insurance plans cover children other than biological and adopted children.

In some states, including New York, California, Connecticut, Florida, Illinois, Iowa, Maryland, Massachusetts, and New Jersey,[18] a guardian suffering from a terminal or progressive illness may designate a standby or springing guardian who will assume the care of the child when the guardian is no longer able to do so.

Foster Care

Children who are abused or neglected by their parents may be placed under the guardianship and custody of the State official charged with the protection of children.[19] Children who have been removed from their parents' home are usually placed in foster homes or placed with relatives.

In most states, a child's relatives may become foster parents.[20] In New York, for example, a child removed from her parents must be placed with a relative in preference to strangers.[21] The relative must be informed about the kinship foster care system and be given the opportunity to apply to become a kinship foster parent.[22] Some grandparents are not informed of the availability of these benefits. As a result, many grandparents are caring for grandchildren who were removed from their parents' homes without the benefit of kinship foster care payments.[23]

If the relative is approved as a kinship foster parent, the child is eligible for kinship foster care payments and Medicaid. Kinship Foster Care payments include payments to meet the food, clothing, shelter, daily supervision, school supplies, personal and special needs of a child. Since foster care payment rates are much higher than public assistance benefit levels, kinship foster care appears to be an attractive alternative for low-income grandparents. However, legal custody of the child remains with the official charged with the protection of children. Department of Social Services staff or staff from a foster care agency supervise the home. The grandparent, therefore, will not have the authority to consent to medical treatment, or make other decisions a guardian or custodian is empowered to make.[24]

Kinship foster care payments are not available to all grandparents. The child must have been removed from the home because of abuse or neglect[25] or must have been voluntarily placed in the care of an authorized agency by the parent or guardian.[26] Grandparents who have obtained custody or guardianship, have adopted their grandchildren, or are caring for their grandchildren informally are usually not eligible for kinship foster care payments.

In most states, foster care, including kinship foster care, is supposed to be a temporary measure while plans are made to find a permanent home for the child by reuniting the parent and the child or freeing the child for adoption.[27] While the practice in some states has been to continue kinship foster care placement for many years,[28] grandparents who become kinship foster parents need to understand that they may be expected to adopt their grandchild or risk having another adoptive family found.

Adoption

Adoption severs all of the rights and responsibilities of the biological parents and the adoptive parents become the child's legal parents.[29] The adoptive parent is able to make all decisions regarding the child's education, medical care, and religious upbringing. In most states, the adopted child will inherit from his adoptive parents, not from his biological parents.[30]

If the biological parents do not consent to the adoption, their rights must be terminated in a legal proceeding, by proving abandonment, permanent neglect or mental illness.[31] The biological parents do not usually have the right to visitation if their children have been adopted by someone else.[32]

Adoptive parents become financially responsible for their adopted children, although adoption subsidies may be available if the child has been in foster care and has special needs.[33] If a grandparent adopts a grandchild, the grandparent obtains all the parental rights and responsibilities of the natural parents. The grandparent's income will generally be counted by public benefit programs.[34]

ECONOMIC SUPPORT FOR GRANDPARENT CAREGIVERS

Grandparents caring for grandchildren are concerned about how to meet the financial needs of the children in their care. This burden becomes overwhelming if the grandparent has assumed the care of more than one grandchild. Some grandparents have to go back to work to help meet the additional needs of caring for their grandchildren; other grandparents have to leave their jobs because of lack of child care, while still others must look to public assistance programs to help meet their needs. Grandparents often need assistance identifying possible additional sources of income.

Temporary Assistance to Needy Families (TANF)

On August 22, 1996, the President signed the Personal Responsibility and Work Opportunity Reconciliation Act (PRA) of 1996. The legislation eliminated the federal entitlement program for poor children, the Aid to Families with Dependent Children (AFDC) program.[35] In its place, the Temporary Assistance to Needy Families (TANF) Program was created. The PRA provides block grants to the states to use to provide cash benefits to poor families with children. Under TANF, states have been given much more discretion to decide how to distribute benefits and benefits will vary from state to state and even, at state discretion, within states.[36] Unlike AFDC, TANF is not an entitlement—there is no guarantee that all poor children will be assisted. It is important for advocates to learn how TANF is being implemented in their own localities and bring the special needs of grandparent caregivers to the attention of local policy makers.

There are several aspects of TANF which will impact negatively on grandparent-headed households. There is a five-year limit per adult-headed household on the receipt of federal benefits.[37] After a family has exceeded the limit, it is up to the individual state to decide what assistance, if any, to provide. After the limit has been reached, assistance to the family *may* be provided in the form of vouchers, rather than cash. While children who previously received TANF benefits while part of their parent's household can receive the benefits when they become part of their grandparent's household, the grandparent and any children residing with her will be subject to the five-year time limit for any time the grandparent received public assistance as an adult.

The PRA also requires that, in order to qualify for TANF benefits, all adults receiving assistance must engage in work or job training no later than 24 months after receiving assistance.[38] States must impose sanctions on recipients who "refuse to engage in work" (such as reducing or limiting the benefits to the family).[39] States have flexibility in deciding good cause exemptions, if any, from the work requirements. States can also elect to require TANF recipients to engage in community service after two months of receiving assistance. Advocates should try to ensure that states use the flexibility given to them under the PRA to assure that grandparent caregivers who, because of their age or disability, cannot engage in work, are exempt from the work requirements.

The PRA provides that federal TANF funds cannot be used to provide assistance to a family that includes an adult who has received TANF assistance 60 months.[40] Grandchildren who are living with a grandparent or other relative (other than a parent or step-parent) can therefore receive TANF benefits as a child-only household, if the caretaker does not apply for assistance for herself.[41] Advocates should assist grandparent caregivers in weighing the benefits of receiving TANF benefits for themselves for a maximum of five years against the need for long-term support for their grandchildren.

Under the PRA, states have the option of deciding whether or not to provide TANF benefits to legal immigrants who have been present in the United States since before August 22, 1996, the date the PRA was passed. Most legal immigrants arriving after August 22, 1996, are subject to a five-year ban on all federal means-tested benefits, including TANF.[42] States may decide to provide state-funded benefits to these families during the five-year period. After the five-year period, states may decide to provide or deny TANF benefits to these families, or may require their sponsors to support them.

Food Stamps

Grandparents can also apply for food stamps for themselves and their grandchildren. A food stamp household is composed of all the people who purchase and prepare food together.[43] In addition, children who are unmarried, under the age of 18, and living under the "parental control" of an adult household member who is not the children's parent or stepparent must be considered part of the caregiver's household.[44] Grandparents and grandchildren are therefore considered one household for food stamps purposes and receive one food stamp grant.[45] This rule penalizes grandparent caregivers because the income and resources of both the grandparents and the grandchildren will determine the amount of food stamps, if any, the household will receive. Because the grandparents' incomes are considered, many grandparent caregiver households will receive little or no food stamps.

Grandparents who receive foster care payments for their grandchildren can elect to exclude the grandchild receiving the benefits from the food stamp household. If they do, the foster care payments will not be counted as household income.[46]

Grandparents who are denied food stamps benefits have the right to appeal that decision by requesting a fair hearing in front of an Administrative Law Judge.[47] A Fair Hearing to appeal a decision made on food stamps benefits must usually be requested within 90 days of the original decision.[48]

Beginning April 1, 1997, legal immigrants are not eligible for food stamps unless they have become naturalized citizens, worked a total of 40 quarters (10 years) and had Social Security taxes withheld from their wages,[49] or are honorably discharged veterans or members of the United States military on active duty and their spouses and unmarried dependent children. Legal immigrants who are refugees, asylees or whose deportation has been withheld are also eligible for food stamps for their first five years in the United States. While a caretaker may be a legal immigrant and not eligible for food stamps, grandparents of children born in the United States, and who are therefore United States citizens, can apply for food stamps on behalf of their grandchildren. Advocates of legal immigrants should refer them to legal services or immigration groups for information on eligibility and assistance.

Social Security Benefits

Grandparents and grandchildren may also be eligible for benefits from the Social Security Administration. Grandparents may be eligible for retirement benefits,[50] disability benefits[51] or survivor's benefits[52] if they (or their spouses) worked long enough to be covered by Social Security.

Grandchildren may be eligible for survivor's benefits if one of their parents has died, worked and paid Social Security taxes, or disability benefits if one of their parents is receiving disability benefits.[53]

Some grandchildren become eligible for Social Security benefits, based on their grandparents' earnings record, when their grandparents retire or die if they have lived with and been supported by their grandparents and if their parents are dead or disabled.[54]

Grandparents who are over 65 or disabled may be eligible for Supplemental Security Income (SSI) if they have low income and resources.[55] Children may also receive SSI if they are blind or disabled.[56]

As with food stamps, SSI benefits are only available to United States citizens and legal immigrants who are naturalized citizens, have worked 40 quarters (10 years) and had Social Security taxes withheld from their wages,[57] or are honorably discharged veterans or members of the United States military on active duty and their spouses and unmarried dependent children. Legal immigrants who are refugees, asylees or whose deportation has been withheld are also eligible for SSI for their first five years in the United States.

In some states, grandparents receiving SSI are penalized when they assume the care of their grandchildren. In New York, for example, grandparents caring for one or more grandchildren will receive a lower SSI amount than they would otherwise receive if they lived alone.

Grandparents can apply for Social Security benefits on behalf of their grandchildren and/or for themselves. Custody or guardianship is not required. Applications for Social Security benefits are available from the nearest Social Security Administration Office.[58] Grandparents may appeal any denial of benefits to the Social Security Administration.[59]

Medicaid

Medicaid provides comprehensive health care coverage for many low-income people. Grandparents and their grandchildren who have low income and resources may qualify for Medicaid.[60] Children in foster care and children who receive adoption subsidies also receive Medicaid.[61] Grandparents' incomes need not be considered if the children only are applying for Medicaid.[62] Grandparents do not need to have custody or guardianship in order to apply for Medicaid for the grandchild.

Under the PRA, states may provide Medicaid to all TANF households, or may set up separate eligibility criteria for Medicaid. States also have the option to provide Medicaid to legal immigrants present in the United States before August 22, 1996. Medicaid will be denied for at least five years to legal immigrants arriving after August 22, 1996.[63] States have the option of providing or denying Medicaid to these immigrants after five years, or deeming their sponsors' income to them.

Some states may provide medical coverage at no or low cost for children who do not qualify for Medicaid.[64] The income of the grandparent is usually not counted when determining eligibility under these state programs.

HOUSING CONCERNS

Housing problems may arise for grandparents who assume the care of their grandchildren. The grandparents' homes may not be large enough to accommodate the grandchildren and it may be difficult to find larger, affordable housing. If grandparents live in public housing, housing authorities usually require notification when someone is added to the household.[65] Leases in private housing may restrict the number of occupants. Generally, discrimination against families with children is prohibited.[66] However, grandparents who live in housing built exclusively for seniors will not be able to remain if their grandchildren move in with them.[67]

ASSISTANCE FOR GRANDPARENT CAREGIVERS

The legal issues confronted by grandparent caregivers are complex and may overwhelm grandparents who have assumed the care of their grandchildren without immediate concern or thought to the legal and financial consequences of caring for them. Responsive legal services and accurate information are needed to assist grandparents with parenting for the second time. Social workers assisting grandparent caregivers should familiarize themselves with the issues confronted by grandparents caring for grandchildren and with programs that may be available to assist them. Such assistance includes grandparent support groups which provide grandparents with an arena where they can share concerns, entitlement information, socialize and receive validation of their feelings.[68] Agencies such as the American Association of Retired Persons' (AARP's) Grandparent Information Center can provide information on support groups, research/statistics and other information on issues affecting grandparent caregivers.[69] In some states, grandparent manuals have been written to provide information on benefits and legal issues to grandparent caregivers.[70] Innovative attempts to address the needs of grandparent caregivers are needed.[71] Responsive legal services and accurate information can assist grandparents with parenting for the second time. A collaboration of the social services, aging, legal, child welfare, health and mental health communities is imperative.[72] Such collaboration will ensure the sharing of information and the provision of services which will best meet the needs of grandparent headed households.

Working together, advocates can provide legal and benefit information, respite, support groups and other services which will alleviate some of the isolation, anxiety and feelings of helplessness that some of these courageous grandparents may face. Grandparents will then be able to concentrate on important things, like enjoying their lives and the grandchildren they love.

AUTHOR NOTE

An elder law attorney and former law school clinical teacher, Margaret M. Flint has worked as a staff attorney with the Institute on Law and Rights of the Older Adult of the Brookdale Center on Aging. Ms. Flint has extensive experience developing *pro bono* programs, training lawyers and social service agency staff on legal issues, and conducting legal information sessions for community residents.

The Grandparent Caregiver Law Center was established to address the legal and financial issues faced by grandparents who are the primary caregivers of their grandchildren through advocate training on legal and financial issues. Melinda Perez-Porter has written a series of booklets in English and Spanish for grandparent caregivers and has recently co-authored an article on state initiatives and kinship care for the special grandparent caregiver edition of the *Clearinghouse Review* (September 1996).

NOTES

1. Levine, C. & Stein, G. (1994). Orphans of the HIV Epidemic: Unmet Needs in Six U.S. Cities. New York: The Orphan Project.

2. Minkler, M. & Roe, K. (1993). Grandmothers as Caregivers: Raising Children in the Crack Cocaine Epidemic. Newbury Park, California: SAGE Publications, Inc.

3. Minkler, M. (1994). Grandparents as Parents: The American Experience. *Ageing International*, 21 (1): 24-28.

4. NY Public Health Law §2504.

5. *Id*. Compare Delaware Parents And Children §707 which permits a minor or a "person professing to be the temporary custodian" of a minor to consent to treatment of conditions which, if left untreated, are expected to threaten the health or life of the minor.

6. NY Education Law §3212.

7. *Id*.

8. CAL. FAMILY CODE §6550 (West 1996).

9. D.C. Code §16-4704 (West 1996).

10. *Stanley v. Illinois*, 405 U.S. 645 (1972).

11. *See, e.g.,* NY Domestic Relations Law §§ 70, 240; CA Family Code § 3040; AZ Marital and Family Relations § 25-332; Colorado Revised Statutes Annotated § 14-10-124. Only five states give preference for custody to the mother. *See Trends in Child Custody Awards: Has Removal of the Maternal Preference Made a Difference?* 28 Family Law Quarterly 247 (Summer 1994).

12. *See, e.g., Matter of Corey L. v. Martin L.*, 45 N.Y.2d 383, 408 N.Y.S.2d 439 (1978); *Bennett v. Jeffries*, 40 N.Y.2d 543, 387 N.Y.S.2d 821 (1979).

13. *See, e.g.,* OCGA § 15-11-43; CODE OF ALA. § 12-15-1 (17)(23); OHIO REV. CODE § 2151.01.

14. See, *e.g.,* NY Surrogates Court Procedures Act § 1704, CA Probate Code § 2251.

15. *See, e.g.,* NY Surrogates Court Procedures Act § 1707. In New York, the Family Court may also appoint a guardian of the person but not of the property of a minor. NY Family Court Act § 661.

16. *See,* MD. JUV. CT. ACT. § 3-820; NEW MEX. STAT. ANN. § 32-1-58.

17. *Id*.

18. SURR. CT. PROC. ACT § 1726 (McKinney Supp. 1996); CAL. PROB. CODE § 2105(f) (West Supp. 1996); CONN. GEN. STAT. ANN. § 45(a)-624 et seq. (West 1996); FLA. STAT. ANN. § 744.304 (West 1996); ILL. ANN. STAT. ch. 755, para. 5/11-5.3 (Smith-Hurd 1996); IOWA CODE ANN. § 633.560 et seq. (West 1992); MD. CODE ANN., EST. & TRUST § 13-901 et seq.; MASS GEN. LAWS ANN. ch. 201, § 2A (West Supp. 1996); N.J. STAT. ANN. § 3B:12-68 et seq. (West Supp. 1996).

19. *See, also,* Ca. Probate. L. § 2105, Fla. Stat. Ann. § 744.304, Conn. Gen. Stat. §§459-624g.

20. Relatives may not be arbitrarily excluded as foster parents. *Miller v. Youakim*, 440 U.S. 125 (1979). Some states require kinship foster parents to meet the

same requirements as non-relative foster parents. In some states, less strict rules apply to kinship foster parents. NY SOC. SER. L. § 384-B; 20 ILCS § 505/7(b); CA. WELF. & INST. CODE §§ 362.7, 368.8. Still other states allow kinship foster parents to choose between standard foster care and programs specifically designed for kinship foster parents. MD FAMILY LAW § 5-501. See also federal law on foster care payments: 42 U.S.C. § 670 et seq.

21. NY SOCIAL SERVICES LAW § 384-b.

22. NY FAMILY COURT ACT § 1017.

23. *Family Assets*, Report of the (NYC) Mayor's Commission for the Foster Care of Children 51 (1993).

24. NY SOCIAL SERVICES LAW § 381.

25. NY FAMILY COURT ACT § 1055.

26. NY SOCIAL SERVICES LAW § 384-a.

27. 42. U.S.C. § 671(a)(16).

28. Schwartz, M. (1993) *Reinventing Guardianship*, New York, Vera Institute of Justice 10.

29. *See, e.g.,* NJ STAT. ANN. § 9:3-50; GEN. LAWS OF RHODE ISLAND § 15-7-7.

30. *Id.*

31. NY DOMESTIC RELATIONS LAWS § 111; GEN. LAWS OF RHODE ISLAND § 15-7-17; NY DOMESTIC RELATIONS LAW § 117.

32. *See, e.g.,* NY DOMESTIC RELATIONS LAW § 117, MD FAMILY LAW § 5-308(b)(2).

33. SOCIAL SERVICES LAW § 450 *et seq.*; 42 U.S.C. § 673.

34. 45 C.F.R. § 206.10(a)(1)(vii)(A); 45 C.F.R. § 230.90; 7 U.S.C. § 202(i); 7 C.F.R. § 273.1(a)(2); 20 C.F.R. § 404.356; 20 C.F.R. § 416; 42 U.S.C. § 1369(a)(17); 42 C.F.R. § 435.602; 18 N.Y.C.R.R. § 360-1.4(b).

35. Pub. L. No. 104-193.

36. For an examination of the implementation issues faced by states, see: *Implementation of the Temporary Assistance for Needy Families Block Grant:An Overview*, November 1996, The Center on Social Welfare Policy and the Law.

37. States may impose a shorter time-limit, if they wish. The five-year time limit begins on the date a completed plan for implementing TANF is submitted by the State to the Department of Health and Human Services. States must submit a completed plan by July 1, 1997, but may do so sooner.

38. Social Security Act § 402(a)(1)(A)(ii) as amended by § 103(a) of Pub. L. No. 104-193.

39. Social Security Act § 407(e), as amended by § 103(a) of Pub. L. no. 104-193.

40. Social Security Act §§ 408(a)(1)(B); 408(a)(7), as amended by 103(a) of Pub. L. No. 104-193.

41. Some states may attempt to count the income of the non-applying caretaker when determining the eligibility of the child-only household. Advocates should work to ensure that only the income of the children are counted in child-only households.

42. Exempted from the five-year ban on federal means-tested benefits are refugees, asylees and those granted withholding of deportation, who are eligible for federal means-tested benefits for the first five years only. Honorably discharged veterans, active duty military, their spouses and unmarried dependents are also exempt from the five-year ban.

43. 7 U.S.C. § 2012(i); 7 C.F.R. § 273.1(a); 18 N.Y.C.R.R. § 387.1(w).

44. *Id.*

45. *Id.*

46. 7 C.F.R. § 273.1(c)(6); 18 N.Y.C.R.R. § 387.16(b).

47. 45 C.F.R. § 205.10; 18 N.Y.C.R.R. § 358-3.0 *et seq.*

48. 7 C.F.R. § 273.15; 18 N.Y.C.R.R. § 358-3.5(a)(2).

49. A legal immigrant can receive credit for quarters worked by himself and his spouse. Unmarried dependent minors can receive credit for quarters worked by their parents.

50. 20 C.F.R. § 404.358.

51. 20 C.F.R. § 404.10 *et seq.*

52. 20 C.F.R. § 404.350 *et seq.*

53. *Id.*

54. *See, i.e.,* NY SOCIAL SERVICES LAW § 209.

55. 42 U.S.C. § 1381 *et seq.*; 20 C.F.R. § 416 *et seq.*

56. 20 C.F.R. § 416.924; 20 C.F.R. § 404.155 *et seq.*Z

57. Legal immigrants may receive credit for quarters worked by himself and his spouse. Unmarried dependent minors receive credit for quarters worked by their parents.

58. 20 C.F.R. § 416.305.

59. 20 C.F.R. § 416.1400 *et seq.*

60. 42 U.S.C. § 1396(a)(10)(A)(i).

61. 42 U.S.C. § 435.115(e); § 435.119; § 435.403; 18 N.Y.C.R.R. § 360-3.3(c)(4).

62. 42 C.F.R. § 36.602

63. Exempted from the five-year ban on federal means-tested benefits are refugees, asylees, and those granted withholding of deportation, who are eligible for federal means-tested benefits for the first five years only. Honorably discharged veterans, active duty military, their spouses and unmarried dependent minors are also exempt from the five year ban.

64. In New York State, Child Health Plus provides medical coverage at no or low cost for children under age 15 who have low incomes and who have little or no medical insurance.

65. See, for example, 9C N.Y.C.R.R. § 1627-6.3.

66. 42 U.S.C. § 3604; NY Real Property Law § 236.

67. See, for example, NY Real Property Law § 236; Executive law § 296.

68. In New York City, the Department for the Aging's Grandparent Resource Center holds monthly meetings for grandparent support group facilitators for the purpose of sharing information and ideas on facilitating grandparent support groups. The New York City Department for the Aging's Grandparent Resource Center also provides trainings on starting support groups and has a telephone re-

ferral line for grandparents. For more information, contact the Director, Rolanda Pyle, at the New York City Department for the Aging, Grandparent Resource Center, 2 Lafayette Street, New York, New York 10007-1392.

69. American Association of Retired Persons (AARP) Grandparent Information Center, 601 E Street, NW, Washington, DC 20049; (202) 434-2296; Advocates with questions on economic and legal issues affecting grandparent caregivers in New York State can contact the Grandparent Caregiver Law Center, Brookdale Center on Aging of Hunter College, 425 East 25th Street, New York, NY 10010; (212) 481-4433.

70. Some of the states that have grandparent caregiver manuals or handbooks include: *Massachusetts*: A Resource Guide for Massachusetts Grandparents Raising their Grandchildren (Printed and distributed by the Massachusetts Executive Office of Elder Affairs, One Ashburn Place, Boston, Massachusetts 02108); *Pennsylvania*: Kids 'n' Kin: A Handbook for Relative Caregivers (Philadelphia Society for Services to Children, 415 S. 15th Street, Philadelphia, Pennsylvania 19146); *California*: Manual for Grandparent Relative Caregivers and their Advocates and Manual for Grandparents and Caregivers of Drug-exposed Infants and Children (both written by Legal Services for Prisoners with Children, 474 Valencia Street, Suite 230, San Francisco California 94103); *New York*: Several booklets addressing issues of concern to grandparent caregivers will be available from the Grandparent Caregiver Law Center, The Brookdale Center on Aging of Hunter College, 425 East 25th Street, New York, NY 10025.

71. For example, in New York City, Volunteers of Legal Services received a grant from the Brookdale Foundation group to recruit, train and supervise volunteer attorneys who assist grandparent caregivers. The Project works collaboratively with social service agency staff who are working with grandparent caregivers. Project volunteers meet with individual grandparents and counsel them about their options. They are available to represent grandparents who wish to become guardians of their grandchildren or legal custodians in uncontested proceedings.

72. An example of such collaboration is the New York City KinCare Task Force. It was established in 1992. The Task Force addresses issues confronted by grandparents and other relative caregivers and is composed of members of the aging, child welfare, social services and legal communities. For more information on the Task Force and its activities, contact Evelyn J. Blanck, Jewish Board of Families and Children's Services, Inc., 120 West 57th Street, New York, NY 10019-3371 or Anna H. Zimmer, The Brookdale Center on Aging of Hunter College, 425 East 25th Street, New York, NY 10010.

SECTION III:
INTERGENERATIONAL EDUCATION

Intergenerational education is a broad term that includes ideas and practices that range from elders and youth taking a college course together to intensive efforts by intergenerational educators to implement formal curricula in schools and programs. It includes informing or training people about relationships between generations, the social concepts that underpin these relationships, and the programs that are based on them. It also develops awareness and understanding in one generation about the characteristics, problems and values of another generation.

Few accredited programs have been established to date, and the first graduate program offering a master's degree in intergenerational studies (at Wheelock College in Massachusetts) is currently closed due to insufficient enrollment. A certificate program established by Generations Together at the University of Pittsburgh trains students about the design, methodology, implementation and evaluation of intergenerational programs, and is focused on the needs of working practitioners rather than full-time students.

The papers in this section represent several views of intergenerational education. The first (Manheimer) describes the process of young and old learning together and from one another. It is the type of learning that takes place in multigenerational classrooms as well as intergenerational programs of all kinds.

In the second, Pine details an intergenerational college course that combines classroom education with "service learning," an approach to education that has become more popular since the establishment of the Corporation for National Service.

The final paper (Friedman) addresses an area of education that deals with the misconceptions the generations hold about one another and the impact of these views on cross-generational behavior. The author argues for the integration of "aging" education into existing curricula throughout the educational system.

Generations Learning Together

Ronald J. Manheimer, PhD

Intergenerational programming has been defined as "activities or programs that increase cooperation, interaction or exchange between any two generations." These programs promote "sharing of skills, knowledge or experience between old and young" (Ventura-Merkel and Lidoff, 1983). While all intergenerational programs have the potential to foster learning across generations, some programs make educational objectives central to their mission. The growing popularity of innovative intergenerational education programs could make them an important and enduring component of lifelong learning in the future.

Intergenerational learning could also play an important role in the evolution of older adult education programs which have expanded rapidly since the mid-1980s (Manheimer, Snodgrass and Moskow-McKenzie, 1995). Intergenerational shared learning opportunities may be a logical next step for some of the hundreds of age-segregated, older adult education programs established in colleges and universities, churches and synagogues, senior centers, public libraries, and department stores.

The educational aspects of intergenerational programs take many forms. This essay is primarily concerned with programs and institutions that identify specific learning goals and aim to enhance educational ventures through multigenerational perspectives.

Ronald J. Manheimer is Director of the North Carolina Center for Creative Retirement, University of North Carolina, Ashville. He will soon publish a book on philosophy and the life course.

[Haworth co-indexing entry note]: "Generations Learning Together." Manheimer, Ronald J. Co-published simultaneously in the *Journal of Gerontological Social Work* (The Haworth Press, Inc.) Vol. 28, No. 1/2, 1997, pp. 79-91; and: *Intergenerational Approaches in Aging: Implications for Education, Policy and Practice* (ed: Kevin Brabazon, and Robert Disch) The Haworth Press, Inc., 1997, pp. 79-91. Single or multiple copies of this article are available for a fee from The Haworth Document Delivery Service [1-800-342-9678, 9:00 a.m. - 5:00 p.m. (EST). E-mail address: getinfo@haworth.com].

INTERGENERATIONAL EDUCATION

Intergenerational education denotes those programs and ventures that bring different generations together to learn from and with one another. There are important learning opportunities in many types of intergenerational programs, such as: (1) helping programs–the young providing help to older persons or vice-versa; (2) mentoring programs in which seniors counsel youth who are at risk of dropping out of school, or unwed and pregnant teenagers, or unemployed youth, or just average students including those in college; (3) intergenerational child care in which older adults are trained to look after young children or where pre-schoolers and frail elders interact in a cooperative day-care facility; and (4) other types of programs with primarily a human service agenda. The learning process in many of these programs concerns better mutual understanding, knowledge about later life, and acquisition of helping skills.

Intergenerational education programs that emphasize transfer or cultivation of knowledge or skills are sometimes called "co-learning programs." They are designed to enable members of different generations to exchange knowledge and experience, and to benefit from different perspectives on time and history in the study of particular topics. Programs that fit this nomenclature range from "Computer Ease," in which elementary school children teach computer skills to older adults at a senior center and experience the responsibilities of being a teacher, while the seniors learn word processing and compose letters to grandchildren (Drenning and Getz, 1992), to a semester-long, intergenerational college course, "1946–the Meaning of A Year," in which undergraduates and senior adults examine the social and cultural history of the post-World War II era (NC Center for Creative Retirement, 1996).

Education–the process of acquiring new skills and information, gaining insight and self-knowledge–is central rather than peripheral to the activity and contents of these programs. Learning about oneself and about the conditions of life of an older or younger person are by-products of all types of programs that bring generations together. Additionally, co-learning programs seek to promote and enhance learning of skills and a body of knowledge by drawing on the fellowship fostered between younger and older persons to illuminate a particular subject matter such as an historical event, social problem, work of literature, or the study of aging and human development. Rationales for establishing co-learning programs are related to the broad goals of intergenerational education.

RATIONALES FOR INTERGENERATIONAL
EDUCATIONAL PROGRAMS

A number of purposes and benefits have been advanced for intergenerational education, including:

- To encourage young and old to overcome prejudice and stereotypes held by the other group;
- To provide opportunities for non-paid or stipend supported services by one group for the other, an exchange of service model designed to foster better understanding and greater care between generations;
- To build common bonds between generations as they discover shared life themes, challenges and problems;
- To gain new conceptual frames of reference and multigenerational perspectives on a wide variety of historical topics and social issues.

These and related rationales can be thought of as forming a continuum with "doing for"–a human service model of program legitimation–at one end, and "learning with"–a communal-developmental learning orientation–at the other. The human service model portrays individuals as a collection of needs, attitudes, and personal desires; the communal-developmental model pictures people as social beings, shaped by, benefitting from and contributing to community ideals. These objectives are not mutually exclusive, though project directors may approach intergenerational learning from an orientation more towards one end of the continuum than the other.

Moody and Disch (1989) argue that most intergenerational programs are too narrowly focused on providing a needed service (e.g., tutoring, chore services), overcoming age stereotypes, or providing companionship and personal contact between old and young. While valid, these instrumental objectives, they assert, lack appreciation for the juxtaposition of old and young in a society scrutinizing issues of equity between generation and facing overwhelming problems of violence, racism, poverty, homelessness, and limited opportunities for minorities and the elderly themselves.

Too often, say Moody and Disch, intergenerational programs are conceived from either a "sentimental" (e.g., life satisfaction, attitude change, good feelings) or strictly utilitarian standpoint. In contrast to sentimental justifications, Moody and Disch urge planners and policy makers to consider how intergenerational programs can contribute to "civic education." They cite four model intergenerational programs that deal with the future of the urban environment, racial and ethnic conflicts, and positive minority role models.

The actual content of the civic education programs highlighted by

Moody and Disch are not that unlike other intergenerational programs that emphasize so-called "sentimental" justifications. Moody and Disch's point is that some programs contribute to ideals of the common good, to an awareness that there is such a thing as a community's welfare as distinguished from special interest group rights and needs, private satisfaction, and strife between generations concerning access to services and resources.

Perhaps it is not that these programs and related research on attitudinal change or life satisfaction are sentimental or philosophically impoverished but that organizers and researchers are constrained by methods acceptable to their particular discipline in designing objectives and drawing "valid conclusions" that avoid (or miss) loftier ambitions and generalizations. Given the large number of variables, the small data collection sets, and the highly subjective nature of interactions between young and old, "proving" the value of intergenerational education or quantifying learning outcomes can easily escape the strictures of good social science research. Some program designers and evaluators may ignore important political implications of age and class differences in a society grappling with the future of Social Security, Medicare, Medicaid or other age-based entitlements.

Adding to the rationale of promoting civic virtue, Paul Nathanson (1989) points to moral and political reasons for intergenerational programs. He urges older adults to educate themselves about the plight of poor children and to become allies and advocates. Nathanson regards this as an "imperative" from the point of view of poor children and wonders whether the elderly and their advocates will accept this perspective. His view is based on a kind of "realpolitik" which recognizes that the social view of competition between young and old could be dispelled if representatives of the elderly joined forces with advocates for poor children to present a united front. It would be "politically expedient for aging organizations to be in the forefront of intergenerational programming," argues Nathanson, and in doing so to "demonstrate to a world skeptical of the aging agenda a sense of caring for the issues important to children."

His second argument promotes an "elders of the tribe" concept: their accumulated years and wisdom should create a sense of duty on the part of older people and their representative organizations, "to lead and guide the society for the betterment of all its members." In this sense, seniors become society's educators.

Clearly, Nathanson would applaud establishment of Generations United in 1986, the national coalition of more than 100 organizations seeking to foster intergenerational harmony and advocacy through an agenda of programs and political reforms.

The changes in orientation advanced by Moody and Disch, Nathanson, and others include developmental, cross-cultural, social and public policy advantages of intergenerational cooperation and collaboration. All are mindful of the advantages of forging an age-integrated form of consciousness. To do this, intergenerational education programs need to help alter conceptions of the life course based on the simile that stages of life can be equated with spaces on a life stage pyramid or traditional staircase motif. The spatial analogy has to be transformed into a temporal-historical consciousness that can imagine the unity of the life course and the linking of generations in a common perception of contemporaneity–i.e., a shared sense of time, history, heritage and destiny.

The theme of common plight or common destiny that would unite people of different ages has parallels with Marx's utopian vision of a classless society dwelling harmoniously at the end of history–that is, at the termination of strife between economic classes, out of which, according to Marx, history is made. Today's economic picture includes not only socioeconomic classes but generational niches of children (e.g., cartoon shows and cereal ads), youth (the Pepsi Generation), yuppies ("You Only Go Around Once"), the middle-aged, and senior citizens ("Where's the Beef?" meets AARP Discounts).

It would be naive to imagine the disappearance of age-cohort difference, whether "natural" or market driven. In addition, the liberation of old age from restrictive stereotypes has also spawned a post-modernist "ageless society" which, for some, means "you're only as old as you feel," you can act youthful all your life. Politically, an ageless society has other implications: that social benefits and entitlements should no longer be distributed on the basis of chronological aging (e.g., Medicare and Social Security which are triggered by turning a certain age) but on the basis of a means test.

Many older adults are caught in the paradox of ageless versus age-based categories. They resist age labels such as senior citizen, older adult, retiree, or senior. They prefer to mix with other age groups and may think of themselves as "one of the gang" not "one of the oldies." But when the opportunity arises to take advantage of senior citizens' discounts or special tax breaks, most would not hesitate to show their membership identity card.

Clearly, there is a difference between an ageless society and an "age-integrated" one. Only by not rejecting the idea of age norms and responsibilities and by recognizing and valuing the strengths and perspectives that it takes a lifetime to learn are mature adults fully capable of joining with other generations in pursuing a vision of the common good.

There are some contexts in which age integration occurs commonly and naturally. Musical groups such as jazz bands, symphonies, choirs, choruses, and folk ensembles are often made up of players spanning a broad age spectrum from those in their 20s to 70s. Their love of music and dedication to collaborative mastery joins them in combining talents, experience and enthusiasm. Frequently, they learn from one another. It is not uncommon, especially among folk musicians, for younger players to revere those more senior, and for the veteran players to encourage and mentor those coming up in talent and ability. Dedication to musical heritages forms the common bond—one that can well serve as an analogy to the common good that is otherwise so difficult to identify in a complex society more polarized by values and allegiances than conjoined by them.

Could intergenerational educational programs actually help bring about a more caring community? The small but growing body of research literature would suggest an answer in the affirmative.

TRANSFORMING EFFECTS
OF INTERGENERATIONAL EDUCATION

Most of the research on intergenerational education focuses on certain narrow indicators and measures. This is typical of social science research, self-contained by criteria of quantitative verification and methodologies. Legitimately, researchers want to know whether such measures as pre- and post-test scores on attitude change as reflected, for example, in semantic differential scales, actually show "improvements" in how one age-cohort views another. A sampling of recent intergenerational studies shows they involve older adults and the following other groups: (1) African-American teenagers (Aday, McDuffie and Sims, 1993), (2) college students (Dellmann-Jenkins, Fowler, Lambert, Fruit & Richardson, 1994; McGowan and Blakenship, 1994), (3) children (McGuire, 1986), (4) pre-medical students (Reinsch and Tobis, 1991), and (5) even middle-aged adults (Glass and Knott, 1982).

One exemplary study (McGowan and Blankenship, 1994) moved beyond attitude-based program assessment by taking a phenomenological approach to describe fundamental changes in the way college undergraduates interpreted the meaning of their experiences during a period of weekly visits with older homebound persons. The students conducted life history interviews, drawing upon social and historical frameworks, and produced a final paper documenting the older person's life. While carrying out this project, the students used journal writing to process, through self-mediation, the meaning of their experiences. Subsequently, these journals were analyzed by the researchers using a content analysis technique.

McGowan and Blankenship found an "ontological change" in students' perceptions of what it means to grow old. Students experienced a conflict between previously unreflective assumptions about old people and those that emerged through the deepening relationships with the real life people they were getting to know. These unsettling experiences prompted critical rethinking of assumptions and a fundamental "repositioning" of role away from the disinterested observer to the involved "friend" or companion.

McGowan and Blankenship's phenomenological approach is a microcosm of how intergenerational learning processes may work. Their students learned how to conduct a life history interview, discovered how social and historical changes may have shaped the lives of the individual subjects, and learned the value of clarifying their experiences through journal writing. The seniors and students got to know one another. The seniors contributed their life histories and received a copy of the final write up.

Most other studies of intergenerational education projects report that programs lead to greater tolerance, increased comfort and intimacy, partial dissolving of rigid stereotypes, and less fear of the other group. Researchers are generally cautious in noting that these changes may be short-term. To date, no longitudinal studies have been reported in the literature.

If building bonds of trust, mutual understanding, and contemporaneity are possible outcomes of intergenerational programs that help foster an age-integrated society, what then of the status of age-segregated programs, which form the bulk of older adult education endeavors?

INTERGENERATIONAL
versus AGE-SEGREGATED PROGRAMS

Education is relatively age-segregated into the college years, although traditional-age students at urban colleges and universities are likelier to be with people ranging in age from 18 to the mid-30s or early 40s. Corporate and other workplace education and training is even more likely to span decades of adult life. Apart from those enrolled in credit-bearing courses in post-secondary education, people in the post-50 age period who seek continuing education are likely to join an age-segregated program like Elderhostel (minimum age 55), one of the institutes for learning in retirement (LRIs), or attend programs at a senior center, Shepherd's Center, a department store-based OASIS program, or a SeniorNet site. Like other ' affinity groups, seniors have a tendency to self-segregate by race, class, religion and, sometimes, gender.

Reasons older adults participate in age-segregated programs are numerous: (1) commonality and greater likelihood of peer support through mutually perceived cohort and life course development tasks; (2) practical matters such as convenient daytime scheduling, length and frequency of courses and semesters, affordable costs, simpler registration procedures; (3) curriculum shaped to meet the intellectual, vocational, recreational, social and, perhaps, spiritual interests of participants; and (4) opportunities for seniors to exercise a degree of control and leadership in influencing organizational and curricular aspects of programs they join on a voluntary basis.

But reasons for intergenerational education may complement these features of age-segregated programs. As Broomall (1992) points out, traditional college-age students may experience phases of adult development focused on appropriating a valid set of beliefs and values (knowing and valuing) that parallel developmental issues in the lives of older adults who also may be challenged by intellectual and emotional reevaluations. For Broomall, the socialization function of higher education provides a "ripe opportunity for adult development to be facilitated by developmental stages."

Based on this reasoning, should age-segregated programs linked to higher education, such as LRIs, be phased out in favor of "mainstreaming" older adults into regular course classrooms through tuition-waiver policies that reduce or eliminate costs to seniors? Mainstreaming of this type already goes on. Hunter College (CUNY) has 800 enrolled senior students and Brooklyn College some 2,000 members. Most states have a policy of reduced or tuition-free enrollment for people over 60 or 65. Nationally, however, the number of seniors participating in higher education is quite modest. And, rarely is there an attempt to take explicit advantage of the presence of older adults in the classroom. In some instances there are reports that younger-aged students resent older class members because they feel intimidated and overshadowed by them. In other instances, the arrangement is mutually stimulating and adds to the learning process.

As Fox and Giles (1993) point out in their review of a multitude of intergenerational projects of many types and with different generational mixes, simply bringing different age groups into contact with one another does not guarantee positive results. Some projects have led to a preponderance of negative outcomes–stereotypes or biases were confirmed rather than overcome. However, where projects were thoughtfully conceived and where mutual educational benefits were involved, results were generally favorable as reflected by both age groups.

Age-segregated and age-integrated educational programs each have their own qualities, values and applications. Hopefully, we will not have to choose between them. More critical is the question concerning the infrastructure that makes both possible. It has taken many decades to establish the validity of campus-based learning in retirement institutes or congregational-based Shepherd Centers with their Adventures in Learning programs. National, state and local coalitions to promote intergenerational education are an even more recent and tentative innovation. What institutions will claim lasting ownership of intergenerational educational ventures? What continuing funding sources will enable them to establish solid foundations?

Elderhostel reported 140 intergenerational educational programs offered in 1994. Most involved grandparents and grandchildren. The May Company's department store-based OASIS program encourages its members to get involved in tutoring children in grades one through three in a special reading program for which training is provided at most of the 29 OASIS sites. Various LRIs have been linking up with local schools for special programs. Public libraries also have played a role in generating intergenerational education programs (Wood, 1995). In most cases, these intergenerational education linkages are sporadic and narrowly conceived.

LRIs are in an ideal position to explore intellectually substantive intergenerational studies at colleges and universities though they will have to overcome a myriad of barriers related to costs, credits, grades, space, scheduling and identification of tangible educational benefits. Would many traditional-age college students want to learn from and with older adults and vice-versa? This is a question yet to be addressed. What would motivate seniors?

THE INTERGENERATIONAL IMPULSE AND IMPERATIVE

Geropsychologist David Gutmann (1987) has argued that across numerous and diverse cultures there is a phenomenon of instinctual grandparenting, not only of children related through kinship but beyond family ties. Until recently, in the United States at least, we have viewed generations of young, old and middle-aged as separated by "gaps" generated from cultural, economic, social, historical, technological and even biological change. Many patriotic veterans of World War II were dismayed by Vietnam protesters but confused about the nature of a war with unclear goals and ambiguous allies. Post-war affluence, the rise of suburban lifestyles, and credit card household economics were a far cry from urban and rural life during the Great Depression. Some historians argue that one reason the Social Security Act of 1935 was so popular was that it meant older parents could afford to live separately from their adult children. Family sitcoms of the 50s and 60s rarely included the presence of grandparents. The generation raised on radio was different from the one raised on television; the computer-entranced child of today may be quite different from his or her parents—at least in some respects.

How does the intergenerational movement of mutual assistance and co-learning make sense given this background of twentieth century American life and the "frozen" conception of life stages as people tagged and separated by cohort characteristics march, unchanged, through time? Has the grandparenting instinct been released from social and cultural suppression? Or is it simply the case that now more people have more time in retirement to think about and help out younger people?

There is no single answer or attributable cause to resolve these questions. Just as there are characteristics that determine which individuals are likeliest to volunteer in earlier and later life, there are probably characteristics of older adults who are drawn to intergenerational service and co-learning programs. Motivations can be summarized by often repeated refrains: (1) "Our kids need help if the U.S. is to remain a strong and competitive nation"; (2) "I want to give something back to society and young people represent its future"; (3) "Working with young people helps me feel young and in touch"; (4) "I'm doing it for the sake of our African-American [Hispanic, Native American, etc.] children"; and (5) "I was a high school drop-out [young offender, unwed and pregnant teen, etc.] and now want to help others in that situation."

While there is an emerging corps of motivated senior adults, any intergenerational program coordinator will tell you that recruiting volunteers for intergenerational programs is difficult and retaining them over time (six months, a year, two years) is even more difficult. Moreover, there is a constant struggle to establish close, well-organized partnerships with institutions that serve younger persons (e.g., schools, juvenile centers, youth clubs). To some degree this administrative stretch may reflect adjustments to increasing use of volunteers in general. But the presence of substantial numbers of the elderly, in many instances of highly skilled and knowledgeable seniors, in the halls of these institutions is still something of a shock to youth and to administrators. Will they truly be useful or are they well-intentioned meddlers who do not really understand the nature of what is going on? There is little question that running intergenerational programs is a labor-intensive activity that usually requires some paid professional staffing or, at least, the support of an institution willing to provide space and the necessary amenities to get the job done.

Intergenerational programs, including educational ones, are unlikely to solve the nation's crime, poverty, drop-out, drug, unwed mother, or low SAT score problems. They will make a difference in some children's lives and in some older adults'. They will make many more older adults aware of these issues as they involve real children and families, not newspaper headlines or politicians' quick fixes.

PROSPECTS FOR THE FUTURE

The growing movement of intergenerational programming—including co-learning—may be a harbinger of change, reflecting closer identification of people in the later years with those in the earlier. Can we imagine a society in which separate age group identification fades and is replaced by orientation to overarching communal values? Older adults may, themselves, seek to shed the nomenclature and identification of elderhood, instead perceiving themselves as individuals who simply organize their days differently than when working.

The motivation to join in intergenerational service and/or educational programs must be related to the dawning awareness of the limits of one's own life and, therefore, of the shape of the life course. Seniors have the gift and burden of time while, for youth, time is endless and measureless. The very personal sense of being part of the life course and of belonging to a generation probably does not occur until one's third decade, intensifying with succeeding decades. Consciousness of aging and of the brief span of our years (for what is human longevity when compared to evolutionary, geological, or cosmic time?) makes some people more sensitive to what they have in common with those in other generations and of whatever class and ethnic make-up. For others, the encounter with finitude and the inevitability of death leads to self-preoccupation and fear and avoidance of those perceived as strangers in time.

Nevertheless, the growing visibility of intergenerational relationships, new emphasis on grandparenting, awareness of the need for whole communities to participate in the education of youth, and innovations in co-learning ventures points to new frontiers of older adult education. As programs and organizations devoted to older learners continue to develop, they are ever likelier to make communal belonging an ideal of lifelong learning. From a political point of view, age-segregated educational programs would do well to scan the broader social scene and to place themselves in the context of change.

It is far from accidental that Congress, for the 1995 White House Conference on Aging (WHCoA), made "increasing public awareness of the interdependence of generations and the contributions of older people" a major focus for policy directions through the end of the century. The subject of intergenerational relationships reflects the sensitivities and subtleties of aging in the United States. Age-based special interest groups have recognized the need for a coordinated agenda around issues of health, safety, poverty, education, housing and work. They understand that young and old will both be losers if their advocacy organizations allow political polarization of their pursuit of goals to improve the condition of each group.

Intergenerational learning is not only an attractive educational idea, it is a socially positive one as well.

REFERENCES

Aday, Ronald H., Wini McDuffie and Cyndee Rice Sims (1993). "The Impact of an Intergenerational Program on Black Adolescents' Attitudes Toward the Elderly." *Educational Gerontology* 19:663-2673.

Broomall, James K. (1992) "Intergenerational Synergy." In *Students of the Third Age*, edited by Richard B. Fischer, Mark L. Blazey, and Henry T. Lipman. New York: Macmillan Publishing Co.

Dellmann-Jenkins, Mary, Lynda Fowler, Donna Lambert, Dorothy Fruit and Rhonda Richardson (1994). "Intergenerational Sharing Seminars: Their Impact on Young Adult College Students and Senior Guest Students." *Educational Gerontology* 20:579-588.

Drenning, Susan and Lou Getz (1992). "Computer Ease" *Phi Delta Kappan* 74: 471-472.

Fox, Susan and Howard Giles (1993). "Accommodating Intergenerational Contact: A Critique and Theoretical Model." *Journal of Aging Studies* 7(4) 423-451.

Glass, J.C., Jr. and E.S. Knott (1982)."Effectiveness of a Workshop in Aging in Changing Middle-Aged Adults Attitudes Toward the Aged." *Educational Gerontology* 8:359-372.

Gutmann, David (1987). *Reclaimed Powers*. New York: Basic Books.

Manheimer, Ronald J., Denise Snodgrass and Diane Moskow-McKenzie (1995). *Older Adult Education: A Guide to Research, Programs and Policies*. Westport, CT: Greenwood Press.

McGowan, Thomas G. and Sara Blankenship (994). "Intergenerational Experience and Ontological Change." *Educational Gerontology* 20:589-604.

McGuire, S.L. (1986). "Promoting Positive Attitudes Towards Aging Among Children." *Journal of Social Health* 56:322-324.

Moody, Harry R. and Robert Disch (1989). "Intergenerational Programming in

Public Policy." In *Intergenerational Programs: Imperatives, Strategies, Impacts, Trends*. Edited by Sally Newman and Steven W. Brummel. New York: The Haworth Press, Inc.

Nathanson, Paul S. (1989). "Political Imperative for Intergenerational Programs?" In *Intergenerational Programs: Imperatives, Strategies, Impacts, Trends*. Edited by Sally Newman and Steven W. Brummel. New York: The Haworth Press, Inc.

North Carolina Center for Creative Retirement (1996). "New Intergenerational Ventures." *The Nautilus* 2, 1, p. 1.

Reinsch, S. and J.S. Tobis (1991). "Intergenerational Relations Pre-med Students at Senior Centers." *Archives of Gerontology and Geriatrics* 13:211-224.

Ventura-Merkel, C and L. Lidoff (1983). "Program Innovation in Aging: Volume 8 Community Planning for Intergenerational Programming." Washington, DC: National Council on the Aging.

Wood, Joan M. (1995). "Intergenerational Work Thrives at Pekin Public Library." *Ohio Libraries*. Fall. Pp. 20-21.

Learning by Sharing:
An Intergenerational College Course

Patricia P. Pine, PhD

SUMMARY. Intergenerational activities involving children and senior citizens in short-term programs generally permit (at most) cursory or fragmented relationships. For example, scout troops or elementary classes may visit a nursing home and entertain the residents in an almost one-way communication activity. Conversely, a senior-citizen barbershop quartet may visit a high school for an annual holiday program in another version of a one-way intergenerational activity. Simply put, intergenerational programs resulting in two-way relationships between members of both generations are unusual.

This paper describes an educational program which uses the nearly opposite paradigm, one based on long-term, highly interactive intergenerational activities. It is based on a coordinated curriculum with educational objectives which involve college students in a semester-long, educational experiential program. The requirements of the course encourage extensive interaction between students and older adults in long-term care settings. This paper also describes three cohorts of students and their responses to the older individuals they met. *[Article copies available for a fee from The Haworth Document Delivery Service: 1-800-342-9678. E-mail address: getinfo@haworth.com]*

BACKGROUND

The project was founded by the Corporation for National and Community Service through the Foundation of Long Term Care of the New York

Patricia P. Pine is Executive Deputy Director, New York State Office for the Aging and Adjunct Professor at the State University of New York-New Paltz.

[Haworth co-indexing entry note]: "Learning by Sharing: An Intergenerational College Course." Pine, Patricia P. Co-published simultaneously in the *Journal of Gerontological Social Work* (The Haworth Press, Inc.) Vol. 28, No. 1/2, 1997, pp. 93-102; and: *Intergenerational Approaches in Aging: Implications for Education, Policy and Practice* (ed: Kevin Brabazon, and Robert Disch) The Haworth Press, Inc., 1997, pp. 93-102. Single or multiple copies of this article are available for a fee from The Haworth Document Delivery Service [1-800-342-9678, 9:00 a.m. - 5:00 p.m. (EST). E-mail address: getinfo@ haworth.com].

93

Association of Homes & Services for the Aging. The purpose was to provide an effective program which would promote interaction with students and the elderly and to attempt to enhance communication and understanding between them (Kendall & Associates, 1990). At the same time, the classroom environment would provide the students with a background to help understand policy choices and their direct impact on individuals (Levison, 1990).

The project disbursed funds to five colleges or consortia of colleges in similar elder care projects in New York State. This paper will focus specifically on the students at the State University of New York at New Paltz over a period of three years. However, based on reports from other faculty members and coordinators of different college programs, it is notable that the findings are consistent. In a nonstatistical but substantively important sense, then, we believe we have fairly reliably portrayed the nature and benefits of this approach.

THE ACADEMIC REQUIREMENT

Students enrolled in the course for academic credit. The students worked as volunteers for over 100 hours per semester in a long-term care setting working directly with residents or clients. The volunteer activities were enhanced by five three-hour seminars in which students shared information and experiences and learned of long-term care policies and financing.

The students were placed in long-term care settings which provide services to the elderly. These included skilled nursing facilities, adult homes, social and medical adult day care programs, and community hospitals throughout a three-county area. As a result, the students' discussion in the classroom provided a description of several types of long-term activities, different levels of care, differing regulations, unique staffing patterns, and differing capabilities of the residents. The range of discussions encouraged the students' understanding of the broad effects of social policy as well as their effects on individual residents (Levison, 1990).

THE INTERVIEW ASSIGNMENT

Among the required assignments was an in-depth interview of an elderly person with whom the student worked. The interview, designed to last at least 2 hours, required that the student learn the life history of the older individual, including birthplace, childhood experiences, family life, occupation, and work history. It also requested a description of the person's physical, mental, and emotional status at the time of interview. This assignment was intended to better acquaint the student with an older person and to enhance relationships and interaction.

After completing this assignment, the students were more sensitized to older people and became more aware of how policies, long-term care situations, and activities can affect an older person's life. It also helped them learn how to communicate more effectively with older people and encouraged them to discuss life histories and other events with other elderly people.

THE JOURNAL

The students maintained daily journals recording experiences, perceptions and observations. This was useful in detailing progress of working with the facility, staff and residents. Increasing responsibility was often noted. It also reflected their changing attitudes toward long term care and older people (Zimmerman, Zawacki, Bird, & Peterson, 1990).

RESPONSES AND REACTIONS

A review of students' papers indicates enthusiasm about this activity and a consistent personalization through these meetings with "my" older person. An analysis of the student reactions revealed three themes which predominated in their reports. The themes were inspiration and respect, education and learning, and interest and enjoyment. The following quotes from their papers are divided into the three themes.

Inspiration and Respect. The students expressed their respect for the difficult lives that their older person had experienced. They also were inspired by the fortitude and strength that many maintained in order to survive or endure difficult times.

One student stated his admiration in the following description:

> Although only five feet tall, S. is the strongest man that I have ever met. More important than physically strong, he is strong willed. The life that he has lived is one nobody deserves to have to experience. But he did, and he has regained his faith in the world.
>
> I will always admire this man. He has made me realize that no matter how bad I think things are, they could be worse. He has taught me to

be able to deal with pressures and made me understand that even if times are tough, they'll get better, and I will be able to get through it.

Two students were encouraged to live their lives to the "fullest" from their encounters.

I feel very fortunate to have met R., a charming man, with a positive outlook on life, whose attitude really encourages me to make the most out of my life no matter what happens.

This walk through the life of A. not only taught me about the past but about life and how to live it. Life is short for some of us, but it can go on and on for others, and we have no control of that. But it is up to us to live it to the fullest and appreciate everyday and every event and every person that comes in and out of it. Because it is from this that we truly learn and pass on to others what life is all about.

One student appreciated the opportunity to meet and respect the older person.

This interview enabled me to meet an extraordinary woman. She has lived through a great deal of hardship, but despite it all, she keeps on smiling. I have a great deal of respect for M., and I have to say she is one of the strongest women I have ever met. I feel very fortunate from this interview, because I experienced something that many of my peers will never experience. I have met a great woman with a history of taking risks and proving her strength time and time again. I truly admire her.

The experience also instilled an appreciation of older people and mutual respect. One student told of how much better the residents responded when treated like individuals who could think, learn, and teach.

C. and F. told me that they like it when I ask them what they think or what they like. They said others do not talk to them this way. This made me really happy because my goal is being achieved–to treat them like individuals! And have them think for themselves.

Overall, the students gained respect for the older people they met, and often that respect was earned because the students learned that the older adults had to cope with many difficult life situations and had not experienced an "easy life" (Levison, 1990). They shared this respect with others and were upset when they heard others being non-respectful. Moreover, emerging from the increased sense of respect also grew the consistent feeling of inspiration.

The students shared their personal life experiences with the older person as well. This interaction created a mutual understanding between the older adults and the students and enhanced a reciprocal feeling of respect for the young by the old. Thus, a beneficial intergenerational relationship developed (Cuoto, 1990).

The administrators of the facilities observed that the student's capabilities increased with their knowledge and respect for the residents. They were more able to cope with differing situations and could better handle difficult residents. Several acknowledged that the students "learned how to relate to those needing special attention." This assisted other staff. Another commented that when a certain student was working that "Mrs. J. didn't complain so much."

Education and Learning. The educational experience taught students about the elderly, how to communicate with them, and how to work with them. It also offered them an opportunity to learn about self-development and life priorities. One student wrote,

> I have learned something about life and what it is like to become older as a woman. I have come to a different understanding about the priorities that we set in life.

Another student stated,

> I feel this gave me great insight into someone's life that I never would have known otherwise. There are so many elderly people out there that would love to share their life and knowledge. Not enough of the younger generation seems to care about the elderly. They are thought of as a burden or a problem.

Prior to this experience, two students held fairly normal stereotypical views of the elderly as demanding, selfish, and boring. The following two quotes explain their views after the course.

> When I first was introduced to Senior Citizens/Elderly, my first impressions were that most of them were selfish, self-centered, and demanded control. However, through this interview I realized not all Senior Citizens are "typical" and that includes M. She will give her time and experience to anyone who wants to receive it. She destroys every prejudice, generality and stereotype that people hold about the Senior Citizens.

. . . It was a pleasure to have interviewed . . . an elder who was very optimistic and enthusiastic. I believe now that age enhances one's being, the way you are at 70 was the same at 17, 27, and all the way up, only emphasizing the qualities and beliefs that you hold in yourself.

Two students explained that they learned social history from their older individuals. One stated,

(The interview) gave A. a chance to reminisce about the past and brought back many memories. For me, I got the chance to hear what life was like through the depression, segregation, the wars, and the first walk on the moon and much more.

Another recalled,

He was telling me things he enjoys and the difference between his generation and mine. I was very interested in hearing what he had to say. This is my favorite part about being there. I love listening about people's lives. It makes history personal and interesting. You can actually listen to experiences rather than just reading them in a book. The history is right there in front of you. It becomes real.

Three students stated that they learned to "put themselves in the older person's place" to get a sense of how it feels to be old and how to deal with older people.

As a result of this field work . . . I was able to put myself in the patient's place. I tried to think about how I might react to some of the situations which the patients must face each day.

This field study also compelled me to think about when I reach an elderly state what situations I might face and how I might react toward them. I think that once I tried to imagine myself in the elderly patient's place, it also assisted me in my communication and behavior with that patient.

This experience also taught me how to deal with different personalities and temperaments. In dealing with these different personalities and temperaments, I learned that I needed to adjust exactly how I approach each patient in the area of encouraging activity.

Another student explained that she developed the feeling that it is important for generations to maintain open communication.

The personal interview made me realize that our society forgets and disregards the wisdom that older people have. Talking with an older person can teach one much more than one can ever imagine.

This course provided both an educational and learning experience for the students. The opportunity for education about older people, their lives, their interests, and their conditions was offered in regular concentrated sessions. The students also learned social history, about dealing with a different generation of people which forced them to question their stereotypes of older people (Wigginton, 1990).

Interest and Enjoyment. Working with the elderly in long-term care settings initially was difficult for most students. However, as they became familiar with the settings and the people, they began to enjoy the experience. These quotes indicate their satisfaction.

I really value the time that I have been able to spend with G. She keeps me on the ball and always remains in good spirits. I have certainly found a friendship that I will treasure dearly, and I will miss her tremendously when the semester comes to an end.

I wish H. would have had children because we need more of her kind in this world. She is really special. I hope when I reach 92 years of age, I'm in as good spirits and as active as H. is. She's touched my heart and I'll never forget her as long as I live.

I'm writing a paper on someone who is real with real problems. I did not take this course with any prior knowledge or interest in future career work in this particular field. But after meeting L. and a group of others, I can't imagine not being with them and learning and enjoying the time they have left–without me!

As noted above, terminating the volunteer work was a difficult transition for many students, and several continued to volunteer or visit after their required hours were finished. The experience was rewarding and one which many students state would affect their career choices and future life plans (Wigginton, 1990).

Providers noted that several students requested information about careers in the field of long-term care. Social workers reported that students who once "wanted to work with children asked about necessary education and training to work in long-term care." Also, nursing home and adult home administrators reported that students expressed interest in those careers as well.

VALUE OF INTERGENERATIONAL EDUCATION EXPERIENCE

The three focused themes of this paper, inspiration and respect, education and learning, and interest and enjoyment, point out specific values encountered in this course. There are some specific built-in guidelines which encouraged these results.

Inspiration and Respect emphasized removing stereotypes and promoting respect and intergenerational harmony. Students should be encouraged to address older adults in respectful terms, that is, addressing them as Mr. or Mrs., until the older person requests a more familiar term. Students also should be warned not to infantilize older people, with terms of endearment, such as "honey," "dear," or "cutie."

Education and Learning promotes communication skills and sensitizes students about individual differences. Students should be encouraged to speak directly to the older person so that person can see as well as hear questions and remarks. They also should maintain eye contact and listen attentively to responses.

Interest and Enjoyment are important to most (if not all) educational experiences, as the more a student enjoys the course, the more effort he or she will expend and the more he or she will retain. Students should be encouraged to be comfortable when talking with an older person and to seek out "common grounds" of interest. Some of these may be familiarity with or commonality of a given community or the same size of family or related work experiences. The older person generally responds to a student who clearly expresses an interest in his or her life.

Long-term care facilities can assist student volunteers in these endeavors by identifying older people with common interests or who are approachable or who might benefit from an intergenerational relationship. The facility's staff also can enhance the experience by suggesting the times of day or day of the week when the experience could be most beneficial for the residents and the students.

Beyond the three themes, the students in these classes experienced an educational activity not previously offered either inside or outside their particular educational institution. The course enhanced their personal lives and possibly their professional lives. It provided personal growth in their ability to understand the older generation. It provided them with many opportunities to communicate with older, often disabled, people.

The experience offered them personal insight into American or social history. The older individuals' accounting of life experiences, work and family activities, and other events, offered an oral history often missed in typical college courses in gerontology.

Finally, the experience offered the student opportunities for risk-taking behavior with interpersonal relationships. Some older residents and patients do not welcome new people in their daily lives. They feel threatened or are not interested in developing new friendships. Students attempted to overcome social and physical barriers to establish contact and new relationships.

Certainly, a major recipient of this program are the facilities where the students volunteered. Although the staff was called upon to provide training and guidance, all acknowledged that they and their residents benefitted from the interaction and assistance the students provided. The administrators and supervisors reported that the students were interested, and as a result of their interest, they were dependable volunteers who "showed up." Their assistance in working directly with patients and residents eased the workload of staff and helped some difficult residents.

CONCLUDING REMARKS

This intergenerational, experiential, educational program proved to be very beneficial to these three cohorts of students. Several of them have continued to work in the field or are pursuing graduate degrees with plans to work with the elderly. They state that this experience changed their career plans.

These students are only a beginning, but the message is resoundingly clear that more intergenerational education is merited. With the increasing number of elderly people anticipated in the 21st century, there will be an increasing demand for more trained professionals, paraprofessionals, and other workers to deal and to work with the elderly. Understanding their needs and knowing how to communicate will be beneficial in practice as well as in establishing policy.

AUTHOR NOTE

Patricia P. Pine has worked professionally in the field of aging since the early 1970s. Her teaching and research interests include long-term care, community organization, and public policy in aging.

BIBLIOGRAPHY

Cuoto, Richard (1990). Assessing a Community Setting as a Context for Learning. In *Combining Service and Learning: A Resource Book for Community and Public Service*. Volume II. Raleigh, NC: National Society for Internships and Experiential Education. pp. 251-265.

Kendall, Jane C. and Associates (1990). Principles of Good Practice. In *Combining Service and Learning: A Resource Book for Community and Public Service*. Volume I. Raleigh,NC: National Society for Internships and Experiential Education. pp. 37-55.

Levison, Lee (1990). Choose Engagement over Exposure. In *Combining Service and Learning: A Resource Book for Community and Public Service*. Volume I. Raleigh, NC: National Society for Internships and Experiential Education. pp. 68-75.

Wigginton, Eliot (1990). Service-Learning and Schools' Three Roles. In *Combining Service and Learning: A Resource Book for Community and Public Service*. Volume I. Raleigh, NC: National Society for Internships and Experiential Education. pp. 493-495.

Zimmerman, Jane, V. Zawacki, J. Bird, and V. Peterson (1990). Journals: Diaries for Growth. In *Combining Service and Learning: A Resource Book for Community and Public Service*. Volume II. Raleigh, NC: National Society for Internships and Experiential Education. pp. 69-79.

The Integration
of Pro-Active Aging Education
into Existing Educational Curricula

Barbara Friedman, MS

SUMMARY. Community service-learning in schools, and increased awareness of the interdependence of generations, has heightened interest in intergenerational programming. While there is agreement that service-learning results in substantial educational opportunities, too often the result is training, or reflection, but not pro-active aging education. Students, therefore, have little sustainable understanding of the older adults with whom they are interacting. This paper addresses what aging education should include, why it is not consistently being taught, and how to integrate aging education into already existing curricula and age-appropriate skill development. *[Article copies available for a fee from The Haworth Document Delivery Service: 1-800-342-9678. E-mail address: getinfo@haworth.com]*

The number of intergenerational programs has dramatically increased in the last decade. Changes in social and family structures, high mobility

Barbara Friedman has been an Intergenerational Educator and Consultant for 13 years. She served as Chairperson of the Massachusetts Intergenerational Network for 3 years and has worked extensively with the youth and aging networks in program and curriculum development. Her teacher's manual for elementary aging education curriculum and program development will be published by Allyn & Bacon, Simon & Schuster Education Group, in 1998.

[Haworth co-indexing entry note]: "The Integration of Pro-Active Aging Education into Existing Educational Curricula." Friedman, Barbara. Co-published simultaneously in the *Journal of Gerontological Social Work* (The Haworth Press, Inc.) Vol. 28, No. 1/2, 1997, pp. 103-110; and: *Intergenerational Approaches in Aging: Implications for Education, Policy and Practice* (ed: Kevin Brabazon, and Robert Disch) The Haworth Press, Inc., 1997, pp. 103-110. Single or multiple copies of this article are available for a fee from The Haworth Document Delivery Service [1-800-342-9678, 9:00 a.m. - 5:00 p.m. (EST). E-mail address: getinfo@haworth.com].

of family members, economic realities, age segregated societies and their psychological effect on young and old, and changing demographics coupled with increasing life-spans and earlier retirements are all contributing factors. The field has also grown in stature from attempting to create warm feelings and change stereotypic attitudes to one that is highly professional and successfully addresses important social issues. Within the schools, intergenerational programming and service learning are rapidly growing because advocates of educational reform recognize that these programs assist communities and help create effective classroom learning situations.

Empirically this is certainly worthwhile. Intergenerational programming has for years proven effective in changing students' negative attitudes about older adults (Seefeldt, Jantz, Galper & Serock, 1981; Cartensen, Mason & Caldwell, 1982; Rick, Myrick and Campbell, 1983; Pratt, 1984; Corbin, Corbin & Barg, 1989; Chapman & Neal, 1990; Dellmann-Jenkins, Lambert & Fruit, 1991; Aday, McDuffie & Sims, 1993). It has also been shown to have significant positive impact on the health, well-being and life-satisfaction of older adults (Erikson, 1951; Wallach, Kelley & Abrahams, 1979; Newman, 1982; Pynoos, Hade-Kaplan & Fleisher, 1984; Newman, 1988; Reville, 1989; Kuehne, 1992).

Although these attitudinal changes are valid indicators of a program's integrity, studies show that when the program design is not carefully planned or does not involve meaningful interaction, negative attitudes are perpetuated (Baggett, 1981; Kocarnik & Ponzetti, 1986; Seefeldt, 1987). Seefeldt (1987) cautioned that children must be exposed to healthy as well as frail older adults in order to develop proper perspectives on the older population. When young children interact only with frail older adults, that become normative frame of reference. In actuality, the majority of older adults are healthy. Thus, taking children to a nursing home without proper preparation, without planned contact with healthy older adults, and without a broader perspective on the aging population can have negative unwanted outcomes.

In addition to proper training, formal education to understand the entire intergenerational experience is an important aspect of program planning. Studies point to the effectiveness of programs that include a curricular component (Glass & Trent, 1979, 1980; Seefeldt, Jantz, Galper & Serock, 1981; Corbin, Corbin & Barg, 1989; Dellmann-Jenkins, Lambert & Fruit, 1991) and advocacy for curriculum is significant (Glass & Trent, 1979; Newman, 1985; McGuire, 1987; Pratt, 1992).

Therefore, what is of concern with the ever-increasing number of intergenerational interactions is not their prevalence, but rather the quality of programs that exist and the quality and depth of aging education that accompanies those programs.

INTERGENERATIONAL PROGRAMMING
versus INTERGENERATIONAL ACTIVITIES

With the growth in intergenerational programming from restoring good feelings between generations and changing stereotypic attitudes and fears to addressing, with the goal of solving, important social issues, we make an undisputed assumption that our society requires generational interdependence. Further, it becomes not simply advantageous, but rather an imperative that intergenerational programs be established (Crites, 1989; Nee, 1989; Kingson, 1989; Moody & Disch, 1989; Nathanson, 1989). Mentoring programs with teenage mothers and fathers, combined day-care facilities, outreach to frail and homebound older adults, intergenerational community service corps, mentoring juvenile offenders, day care centers partially staffed by older adults, latchkey projects, violence prevention programs initiated by intergenerational groups and support to disabled children are examples of important social issues being addressed intergenerationally.

The high expectations for intergenerational programming require that it be significantly different from a simple combination of intergenerational activities. According to Vickery (1972) and quoted by Brummel (1989), intergenerational programs provide a way for experiences and interactions to take on meaning relevant to one's life. Intergenerational activities alone do not allow that level of meaning to exist because they lack depth and long term significance. Attitudinal changes may not be sustainable without meaningful, knowledgeable, interactions. The requirements for good, lasting programming have been well documented (Seefeldt, 1987; Brummel, 1989; Henkin & Sweeney, 1989; Ventura-Merkel, Liederman, Ossofsky, 1989; Lyons, 1992; Angelis, 1992) and most agree that programs must at least include the four essential criteria:

- programs should be beneficial to all;
- programs should be on-going, lasting for a significant length of time to establish relationships;
- programs should serve the community;
- programs should include a curricular and reflective component.

There are many factors involved in the planning of programs in order to meet these four criteria and the above references discuss them in detail. It is the curricular issue that this paper attempts to address.

CURRICULUM ENHANCEMENT
versus PROACTIVE AGING EDUCATION

Just as programming needs to be more than a set of activities, so too should aging education become proactive.

Most educators interested in service learning recognize the need to prepare students for intergenerational interactions and to teach them about aging. According to the Alliance for Service Learning in Education Reform (1993), community service learning occurs when:

> there is a deliberate connection made between service and learning opportunities which are then accompanied by conscious and thoughtfully designed occasions for reflecting on the service experience.

Older adults also need to be prepared for the interaction since raising a family years ago is no longer proper preparation for understanding today's youth.

But, despite good intentions, what most frequently occurs is training, not education. The training usually takes the form of a class, or a few classes, that are specific to the skill or knowledge development the student or older adult needs in order to interact effectively in the program. Education, on the other hand, is long-term, broader in its scope, sequence and critical thinking skill development, and raises one's general knowledge base. This does not negate the effectiveness of proper training; indeed it is crucial. But too often participants are left without a true understanding of the people with whom they are interacting.

What often occurs in schools in place of aging education is the enhancement of the existing curriculum by using the resources of older adults to meet class needs. Examples of this would be an oral history project in a social studies class studying World War II; an intergenerational chorus in a music class; a retired scientist coming to a science classroom to do experiments with students; reading intergenerational literature; and reflecting about service projects such as friendly visiting in a nursing home, phone pals for latchkey children or pen-pal programs in language arts classes.

Although the examples above do incorporate academic disciplines into the intergenerational interactions, and are valuable, they cannot be considered aging education. The normal process of aging and all the ramifications of that in our society should be studied as well as the recognition of the value and contributions of older adults. Aging education should not be relegated to a health curriculum or even a biology curriculum but should stand on its own, in any classroom, with age appropriate content for any grade level (Glass & Trent, 1979; McGuire, 1987).

In terms of student outcomes, the goals for aging education should be that students will:

- understand that aging is a natural, normal, lifelong process;
- understand the physical and psychosocial elements of aging;
- empathize with older adults who are challenged by illness, frailty and difficult aging;
- recognize the changing demographics of society and the subsequent need for adjustments;
- identify the sources of ageism that can plague society;
- recognize the realities in the lives of older adults that will affect their living styles and behavior;
- become aware of the valuable historic perspectives that older adults offer.

It is clear that educators need to recognize the impact our ageist society has had on everyone and overcome their own discomfort with the subject. It is also clear that as intergenerational programming becomes more prevalent, curricular information must be published for use in the classroom. But to make aging education infinitely more accessible to classrooms, and educators more willing to adopt it, there will need to recognize the connections that can be made between aging information and their already existing skills and grade content requirements.

To be specific about this incorporation into already existing curricula and skill development, let's use as an example the fact that many elementary curricula focus on communities or neighborhoods and the elements that create those communities. Housing, therefore, is a common area of study. To pair this with teaching skills in academic subjects, students would:

- *Observe* their communities for types of housing alternatives available and their physical connections to the community.
- *Graph* the demographics of the community after obtaining data from local officials. Recognize the need for older adult housing options.
- *Interview* people about housing for the elderly versus home care and then explore the positive and negative aspects of each using problem solving skills development to determine how to allow older adults to stay at home and still maintain services for them.
- *Read* fiction about older adults living in different housing options and discuss the realities.
- *Write* to local government officials for local older adult advocacy agencies to report their findings and advocate for solutions.

- *Develop budgets* for people living on limited incomes and explore the feasibility of their staying in their own home.
- Do *oral histories* with older adults to determine how living alternatives were different for older adults years ago.
- *Write poetry* about how it feels to leave a home you've been in so much of your life, exploring the memories that are associated with that home.
- Explore *cultural differences* in housing for older adults in different countries and the role of older adults in different societies.
- *Analyze* the media for examples of ageism and recognize why older adults live isolated from the community.
- *Design and draw* an ideal home for older adults.
- *Critique* the nursing home being visited in the service project and the well-being of the residents. Advocate for change or applaud the service.

When this kind of interdisciplinary aging education is coupled with an intergenerational service-learning project, the education becomes relevant and personal and important learning occurs. As teachers begin to incorporate education reform objectives into their classrooms, this approach will become easier to implement. Some techniques for teaching about aging have already begun to be published for use by teachers (Tiemann & Stone, 1992).

Aging education needs to be an imperative, not an option. Students must truly understand the people with whom they are interacting in their intergenerational service programs in order for those programs to be meaningful. As intergenerational programs continue to address social issues, that education becomes more relevant. Today's students will later be caring for a larger generation of older adults than ever before. Understanding and empathy will make a huge difference in the character of our communities. And future adults' acceptance of their own aging will occur more easily.

REFERENCES

Aday, R.H., McDuffie, W., & Sims, C.R. (1993). Impact of an Intergenerational program on Black Adolescents' Attitude Toward the Elderly. *Educational Gerontology*, 19, 663-673.

Angelis, J. (1992). The Genesis of an Intergenerational program. *Educational Gerontology*, 18, 317-327.

Baggett, S. (1981). Attitudinal Consequences of Older Adult Volunteers in the Public School Setting. *Educational Gerontology*, 7, 21-31.

Brummel, S.W. (1989). Developing an intergenerational Program. In S. Newman, & S. Brummel (eds.). *Intergenerational Programs: Imperatives, Strategies, Impacts, Trends*, 119-135. New York, N.Y.: The Haworth Press, Inc.

Cartenson, L., Mason, S.E., & Caldwell, E.C. (1982). Children's Attitude Toward the Elderly: An Intergenerational Technique for change. *Educational Gerontology*, 8, 291-301.

Chapman, N.J., & Neal, M.B. (1990). The Effects of Intergenerational Experiences on Adolescent and Older Adults. *The Gerontologist*, 30(6), 825-832.

Corbin, D.E., Metal-Corbin, J., & Barg, C. (1989). Teaching about Aging in the Elementary School: A One-Year Follow-Up. *Educational Gerontology*, 15, 103-110.

Cites, M.S. (1989) Child Development and Intergenerational Programming. In S. Newman, & S. Brummel (eds.). *Intergenerational Programs: Imperatives, Strategies, Impacts, Trends*, 33-45. New York, N.Y.: The Haworth Press, Inc.

Dellman-Jenkins, M., Lambert, D., & Fruit, D. (1991). Fostering Preschoolers' Prosocial Behaviors Toward the Elderly: The Effect of an Interational Program. *Educational Gerontology*, 17, 21-32.

Erikson, E. (1951). *Child and Society*. New York: Norton.

Glass, J.C., & Trent, C. (1979). Teaching About Aging. *The High School Journal*, 63(2), 80-82.

Glass, J.C., & Trent, C. (1980). Changing Ninth-Graders' Attitudes Toward Older Persons. *Research on Aging*, 2(4), 499-513.

Henkin, N.Z., & Sweeney, S,W. (1989). Linking Systems: A system Apprroach to Intergenerational Programming. In S. Newman, & S. Brummel (eds.). *Intergenerational Programs: Imperatives, Strategies, Impacts, Trends*, 165-173. New York, N.Y.: The Haworth Press, Inc.

Kingdom, E.R., (1989). The Social Policy Implications of Intergenerational Exchange. In S. Newman, & S. Brummel (eds.). *Intergenerational Programs: Imperatives, Strategies, Impacts, Trends*, 91-101.

Kocarnik, R.A., & Ponzetti, J.J. (1986). The Influence of Intergenerational Contact on Child Care Participants' Attitudes Toward Elderly. *Child Care Quarterly*, 15, 244-250.

Kuehne, V.S. (1992). Older Adults in Intergenerational Program: What are their Experiences Really Like? *Activities, Adaption & Aging*, 16(4), 49-65.

Lyons, M. (1992). *A Guide to Developing Intergenerational Programs*. Glenn H. Woods Corp.

McGuire, S.L. (1987). Aging Education in Schools. *Journal of School Health*, 57(5), 174-176.

Moody, H.R., & Disch, R. (1989). Intergenerational programming in Public Policy. In S. Newman, & S. Brummel (eds.). *Intergenerational Programs: Imperatives, Strategies, Impacts, Trends*, 101-11. New York. N.Y.: The Haworth Press, Inc.

Nathanson, P.S. (1989). Political Imperative for Intergenerational Programs? In S. Newman, & S. Brummel (eds.). *Intergenerational Programs: Imperatives, Strategies, Impacts, Trends*, 111-117. New York, N.Y.: The Haworth Press, Inc.

Nee, D. (1989). The Intergenerational Movement: A Social Imperative. In S. Newman, & S. Brummel (eds.). *Intergenerational Programs: Imperatives, Strategies, Impacts, Trends*, 79-91. New York, N.Y.: The Haworth Press, Inc.

Newman, S. (1992). The Impact of Intergenerational Programs on Children's Growth and on Older Persons' life Satisfaction. Unpublished paper at a Symposium: *Innovations Within Educational Gerontology.*

Newman, S. (1995). A Curriculum on Aging in Our Schools: Its Time Has Come. *A paper presented at Bridging the Gap Conference, Brookdale Institute and NYC Public Schools.*

Newman, S. (1988). The Impact of the School Volunteer Experience on the Well-Being of Older Persons. *A paper presented at The Gerontological Society of America.*

Pratt, F. (1984). Teaching Today's Kids–Tomorrow Elders. *Aging*, U.S. Dept of Health 7 Human Services, 346, 19-26.

Pratt, F. (1992). Why Teach About Aging? *Schools in an Aging Society*, Center for Understanding Aging, 55.

Pynoos, J., Hade-Kaplan, B., & Fleisher, D. (1984). Intergenerational Neighborhood Networks: A Basis for Aiding The Frail Elderly. *The Gerontologist*, 24(3), 233-237.

Reville, S. (1989). Young Adulthood to Old Age: Looking at Intergenerational Possibilities From A Human Development Perspective. In S. Newman & S. Brummel (eds.). *Intergenerational Programs: Impreative, Strategies, Impacts, Trends*, 45-53. New York, NY: The Haworth Press, Inc.

Rich, P.E., Myrick, R.D., & Campbell, C. (1983). Changing Children's Perceptions of the Elderly. *Educational Gerontology*, 9: 483-491.

Seedfelt, C. (1987). The Effects of Preschoolers' Visits to a Nursing Home. *The Gerontologist*, 27 (2), 228-232.

Seedfelt, C. (1987). Intergenerational Programs: Making them Work. *Childhood Education*, 14-18.

Seedfelt, C., Jantz, R.K., Galper, A., & Serock, K. (1981). Healthy, Happy and Old: Children Learn about the Elderly. *Educational Gerontology*, 7, 79-87.

Tiemann, K.A., & Stone, M.D. (1992). Projective Aging: An Engaging Technique for Teaching Issues in Growing Older. *Educational Gerontology*, 18, 645-649.

Ventura-Merkel, C., Liederman, D.S., & Ossofsky, J. (1989). Exemplary Intergenerational Programs. In S. Newman, & S. Brummel (eds.). *Intergenerational Programs: Imperatives, Strategies, Impacts, Trends*, 173-183. New York, N.Y.: The Haworth Press, Inc.

Wallach, H.F., Kelly, F., & Abrahams, J.P. (1979). Psychosocial Rehabilitation for Chronic Geriatric Patients: An Intergenerational Approach. *The Gerontologist*. 19(5), 464-470.

SECTION IV:
INTERGENERATIONAL
PROGRAM MODELS

Intergenerational programs are normally thought of as intentionally created or planned efforts to link generations for the purpose of benefiting the participants, their institutions, and the community at large. Social commentators from the 1960s on have argued the demise of the extended intergenerational family, noted the negative social consequences of the latchkey phenomenon, and shown how the generations have become segregated by changes in the ways people live and work. Whatever the truth in these analyses, they have become convenient rationales to justify (and fund) a wide variety of intergenerational programs. The analyses of intergenerational problems, it should be added, were often accompanied by the identification of the elderly population as a great "untapped resource" that could be mobilized to help repair social dislocation through interaction with youth.

When carefully conceived and implemented, intergenerational programming can provide needed services to different age groups while simultaneously incorporating the special qualities and strengths that the generations can give to one another. And, because they meet the needs of more than one population, intergenerational services can be cost effective and socially unifying, strengthening family and community while conserving resources.

In this section we have included examples of the main types of intergenerational programs mentioned in the Introduction. The first (Sherman) deals with an intergenerational arts program serving a special needs population (a paper that could have been included in the community-building section of the volume since it illustrates the role that arts programming can play in building a community of common interests). This is followed by an argument in favor of establishing older/younger mentoring relationships to help meet the needs of vulnerable youth (Rogers & Taylor). In the third paper the author looks at innovative school-based programs that demonstrate how intergenerational reminiscence/life review programs can help children realize their educational potential while building a sense of shared communal history between generations (Lubarsky). The application of traditional social work methodologies to deal with the increasing alienation of some grandparents from their grandchildren is the subject of the next paper (Fields). While the support group methodology in this case is innovative, such groups have become widely used to address the needs of grandparents who are primary caregivers for their grandchildren. In the final paper, the author (Baecher-Brown) describes a multifaceted award-winning program in a New York City geriatric center that could be typical of any large geriatric center, since the programs draw on strengths intrinsic to such facilities.

A Case Study
of Intergenerational Relations
Through Dance
with Profoundly Deaf Individuals

Andrea Sherman, PhD

SUMMARY. In this study, the medium of dance was used to explore intergenerational relationships between profoundly deaf young children and profoundly deaf older adults. The specific purposes of the researcher were to explore interaction between a group of profoundly deaf older adults and profoundly deaf young children in an intergenerational dance program setting; to examine the extent to which individuals of one age group act as grandparents or grandchildren for those of another age group; to examine the dance elements of warmups, partnering, touch, and line versus circle; and to investigate whether dance can act as a catalyst for social interaction between these two age groups. *[Article copies available for a fee from The Haworth Document Delivery Service: 1-800-342-9678. E-mail address: getinfo@haworth.com]*

A synthesis of ethnographic case study techniques was employed for data collection: participant observation, informal and formal in-depth interviewing, and movement rating.

Andrea Sherman is Project Director of the Columbia University-New York Geriatric Education Center.

[Haworth co-indexing entry note]: "A Case Study of Intergenerational Relations Through Dance with Profoundly Deaf Individuals." Sherman, Andrea. Co-published simultaneously in the *Journal of Gerontological Social Work* (The Haworth Press, Inc.) Vol. 28, No. 1/2, 1997, pp. 113-123; and: *Intergenerational Approaches in Aging: Implications for Education, Policy and Practice* (ed: Kevin Brabazon, and Robert Disch) The Haworth Press, Inc., 1997, pp. 113-123. Single or multiple copies of this article are available for a fee from The Haworth Document Delivery Service [1-800-342-9678, 9:00 a.m. - 5:00 p.m. (EST). E-mail address: getinfo@haworth.com].

113

The study consisted of two groups of participants, with each group composed of 10 profoundly deaf individuals who resided in a large urban area. One group consisted of 10 older adults, all over 60 years of age and living at a residence for elders; the other group was composed of 10 children, aged 9 to 12, all enrolled in a school for the deaf. Both groups of participants used American Sign Language, signed English, lipreading, and oral communication.

A dance teacher was selected to teach the dance classes, and each class was structured into four segments: the first to build trust, the second to provide warm-ups, the third to encourage creative improvisation, and the fourth to facilitate closure.

The study itself was divided into two phases. In Phase I, the dance teacher taught one weekly class for the older adults at the center for elders and one weekly class for the children at the school for the deaf over a five-week period. In Phase II, she taught weekly intergenerational dance classes for both the children and older adults at the school for the deaf over a ten-week period. All classes were observed by the researcher. Five older adults and five children were interviewed. A field log was developed, which included a description of the events, typed transcripts of the interviews, and the researcher's impressions.

A coding system was developed to organize the data. Words and phrases (meaning units) from the descriptive data were noted. Personal and analytic memos summarizing the research process as it proceeded were used to focus and funnel the study. Themes were then analyzed and supported by observation and interview data. Interpretations were validated through triangulation (use of numerous data sources) and discussion with a peer support group and an auditor who independently coded the fieldwork log and reviewed interpretations. Support group and auditor codes and analyses were compared to those of the researcher and alternative interpretations were discussed.

Four major themes were identified:

1. *Kinesthesia*: This theme describes the use of a kinesthetic framework to discuss the researchers' choreographic process, the kinesthetic snapshots used to relay the findings, and the mirroring that occurred between the dance and the intergenerational relationships. The subthemes of dance as a catalyst for the intergenerational interaction, dance warm-ups, touch, and line versus the circle were also discussed.

2. *Relationships*: This theme refers to the spectrum of interactions that occurred between the children, between the children and the dance teacher, between the elders, between the elders and the dance teacher, and between the children and elders. It includes the subthemes of beginning

socialization for the children, beginning socialization for the elders, and intergenerational socialization. The subthemes of partnering, grandparenting and grandchilding, and attitudes within each group are also a part of this theme.

3. *Deaf Individuals and Communication*: This theme discusses the common ground of deafness between the generations. Subthemes include deaf culture/deaf community, conceptualization, and expressiveness.

4. *Program Implementation: What a Production!*: This theme describes the researcher's dual role as researcher-observer and project director-participant. The subthemes of scheduling, transportation, insurance, recruitment, personnel, space, frailty of seniors, and closure are examined in light of this dual role.

INTEGRATION OF THE STUDY FINDINGS WITH THE LITERATURE

For discussion purposes, the literature pertinent to the study has been divided into the following areas: intergenerational relations, dance, and deafness.

Intergenerational Relations

Brummel (1989) believes that an intergenerational program operates on the premise that both age groups are capable of being active contributors; the importance of such a program lies not only in its activities, but also in the meaning that the program gives to both age groups.

The researcher in this study examined the meaning that the intergenerational program had for its participants by using a symbolic interactionist perspective. Stryker (1980) defines action as the product of a person's having taken into account and interpreting the significance of future actions, and he believes that the manner in which individuals view themselves in relation to others is a primary focus of symbolic interactionism. Symbolic interactionist Blumer (1969) elaborates on how society consists of acting people and their actions in situations and notes that it is through the social process of language, use of symbols, role taking, and patterns of interaction that individuals define, interpret, and share meaning.

In discussing the necessity of an intergenerational approach to public policy in response to our aging society, Kingson (1989) states that individuals and society must come to terms with the changes and life choices that result from aging. Such changes must involve meaning in the lives of the elders and improve their quality of life. The present researcher's findings support Kingson's concept that intergenerational programs build community, respond to the new challenges presented by an aging America, develop productive roles, and bridge aging stereotypes. As the interaction occurred, each age group gained an awareness and understanding of the other. The children viewed the elders as active, imaginative, and able; the elders viewed the children as caring, helpful, and imaginative.

Moody and Disch (1989)–who agree with Kingson that intergenerational programs must be thought of in terms of how they contribute to building community and resolving social issues that affect all generations–speak of the

> . . . ideal of citizenship as a collaborative task within life span development. This ideal means that young and old are joined in a common historical task of shaping the public world and understanding themselves as participants in that world. (p. 102)

Ventura-Merkel, Liederman, and Ossofsky (1989) also agree that exemplary intergenerational programs should address a major social problem or issue:

> Intergenerational programs can provide a renewed sense of community and continuity by reminding people of diverse ages, interests, and backgrounds that the community is an interdependent environment that relies on a delicate balance among all segments of the population. (p. 176)

This study was conceived with such vital social issues in mind, specifically the isolation of the two deaf age groups from each other (age segregation) and the lack of children's understanding of deaf culture. The intergenerational program showed the two aged groups (deaf elders and deaf children) that together they constituted a community and a culture. In the intergenerational classes, they were no longer "outsiders in a hearing world," but were "insiders in a deaf world." It was a positive and enriching experience, providing each age group an opportunity to care for the other.

The young and old defined themselves in relationship to each other during the course of their interaction in the dance classes. The elders made a commitment to come to the intergenerational classes, to be with the children and dance teacher, and for some to teach the children. They began to pass on some of their learning and wisdom to the children. Through their humor, ability to play, and expressiveness, the elders nurtured and cared for the children, and at the same time regenerated themselves.

E. Erikson's (1986) study of octogenarians refers to the second chance of generativity that grandparenting often offers, an opportunity to serve as guides or role models for future generations. Here, the elders developed grandparenting attitudes toward the children through their disciplining, creativity, listening, and deaf awareness.

As the children learned more and more about aging through direct contact with the elders, they developed attitudes of grandcaring. As they became aware of the elders' physical abilities and disabilities, they set up their chairs and were tender and nurturing to their needs. This finding is consistent with S. Newman's (1986) study of elementary school children and D.J. Lambert, J. Dellman-Jenkins, and D. Fruit's (1990) study of nursery school children and older adults. In each case, direct contact with elders promoted more positive attitudes toward older adults. This finding is also consistent with Erikson's (1986) view of the generativity of the life cycle and the assistance that flows down from older generations to younger ones and up from younger to older.

Participants in the study experienced a sense of renewal ("more energy") through the intergenerational classes. Eighty-five-year-old Anna became more aware, interactive, and vital in her 80s. Elder Herman became increasingly motivated, expressive, and sociable. It is interesting to view this finding in terms of E. Cumming's (1961) disengagement theory, which holds that the number of people an older person interacts with varies with the amount and purpose of interaction; qualitative changes occur in the style or pattern of interaction; and increased isolation or disengagement may lead to personality changes. Yet no evidence of disengagement was seen during the intergenerational classes. In fact, for some like Anna and Herman, the intergenerational interaction provided new meaning and re-engagement. Perhaps long-term intergenerational programs may begin to address problems of disengagement and provide an opportunity for elders to reengage themselves and provide new meaning in their lives.

Findings also indicate that an age-specific socialization process occurred at each separate site (school and elders' residence), where a core group of participants was formed. The elders socialized among themselves and with the dance teacher, and the children did the same. Social ties with the dance teachers grew as participants began to learn the language of dance through partnering, touch, and imaginative improvisation. The intergenerational socialization process was crossgenerational and introduced the children to deaf culture.

Consistent with Blumer's (1969) concept of society's composition of acting people, the intergenerational group consisted of acting unites, developing acts to meet the intergenerational situation. The children began to assess the elders' friendship, grandparenting, and caring attitudes and responded by caring and creating together with the elders. Likewise, the elders proceeded with caution and curiosity upon first meeting the children and assessed the children's caring attitudes and began to warm up to and grandparent the children. Together, a community was built.

The abilities and disabilities of the elders in the study covered a wide range, and a programmatic issued developed because of the frailty of some participants. Initially, it had been determined that the participants would be "well-elderly"; however, because a core group of participants was desired, beginning sessions at the residence for elders were open to anyone who wished to attend the classes. Residents such as 93-year-old Clara and 85-year-old Bertha attended the classes at the residence for the elders, but after their first visit to the school, they withdrew because the intergenerational phase was too demanding. Thus, diverse intergenerational programs should be developed for both the well-elderly and the frail elderly.

Dance

According to G. Mead's (1934) symbolic interactionist theory, gestures are the foundation of communication, the earliest stages of social acts that indicate those stages yet to come. For Mead, communication between people involves a "conversation of gestures." In the present study the participants communicated through American Sign Language (ASL) and dance, both symbolic and visual gestural languages. Both dancers and ASL users communicate through their bodies. In sign language, the hands are shaped into symbols to illustrate concepts; facial expressions and overall body language add meaning to the sign.

Dance served as a common vocabulary, a powerful communicative tool, between the two age groups. As they began to learn its language symbols (i.e., warming up the body, partnering, and touch), they used them to interact and define meaning. Concurrently, the groups used ASL, often seen signing together before and after the dance classes. (Interestingly enough, sometimes signing differences occurred due to the age span between the two groups.)

S.E. Oosterhouse (1985) points to the natural relationship between dance and ASL, that both are nonverbal languages that use the body for expression and communication. Oosterhouse believes that dance provides one with an opportunity to sign with the whole body and achieve emotional and physical integration. She believes that the body is the basic tool of sign language, whether using the hands or the face, and that the entire body is used in a dance therapy session to express feeling. By integrating ASL and dance, body moving and feeling become one.

Oosterhouse assumes that movement reflects personality and sign language is essential in doing dance therapy with the deaf, assumptions she explored while teaching dance as therapy for deaf psychiatric adolescent and adult patients. Oosterhouse found that the sessions began with signing in ASL (to help develop a symbiotic relationship), moved to warm-ups reflecting the patient's movement style (developing kinesthetic empathy), and were then followed by an integration of body movement and signing. Emotional themes were developed through movement improvisations.

Similarly, in the present study the dance teacher used her knowledge of ASL to gain trust and respect from the participants and to build upon through improvisation. At times the dance teacher extended a sign into movement, perhaps exaggerating it, changing its tempo, or modifying it with mime and gesture. For example, she had the group mime opening a box, carrying a heaving object, and feeding an animal, and then participants enlarged these movements into a dance. Oosterhouse also found pantomime and ASL helpful for the deaf, who are accustomed to expressing their feelings through gesture.

The warm-up process provided an ideal structure for the intergenerational program, allowing learning to occur on both physical and socially interactive levels. Through exercises like intergenerational massage, both groups not only learned the physical activity of massage, but also what an elder or younger person's body felt like.

At times the classes were held in a circle formation, and at other times in a line format. The circle offered more visual awareness, important in both dance and sign language. The use of the circle in working with the elderly is supported by the teachings of E. Garnet (1982), Caplow-Lindner (1979), and Lerman (1984).

E. Garnet (1982) arranges chairs in a "gentle circle" for her dance classes with the elderly so that attention is focused on the teacher, who can also use eye contact to give individual attention. In this way, the teacher can read changes in facial expression, "whether it is the pallor of dizziness, flush of exertion, or the relaxed expression and smile of pleasure" (p. 129). In the circle, an individual is also given attention and recognition within the form of group activity.

Caplow-Lindner (1982) believes a circle develops group solidarity, allows greater visibility, and reduces anxiety. Its encouraging and accepting atmosphere decreases an elder's sense of isolation.

Lerman (1984) also suggests that a circle allows for greater visibility so that participants can follow each other, and it also increases group cohesiveness. In addition, Lerman uses a circle in standing improvisations;

allowing the group to maintain balance by holding hands makes them feel supported, both physically and emotionally.

Because the participants in this study were profoundly deaf, the data revealed rich visual images, symbolic pictures of interaction, and strong gestural images. These "kinesthetic snapshots" were memorable images and symbols of the interaction that occurred in the intergenerational program. As dancer Mary Wigman (1966) so aptly states, "It might very well be that, above all, the dance asks for direct communication without any detours" (p. 10). Certainly these words were true in this study, where dance was a clear vehicle for communication between two generations of profoundly deaf individuals.

Deafness

Interesting cultural distinctions existed between the two age groups who participated in the study. The children attended a school for people with a variety of disabilities, whereas the elders had attended residential and deaf day public schools. The children also lived at home, in hearing families who did not sign, while the elders lived in a residence predominantly for deaf elders who use ASL.

For the deaf elders, the group was the socializing element in their lives. They lived in the same residence, often ate together, and spent time together in the lobby and community room. This observation is consistent with G. Becker's (1980) findings in her study of 200 deaf elders: "The world view of deaf people is of people in groups rather than as individuals. Therefore the group becomes an organizing element in the social world of deafness" (p. 38).

The deaf elders and children communicated effortlessly in ASL–a symbolic bond that the young and old shared together. This sense of community, of a shared language and beginnings of a shared culture, was symbolized in the self-expression, language, and storytelling that occurred between the two age groups.

B. Myerhoff's (1978) study of Jewish elderly and their culture in a California community suggests how the fabric and meaning of specific cultures occurs through the stories that the people tell and the rituals that they enact. In this study, the deaf participants' sharing of deaf culture and stories had meaning for both the children and the elders. The children began to see a future, a continuity in the generational cycle, while the elders passed on some of their wisdom and life experiences.

Overall, in the intergenerational dance classes, the group became insiders in a deaf world where deafness was the central point of reference. This finding is consistent with the work of C. Padden and T. Humphries (1988), who believe there is a different center for those who are deaf: "For deaf people the greatest deviation is hearing . . . in this case Deaf, not hearing, is taken as the central point of reference" (p. 41). They believe that a widespread misconception among hearing people is that deaf people live in a world without sound. This metaphor of silence, portrayed by hearing people as the dark side of deafness, is different for those who are themselves deaf. Silence is not, in fact, at the core of deaf people; rather, they are filled with the sounds of rich layers of sign language and poetry that create a counterpoint and a music–and a different center.

In speaking about deafness, B.L. Benderly (1980) notes Helen Keller's observation that blindness separates people from things, but deafness separates people from people and is a disorder of communication. Unlike other communities, the deaf children in this study had little previous contact with deaf adults. There is little continuity from generation to generation for deaf communities and their members (Becker, 1980), and this study notes the significance of such intergenerational interaction, particularly for the children who began to learn from the elders about the deaf community and Deaf culture.

IMPLICATIONS FOR EMERGING TERMINOLOGY

The following glossary was developed in response to the need for a language that appropriately describes concepts and phenomena that emerged during the course of the study. This emerging language developed during the interaction between the two age groups.

Age Information Exchange: An interaction whereby the children gained information and awareness about the elderly and the elderly learned about the children.

Dance Warm-Up: This refers to the process whereby the children and elders through physical movement exercises broke the ice, warmed up muscles and joints, and socially interacted.

Generational Isolation: Separation between the generations.

Grandcaring: The children's sensitivity, nurturing, and sharing attitudes toward the older generations as a group as well as for individual older adults.

GrandParenting: The caring, nurturing, listening, and creativity of the elders toward the children.

Kinesthetic Mirroring: The simultaneous reflection that often occurred between a dance (movement) activity and the intergenerational relationships.

Kinesthetic Snapshot: Memorable and colorful images or pictures of the interactions.

Partnering: The interaction of one child and one older adult participating in intergenerational dance classes.

FINAL COMMENTS

In this study, the researcher observed the elderly become reintegrated with their youth as they imitated various dance moves of the children, mimed animals, and transformed themselves during thematic improvisations. The children began to understand aging through caring for the elders and became sensitive to aging. Through dance, age receded and reappeared. Through dance, one of the oldest forms of communication of humankind, the children and elders together shared a life-renewing and regenerating experience.

AUTHOR NOTE

Andrea Sherman was the national representative for the Arts and Humanities at the 1995 White House Conference on Aging and is a member of the Executive Committee, New York State Intergenerational Network.

BIBLIOGRAPHY

Becker, G. (1980). *Growing old in silence.* Berkeley,CA: University of California Press.

Benderly, B. L. (1980). *Dancing without music.* Washington, DC: Gallaudet University Press.

Blumer, H. (1969). *Symbolic interactionism.* Englewood Cliffs, NJ: Prentice-Hall, Inc.

Brummel, S. W. (1989). Developing an intergenerational program. In S. Newman & S.W. Brummel, Eds. *Intergenerational programs.* New York: The Haworth Press, Inc.

Caplow-Lindner, L. (1982). Dance as a therapeutic intervention for the elderly. *Educational Gerontology,* 8(2), 167-173.

Cumming, E., & Henry, W.E. (1961). *Growing old.* New York: Basic Books.

Erikson, E., Erikson, H., & Kivnik, H. (1986). *Vital involvement in old age.* New York: W. W. Norton & Co.

Garnet, E.D. (1982). *Movement is life.* Princeton, NJ: Princeton Book Co.

Kingson, E. (1989). The social policy implications of intergenerational exchange. In S. Newman & S. W. Brummel, Eds. *Intergenerational programs,* pp. 91-99. New York: The Haworth Press, Inc.

Lambert, D.J., Dellmann, J., & Fruit, D. (1990). Planning for contacts between the generations: An effective approach. *Gerontologist*. Washington, DC: Gerontological Society of America.

Lerman, L. (1984). *Teaching dance to senior adults*. Springfield, IL: Charles C. Thomas Publisher.

Mead, George H. (1934). *Mind, Self and Society*. Chicago, IL: University of Chicago Press.

Moody, H.R., & Disch, R. (1989). Intergenerational programming in public policy. In S. Newman & S.W. Brummel, Eds. *Intergenerational programs*, pp. 101-110. New York: The Haworth Press, Inc.

Myerhoff, B. (1978). *Number our days*. New York: Simon & Schuster.

Newman, S. (1986). *Senior citizen school volunteer program*. Pittsburgh: Generations Together.

Oosterhouse, S. E. (1985). Dance/movement therapy with the deaf. Unpublished master's thesis, Gaucher college, Towsen, MD.

Padden, C., & Humphries, T. (1988). *Deaf in America*. Cambridge, MA: Harvard University Press.

Stryker, S. (1980). *Symbolic interactionism*. Menlo Park, CA: The Benjamin/ Cummings.

Ventura-Merkel, C., Liederman, D.S., Ossofsky, J. (1989). Exemplary intergenerational programs. In S. Newman & S.W. Burmmel, Eds. *Intergenerational programs*, pp. 173-180. New York: The Haworth Press, Inc.

Wigman, M. (1966). *The language of dance*. Middletown, CT: Wesleyan University Press.

Intergenerational Mentoring:
A Viable Strategy for Meeting
the Needs of Vulnerable Youth

Anita M. Rogers, PhD
Andrea S. Taylor, PhD

INTRODUCTION

Over 14 million youth are growing up at risk of dropping out of school, abusing drugs, becoming involved in criminal activities, or exhibiting other problem behaviors. Many young people are isolated from the range of caring and consistent adult relationships that are so important for navigating the treacherous course from adolescence to adulthood. Research suggests that a good mentoring relationship can build a young person's skills and self-esteem as well as help buffer the inevitable stresses of adolescence. Mentors act as advocates, challengers, nurturers, and role models. Older adults, in particular, are an untapped resource for mentoring youth. Older Americans make up the fastest growing segment of the population

Anita M. Rogers is Principal Investigator of two Center for Substance Abuse Prevention grants, *Grandma's Kids*, a Temple University support program for children and kinship care providers and *Thank Goodness I'm Female*, a project of the Philadelphia Anti-Drug/Anti-Violence Network for middle school girls. Andrea S. Taylor is affiliated with the Center for Intergenerational Learning, Temple University, and is the Principal Investigator of the *Across Ages Project*, an intergenerational mentoring approach to drug prevention coordinated by the Center for Substance Abuse Prevention.

[Haworth co-indexing entry note]: "Intergenerational Mentoring: A Viable Strategy for Meeting the Needs of Vulnerable Youth." Rogers, Anita M., and Andrea S. Taylor. Co-published simultaneously in the *Journal of Gerontological Social Work* (The Haworth Press, Inc.) Vol. 28, No. 1/2, 1997, pp. 125-140; and: *Intergenerational Approaches in Aging: Implications for Education, Policy and Practice* (ed: Kevin Brabazon, and Robert Disch) The Haworth Press, Inc., 1997, pp. 125-140. Single or multiple copies of this article are available for a fee from The Haworth Document Delivery Service [1-800-342-9678, 9:00 a.m. - 5:00 p.m. (EST). E-mail address: getinfo@haworth.com].

125

and many are seeking opportunities for continued productive activity and meaningful human contact. The Center for Intergenerational Learning at Temple University joined these two burgeoning groups through two programs, *Linking Lifetimes*, a national program that utilized older persons as mentors to at-risk middle school students and young offenders in nine cities and *Across Ages*, a school-based Philadelphia project that matched older mentors with middle school students.

Linking Lifetimes started in 1989 as a research and demonstration initiative created to systematically promote the development of programs that provide support to vulnerable youth while simultaneously enabling older adults to remain productive members of our society. Today, seven of these programs are still operational. Across Ages was initiated in 1990 as an intergenerational drug prevention program under federal funding from the Center for Substance Abuse Prevention. Across Ages augmented elder mentoring with a child-centered life skills curriculum, elder-youth community service activities and workshops for parents and family members.

Unlike many corporate-based mentoring programs that match middle-aged persons with youth, Linking Lifetimes and Across Ages target persons 55 years and older to serve as mentors. Many of the mentors are older community residents who have experienced the same marginal status as the youth and therefore understand well the problems facing the young people in this program.

Traditionally, mentoring has occurred naturally when a younger or more inexperienced person and a mentor find each other, somewhat accidentally, through the identification of mutual needs and desires. Such natural mentoring progresses purely at the will and ease of the mentor and the youth. The resurgence of mentoring in a "planned" or "programmatic" format entails the matching of participant pairs, often strangers, within structured institutional settings. Such mentoring is spurred by the increased isolation and limited resources of disadvantaged youth and the recommitment of social structures to finding new intervention strategies to address the problems of this population. These programs are integrated with other interventions in order to have a significant impact on the high-risk youth. Mentors, in conjunction with agency staff, help youth set specific goals that guide them through school, work, and life decisions. Mentors and youth also enjoy sports/cultural activities together.

Although the growth in mentoring programs has spurred a number of research studies, very few have examined the experiences of older people as mentors. The preponderance of research about mentoring focuses on mentors from the corporate sector, business sector and nursing education areas. Also, the mentors studied are primarily middle aged and Caucasian while the youth are often gifted students or those who have B/C grade averages. Similarly, research on intergenerational programming, though more extensive, has focused primarily on relationships between elders and young children rather than those with at-risk adolescents. As the aging network becomes more involved in the challenge of helping America's troubled youth, it is essential that it identify which elders are most likely to get involved with at-risk youth and what factors are important in designing effective mentoring initiatives.

WHY ELDERS AS MENTORS TO YOUTH?

Although programmatic mentoring is gaining increased popularity across the country, most of the organizations promoting this concept focus on recruiting middle-aged, middle class and "corporate America" adults. Time constraints, competing responsibilities and commitments, and value differences often interfere with the ability of these mentors to develop and maintain meaningful relationships with vulnerable youth. Elders are a rich resource for the mentor pool. As the fastest growing segment of the population, older adults constitute a community resource with tremendous potential. During the past 30 years, the health and longevity of older Americans has improved substantially due to major advances in biomedical technologies and drug interventions that treat diseases, ameliorate their effects and often prevent their occurrence. When people talk about the growing population of elderly, they often couch such discussions in negative terms—greater numbers mean more societal problems. Rather than see the projected number of over 35 million older persons over 65 by the turn of the century as a problem, one could alternately see such growth as an opportunity. With the aging of the world's population, knowledge about elders and their volunteer patterns could assist policy makers in responding to the challenges of an aging productive society. According to a 1988 AARP survey, the 60-plus age group appears to give more time per month for their volunteer activities than those under 60. Kouri (1990) found that persons, age 65 to 74, volunteer an average of 6 hours a week, compared to 4.7 weekly hours for younger volunteers. As competition for volunteers increases, it is important to develop effective strategies for elder volunteer recruitment that are sensitive to the elderly and its many demographic characteristics.

A study by Lee and Burden (1991) explored the reasons older adults do and do not participate in volunteer activities. Their main findings of 258 residents over age 55 were as follows: 34.9% had been active in organized volunteer work, while 65.1% volunteered informally; 76.6% of volunteers donated their time to a single organization; and the most frequently mentioned volunteer work was care, companionship and visiting (28.9%). The frequent reason given for volunteering was "to help others," reported by 33.3%. Elders not involved in volunteer activities said they were too busy (30.4%) or poor health prohibited them (25%). These findings suggest that elder volunteers are available but often are not found in formal organizational structures. It would also appear that the motivation for elders volunteering may be very altruistic, for many give without a lot of fanfare and are not included in volunteer statistics.

A study by Newman, Vasudev, and Onawola (1985) found that older volunteers who worked with school youth felt that their intergenerational experience had given their lives meaning, structure and a sense of feeling needed. Elders in this program also felt that they were enriched and rejuvenated by the experience which helped them cope with their own personal traumas. Tierce (1987) identified older adults as valuable school volunteers who could fill in the void left at schools by the overwhelming number of women returning to the workplace. He notes that the elders bring a lifetime of experiences to the classroom setting and dispel many negative stereotypes about old people. Elder volunteers have time to give youth the attention they need, as well as valuable skills and experiences to share. For young people who lack a future orientation and perceive they have few choices, an older adult who has experienced significant changes can offer a life perspective that is rooted in survival. For elders, mentoring provides an opportunity to feel needed and to pass on the knowledge they have accumulated over a lifetime. Elder mentors can perform many roles including the following:

- Companion–interacting with the youth;
- Social Supporter–showing concern, respect, encouragement;
- Teacher–teaching or expanding the youth's horizons;
- Role Model–modeling values and behavior;
- Challenger–encouraging goals, plans;
- Resource Supporter–providing explanations, advice, resources.

In a report entitled *Partners in Growth*, Marc Freedman (1988) describes elder-youth relationships in five programs across the country. He indicated that in many cases older adults established genuine relationships with youth that closely paralleled extended family. Often elders used their personal connections to help their partners obtain work and provided youth entry into social networks that were formerly closed to them. Elders promoted youth's stability and sense of competence by giving unconditional support, appreciating the abilities they possessed, and taking them seriously.

Many elder mentors become powerful advocates for their mentees, teaching them how to navigate the system. Freedman suggests that older people who had experienced the same marginal status as high-risk youth were especially resourceful and effective in reaching vulnerable youth.

Elders can and have made a significant difference in the lives of young people. Considering the fact that there are millions of older adults in the United States today, can we afford not to look to this group to help us address the problems of troubled youth?

PROJECT GOALS

The overall mission of intergenerational mentoring initiatives is to help vulnerable youth become productive and self-reliant members of society. Specifically, the goals of Across Ages and Linking Lifetimes are to:

1. Demonstrate the efficacy of utilizing elder mentors as a viable strategy for helping youth-at-risk;
2. Foster collaboration among agencies serving youth and elders;
3. Influence public policy regarding the value of intergenerational mentoring as an effective social intervention;
4. Broaden the theoretical and empirical knowledge base on intergenerational mentoring; and
5. Facilitate the replication of effective intergenerational mentoring models.

Program Guidelines for Intergenerational Mentoring

The Linking Lifetimes and Across Ages initiatives established and tested some basic guidelines that can be utilized to help other organizations develop successful intergenerational mentoring programs. The following are the basic features of intergenerational mentoring:

- Mentors receive 8-10 hours of preservice training on mentoring, adolescent development, communication skills, problem-solving techniques, and other relevant topics.
- Youth and their families receive orientation about the requirements for participation in the program.
- There is one-to-one contact between mentors and youth for a specified minimum number of hours per week (usually 2-6 hours).
- Mentors are asked to commit themselves to a youth for at least one year.

- A mentor can be matched with more than one youth as long as each youth receives one-on-one contact for the minimum required hours.
- Specific mentoring activities are determined by individual mentor-youth pairs and driven by the specific needs of youth. There is a general goal of developing the youth's social competence, productivity, and self-reliance as it relates to clearly identified programmatic outcomes (e.g., school performance, employment, effective parenting skills).
- Mentors and youth mutually agree to the general purposes of their relationship in terms that are understandable, acceptable, and consistent with the goals of the initiative and operating sites.
- Mentoring activities complement general agency services and are integrated into the case management plans for the youth.
- Ongoing support of the mentor-youth relationship is provided through personal contact with mentors and youth, regularly scheduled mentor in-service training, youth and parent group meetings, and large group mentor-youth activities, as well as interaction with other professionals who relate to the participants.
- Mentors receive stipends and/or are reimbursed for expenses.
- Agencies work with other community agencies serving children and/ or older adults.
- Sites procure consent forms signed by all elder mentors, youth, and their parents or legal guardians (when the youth is under 18 years) stating that they agree to participate in all program and research activities.

These guidelines should be adapted to meet the specific needs of each program's targeted population.

Key Implementation Issues

Linking Lifetimes and Across Ages provided an opportunity to identify strategies that could facilitate solid mentor-youth matches and programmatic structures. The following are recommended program practices that can help program operators institute effective intergenerational mentoring projects.

Creating Partnerships: If the goal of the project is successful relationships between mentors and youth, it is important to model and emphasize relationship-building at all levels of the project. Intergenerational approaches to program development, by definition, tend to involve a great deal of interagency cooperation; extra time and effort are often required to establish trust and clear communication between project partners, particularly if they have never worked together before.

Staffing: A single coordinator, serving a case management role, should be given the responsibility for primary contact for both mentors and youth. A program usually needs at least a 50% time coordinator to manage a 20 mentor-10 youth complement. Cultural sensitivity and understanding should be primary considerations in staff selection. Additionally, program coordinators and other related staff should have opportunities to be updated about the latest developments in their own program as well as the general field of mentoring.

Client Orientation: Information and orientation sessions should be provided for the targeted youth and their families to maximize the benefits they can receive from the mentor-youth relationship. If young people are to be prepared for their own aging and be sensitive to their elder partners, they must be taught about aging. According to Pratt (1982), this teaching falls into three areas: informing the young about what happens to people when they age; dispelling myths about the elderly; and enlightening youth about social issues that will impact upon all people, no matter what age. Preparing youth in these latter areas will help them be more receptive to older volunteers as well as provide services to elders with more sensitivity and understanding. Youth orientation prior to matching them with elders is essential.

Agency Linkage: The sponsoring organization should integrate the mentoring program into their general agency offerings and planning process to stabilize the program, particularly when start-up funds diminish. Placing the mentoring project within a unit that has a higher likelihood of sustaining it is paramount. Besides the intra-agency linkages, it is essential for the project to create and sustain relationships with outside agencies whose sanction of the project and resources can foster its success.

Elder Mentor Recruitment: Mentor recruitment is a labor intensive process. Targeted mentor recruitment should focus on mentors who are more likely to meet the needs of the selected youth population. Since a large majority of the at-risk youth in mentoring programs are from African-American and Hispanic communities, recruiting and maintaining elders of similar cultural backgrounds to serve as mentors is an important task. Attention should also be given to recruiting culturally sensitive elders mentors who may reside in the "backyards" of the targeted youth. Morrow-Howell and Mui (1990) in a study on the impact of race on elder volunteers in helping relationships found that clients rated racially mixed dyads as less helpful and felt the elders committed less time to the relationship than when the volunteers and client were of the same race. Such a finding may address the predilection of the participants for sameness and expectation of cultural similarities. This study also suggests, however, that more energy may need to go into matching volunteers with same race clients. It would appear that, too often, little effort is exerted to find volunteers who are from the same cultural background of clients. Other studies have demonstrated that older Americans are under-utilized as volunteers, and that many would welcome the opportunity to become productive again but need to be actively recruited and welcomed by program staff (Wolozin, 1985; Stevens, 1990; Morrow-Howell and Mui, 1989). These authors suggest that personal contact was essential for successful recruitment of elders and the creation of social opportunities among the elderly and appropriate placement were key to maintaining them as volunteers. Thus, successful outreach to this population might be affected less by formal techniques, such as letters, than face-to-face contact that allows for discussion with potential older volunteers. Such contact could also serve to convince the elders of their worth to serve, which has been greatly minimized in western cultures.

Mentor Screening: In addressing potential volunteers, a balance must be struck between presenting the program as an exciting opportunity for a positive experience and describing in a realistic manner the difficult challenges in working with high-risk youth. It may be tempting to oversell the program in order to meet the projected number of volunteers, but careful screening will avoid difficulties later on. This can be handled through personal interviews, preservice training, talking with references and more formal background checks.

Elder Incentives: Inducements for increasing elder volunteerism are suggested by Costello (1991) which include: decreased organizational barriers, targeted recruitment strategies, on age sensitive working environment, and a system of incentives or fringe benefits. Such inducements suggest the need to develop and implement more succinct elder volunteer policies by public, private and independent sectors on the local, state and national levels. These policies would consider making buildings more easily accessible, conducting age sensitivity training with staff who would be in contact with elder volunteers, and planning recruitment that would emphasize benefits meaningful to this population. Incentives for mentor participation include reimbursable expenses or stipends, college credits, free meals, employee recognition and practicum placement. The importance of the stipend was underscored in a teen parenting program in which mentors dropped out when funds were no longer available to support their mentor activity (Branch, Riccio & Quint, 1984). Money as the sole inducement for a mentor's participation certainly raises the issue of the mentor's reasons for volunteering or their inability to support their mentor efforts without funds. This certainly has implications for low income persons who would like to mentor but cannot afford the cost of volunteering.

Elder Mentor Training/Support: The training of both mentors and mentees is an extremely important component in planned mentoring programs. The training enables the pair to get to know one another and understand their roles with each other, facilitates their communication and helps them develop realistic expectations. Elders must also become familiar with the youth culture so that they can adequately relate to the issues confronting their younger friends and provide support. Ongoing mentor training and contact provide the opportunity for empowering the mentor to assume greater responsibility in the development and maintenance of the relationship as well as diminishing the oversight role of the coordinator. Regularly scheduled mentor meetings usually serve a support group function and encourage mentors to assume leadership roles for the entire mentor program as well as provide opportunities for mentors to express their concerns and problem-solve.

Elder Mentor/Youth Matches: Clear cut guidelines must be established to insure that match terminations are smooth transitions for both the mentor and the youth. A wide variety of issues must be considered when forming mentor-youth pairs, including transportation/scheduling issues, health, gender, race, cultural background, interests/hobbies and stated personal preferences. Training and/or informal workshops for elders and youth go a long way toward breaking down age-related stereotypes on both sides and provide project staff a chance to observe interactions between them. If a match needs to be terminated prior to the committed time period, mentors and youth must have an opportunity to talk with one another so that both understand the reasons for termination. The process for termination should be explained during training and orientation.

Mentor-Youth Activities/Relationship: In 1992 (Styles & Morrow) Public Private Ventures (P/PV) completed a study of four Linking Lifetimes intergenerational mentoring sites in which several characteristics of successful mentoring relationships between older adults and at-risk youth were identified. P/PV found that successful adult/youth relationships were characterized by the mentor being able to identify and address the youth's needs. The seven effective patterns of mentor interaction identified were:

1. patience in allowing trust to develop in the relationship;
2. identification of youth's interests and taking those interests seriously;
3. the offering of constant reassurance;
4. mentors not forcing disclosure;
5. offering of help in solving problems on the youth's terms;

6. acceptance of the youth's family, social class, and culture; and
7. understanding of mentor role of giving.

Program goals at both the agency and mentor-youth levels should be clearly articulated and formalized so participants can identify and attain tangible successes. Beyond the goal of establishing a personal relationship, it is strongly recommended that the mentor-youth pairs have identifiable, well-defined goals to reach.

Meeting Facilities: If possible, programs should identify a meeting space(s) that both mentors and youths can clearly identify as "their" place. The space(s) should be large to accommodate the range of program activities. A program space also provides turf where both mentors and youth can feel safe.

Project Evaluation

Evaluation is a critically important component of program development. It enables practitioners to determine the extent to which project goals have been met and to identify hard evidence that a program is successful. For programs which depend on funding from federal, state or local agencies, a solid evaluation plan is essential.

Program evaluation includes both process and outcome data. Process evaluation refers to data that is collected to assist program staff in understanding the context in which a project is developing and the way it is being implemented, the characteristics of the population being served, the amount and types of services being provided and the costs involved (King, Morris and Fitz-Gibbon, 1987; Scheirer, 1987). Process data also serves to illuminate the outcome findings and to interpret results which, taken alone, might have little meaning. Examples of process data include on-site and telephone interviews conducted with project participants and staff; observations of program activities; attendance and extent of participation in program activities; information from focus groups; school records; and logs, progress reports or intake forms completed by participants.

Outcome evaluation provides empirical evidence that a program is having an impact on its target population. A randomized pretest/post-test control group is the classic model of experimental design (Campbell and Stanley, 1966). Each experimental group is exposed to one "treatment" condition while others in a comparison group receive no treatment. The results are then compared by means of analyzing a survey completed by participants at the beginning and conclusion of the program. Ideally, treatment and control group populations are identical and control group participants have not been exposed to any experimental conditions.

The evaluation results of *Across Ages* and *Linking Lifetimes*, when examined together, render a comprehensive picture of intergenerational mentoring and its positive impact on youth. Process data provided valuable documentation about the nature, progression and intensity of the mentor relationships, as well as information for interpreting the results of the outcome evaluation. The outcome evaluation demonstrated the importance of intergenerational mentoring as a powerful intervention for supporting high risk youth.

WHO ARE THE MENTORS?

Some tendency toward female participants. Slightly more than half the youth were female, reflecting the demographics among the general population in this age group. Approximately $2/3$ of the mentors, however, were female. It would appear that the greater longevity of older women and the likelihood that women volunteer more often than men contribute to this phenomena.

Greater tendency toward African-American participants. Over 75% of the older mentors were African-American. A majority of the youth involved were African-American. The projects had less success in recruiting mentors of other races and ethnicities. Recruitment is definitely influenced both by the individual doing the recruiting as well as the norms operating in a particular culture and/or community. For example, the concept of caring for all the children, regardless of kinship, is more acceptable in some communities than in others.

Truly intergenerational. Mentors ages ranged from 51-93 years, while youth ages range from 9-20 years. The average difference in age for a mentor-youth pair was 50 years.

Varied educational levels. Approximately $3/4$ of the mentors had completed high school. Of these, a few had completed a year or two of college and a few held a Bachelor's degree. Of the $1/4$ who had not completed high school, a small number had returned to school to work toward a GED.

Mentor health generally good. More than $3/4$ of the mentors reported good health that was "rarely a problem." Even those whose health was not the best reported their involvement as a mentor motivated them toward increased activity because of their commitment to the youth.

Most pairs were same-gender. Over half the matches were comprised of a female mentor and youth. Another third matched a male youth with a male mentor, while some paired a female mentor with a male youth. Male mentors were not paired with female youth.

Most pairs were same-ethnicity. Three quarters of the pairs (75%) were of the same racial or ethnic background. These included: African-American, Latino, Asian, Caucasian and Native American Indian.

WHAT MAKES A SUCCESSFUL RELATIONSHIP?

The research indicates that there are distinct behavioral patterns of interaction between elders and youth in "satisfied" versus "dissatisfied" relationships. Satisfied relationships were youth driven in their content and timing whereas dissatisfaction often resulted when the mentor failed to take the youth's interest into account and were prescriptive in how they would work with the youth (Styles & Morrow, 1992).

For Youth

Was the activity fun? The mentoring relationship was largely seen in terms of whether the activities they shared together were "fun" for them. There was no higher praise for a mentor than being described as "a lot of fun." Youth wanted mentors to take part in the recreational activities they enjoyed or be willing to accompany them on an outing such as roller skating even if the mentor might not be able to fully participate. Youth enjoyed going to places that were familiar to them, but were also excited to try out new things. Resentment occurred if a mentor consistently planned something without input from the youth.

Was the mentor a good listener? The worst thing a mentor could do was talk to the youth in terms of "shoulds" and "oughts." When mentors saw their role as educators rather than friends, the youth perceived them as nagging. If a young person approached the mentor with a problem to be solved, either personal or school related, the adult who could listen and help the youth generate solutions was greatly appreciated.

Did the youth learn something new? Many youth appreciated the help they received from their mentors in finding job opportunities, filling out applications and in doing something new like baking a cake or building a bookshelf. The mentor's ability to support the youth's interest and need to learn new skills, rather than impose his/her own agenda, was a significant impetus in driving a successful relationship.

For the Mentors

Did the youth appear to be trusting? Many mentors in unsatisfying relationships described an initial situation that seemed daunting: the youth seemed to mistrust them from the start, just because they were adults, frequently failed to keep appointments and were often unresponsive. In contrast, youth who were particularly interested in having a supportive adult relationship often shared more at the first meeting than the mentor was comfortable with. Successful mentors were usually able to resist the temptation to force the relationship, instead taking it more slowly. Most started with mutually agreed-upon recreational activities, and offered youth counsel or an opportunity to talk only when asked.

Did the mentor understand the youth's background? One of the biggest problems for many mentors was coming to terms with the youth's background. Some had a difficult time understanding their youth's culture and experience even if they had been raised under similar circumstances. Some had difficulty because they feared the neighborhood in which the youth lived and allowed their own perceptions to affect their ability to support the youth and take part in his/her life.

What was the nature of the relationship with the youth's family? Perhaps the most troubling problem for mentors was their relationship with the youth's family. Some said the youth's family opposed the relationship. Others felt the youth's family had become too close–in some cases the parents expected the mentor to be their confidant. Many mentors described a difficult balancing act between understanding and appreciating the youth's family, and maintaining the one-on-one mentoring relationship as the centerpiece.

WHAT ARE THE OUTCOMES FOR YOUTH?

A classic experimental research design was conducted with students in classrooms participating in *Across Ages*. The results indicate positive outcomes for youth on a variety of measures. Experimental and control group classes were randomly assigned from a pool of 6th grade teachers who had all agreed to participate after classes for special education or mentally gifted were eliminated from the selection. Three classes were randomly selected in each school and assigned to one of three groups.

Group 1: This group received all experimental conditions. This included: (1) mentoring; (2) participating in a life skills curriculum taught by the classroom teachers; (3) performing community service activities; and (4) engaging parents and family members of the targeted youth in workshops designed to support and enhance positive parenting and involvement in school activities.

Group 2: This group received all experimental conditions except mentoring.

Group 3: This group received no experimental conditions but served as a comparison group.

Hypothesis: The major hypothesis was that all students participating in the project would show positive changes in outcome measures over those in the control group. The most positive changes, however, would be seen for those students who had mentors. Furthermore, the more intense the mentoring relationship, the more significant the change.

Results: Students in both experimental groups, those with mentors and those without, demonstrated statistically or marginally significant differences on 7 of the 9 measurement scales over students in the control group. Measurements included: (1) reactions to stress and anxiety; (2) self-perception; (3) the Rand well-being scale; (4) attitudes toward school, elders and the future; (5) problem-solving efficacy; (6) attitudes/knowledge about older people; (7) overall frequency of substance use (for specific substances) during the past two months; (8) persuasion to use specific substances; and (9) knowledge about substance abuse.

Scores were most favorable, however, for those students who received mentoring in addition to other program interventions (Group 1). Significant results favoring Group 1 over Group 2 included measures of attitudes toward school, future and elders; feelings of well-being; frequency of drug use; and reactions to stress and anxiety.

A variable of particular interest to practitioners and researchers is school attendance. The results of the study are clear and notable. Those students in Group 1, those with mentors, had fewer days absent than those in both Groups 2 and 3. Group 2 students, in turn, had fewer absences than those in Group 3. Within Group 1, it was also found that those students identified by staff as being highly involved with their mentors were absent even less than those identified as involved at an average or marginal level.

The evaluation results support the initial hypothesis that a multifaceted approach in working with high-risk youth results in positive changes. Mentoring, however, appears to result in even more significant changes by: (1) enhancing youth's knowledge and refusal skills regarding alcohol, tobacco and other drugs; and (2) increasing youth's reported sense of self-worth, promoting feelings of well-being, and reducing feelings of sadness and loneliness.

CONCLUSION

These findings add to the conclusion that interventions for high-risk youth must unite them and the important adults in their lives in a collaborative effort to develop positive coping skills and strategies for staying in school, abstaining from risky sexual behavior and resisting drugs. Mentoring must be viewed as part of a broad social strategy that recognizes the importance of adult relationships in the lives of young people. Specifically, older mentors, because they have the time, patience and experience, are in an ideal position to be a valuable support to youth.

AUTHOR NOTE

Previously, Anita M. Rogers coordinated *Linking Lifetimes* Center for Intergenerational Learning at Temple and has co-authored several intergenerational mentoring publications and videos.

Andrea S. Taylor provides training and technical assistance for replication of the *Across Ages Project* model and is the author of several articles about the benefits of intergenerational mentoring for youth-at-risk, including (as co-author) "An Outcome Evaluation of *Across Ages*" in the *Journal of Adolescent Research* Vol. 11, No. 1 (January, 1996).

REFERENCES

Branch, A., Riccio, J., and Quint, J. (1984). Building Self-Sufficiency in Pregnant and Parenting Teens. Final Implementation Report of Project Redirection. New York: Manpower Demonstration Research Corporation.

Campbell, D.T., and Stanley, J.C. (1966). *Experimental and quasi-experimental design for research.* Chicago, IL: Rand-McNally.

Costello, Cynthia B. (1991). Executive summary and commentary. In AARP & Cornell University Department of Rural Sociology (Eds.). *Resourceful Aging: Today and Tomorrow,* pp. 15-29. Washington, DC: Families USA Foundation.

Freedman, M. (1988). *Partners in Growth: Elder Mentors and At-Risk Youth.* Philadelphia: Public/Private Ventures.

King, Jean A., Morris, Lynn L., and Fitz-Gibbons, Carol, T. (1987). *How to assess program implementation.* Newbury Park, CA: Sage.

Kouri, Mark (1990). *Volunteerism and Older Adults.* ABC-CLIO, Inc., Santa Barbara, CA

Lee, Alec J., and Burden, Catherine (1991). Understanding the needs of the senior volunteer. *Journal of Volunteer Administration,* 9(2), 13-17.

Morrow-Howell, Nancy, & Mui, Anita (1989). Elderly volunteers: Reason for initiation and terminating services. *Journal of Gerontological Social Work,* 13(3-4), pp. 21-34.

Newman, Sally, Vasudev, Jyotsna, & Onawola, Roland (1985, December). *Older volunteers' perception of impact of volunteering on their psychological well being,* 4 (2), pp. 123-127.

Pratt, Fran (1982, February). What should we teach the young about growing old? *Massachusetts Council for Social Studies Newsletter.* pp. 2-3.

Scheirer, Mary A. (1987). Program theory and implementation theory: Implications for evaluators. In Leonard Bickman (ed.) *Using program theory in evaluation, new directions for program evaluation.* No. 33. San Francisco: Jossey-Bass.

Stevens, Ellen S. (1990). Utilizing a "rich" resource: Older volunteers. *Journal of Volunteer Administration,* 8 (2), 38.

Styles, Melanie B., & Morrow, Kristine (1992). *Understanding how youth and elders form relationships.* Public Private Ventures, Philadelphia, PA.

Tierce, Jerry Wood and Sielbach, Wayne C. (1987). Elders as school volunteers: An untapped resource. *Educational Gerontology,* 13 (1), pp. 33-41.

Wolozin, Harold (1985, Winter). Volunteer work and the retired: Road to renewed productivity. *Retirement Planning,* pp. 13-15.

Rememberers and Remembrances:
Fostering Connections
with Intergenerational Interviewing

Nancy Lubarsky, EdD

Life review is the ground on which the old wage the struggle for
integrity; it is here that they reexamine and come to terms with the
Was. . . . the old are free to remember, to regret, to look reflectively
at the past and try to understand it. And we are free to listen and to
treat rememberers and remembrances with the respect they deserve.
(Dobrof, 1984, p. xviii)

In *The Uses of Reminiscence: New Ways of Working with Older Adults*
(1984), Marc Kaminsky (Ed.) and other researchers and theorists who
work with the elderly discuss a powerful method, the life review, that
enables older people to access their personal stories. The emphasis in this
work is on enabling participants to get in touch with those stories which
have given or will give their lives meaning, value and completeness.

Kaminsky sees this reflective process as a way for older people to piece
together seemingly unconnected ideas and events among their experiences
and to find threads that will link and develop them into some overarching
themes or 'answers.'

We can discern the life review process in action when we find, amid
fragments of reminiscence, a recurring configuration of images that

---

Nancy Lubarsky is an English/Social Studies Supervisor at Abraham Clark
High School in New Jersey.

[Haworth co-indexing entry note]: "Rememberers and Remembrances: Fostering Connections with
Intergenerational Interviewing." Lubarsky, Nancy. Co-published simultaneously in the *Journal of Gerontological Social Work* (The Haworth Press, Inc.) Vol. 28, No. 1/2, 1997, pp. 141-149; and: *Intergenerational Approaches in Aging: Implications for Education, Policy and Practice* (ed: Kevin Brabazon,
and Robert Disch) The Haworth Press, Inc., 1997, pp. 141-149. Single or multiple copies of this article
are available for a fee from The Haworth Document Delivery Service [1-800-342-9678, 9:00 a.m. - 5:00
p.m. (EST). E-mail address: getinfo@haworth.com].

> manifest a question and a partial answer to it. This description im-
> plies that the repetition of the configuration of images is the result of
> a normative problem-solving process . . . Each recurrence may be
> seen as another attempt to answer the question which the life review
> manifests and addresses; the process is of necessity repeated until the
> pieces of the configuration have been put together in a new way, one
> that provides illumination, wholeness, and harmony. (Kaminsky,
> 1984, p. 14)

The continual review of and return to these images and ideas through
reflection and conversation is the heart of the process. Kaminsky also sees
writing about these experiences as a way to enhance and extend them. He
describes two different life review projects in which writing played a key
role. In one, the participants kept a journal and that significantly affected
the way they perceived themselves and their own ideas. "[They] began to
approach the world as writer[s]: predatory, receptive, curious, curatorial;
they sought to find in their everyday lives the raw materials for stories and
poems" (p. 3). Others engaged in autobiographical writing and were able
to explore memories and ideas that were perhaps once off-limits, document them, and discover where the meaning was hidden (p. 18).

Unfortunately, according to Harry R. Moody in "Reminiscence and the
Recovery of the Public World" (1984), traditional storytelling, particularly those stories passed down from society's elders, is not valued as much
as it once was. He argues that telling stories is not just for amusement but
functions as important guidance for future generations.

> One of the greatest dangers we face is that the whole activity of
> storytelling may seem irrelevant. Modern societies discard the past
> and thus abolish the possibility of collective memory, the history of a
> unified social order in which old people have a function–the function
> of storytellers, carriers of tribal lore, initiates into the world of ances-
> tors. (Moody, 1984, p. 158)

There also seems to be a de-emphasis on narrative and storytelling in
school curricula, particularly at the higher grade levels. Barbara Hardy, in
her essay "Narrative as a Primary Act of Mind" (1977), argues against a
simplistic, short-sighted view of narrative. She feels that many educators
operate under the false assumption that growth and maturation means
moving away from stories and toward a more fact-oriented, realistic curriculum. She emphasizes that storytelling doesn't come to an end at age
eighteen but rather remains intertwined with the more "life-oriented modes
of planning, faithful remembering, and rational appraisal" (Hardy, 1977,
p. 13).

Many educational theorists would argue that not only is this life review process a good tool for reflecting and synthesizing one's past but the very act of constructing narratives about one's world is the primary way individuals of any age think and learn.

John Dewey believed that every experience that humans learn from calls for a synthesis of past experience in light of present experience, subject to revision with future experience.

> . . . we live from birth to death in a world of persons and things which in large measure is what it is because of what has been done and transmitted from previous human activities. (Dewey, 1938, p. 39)

The experiences of other people become part of a single individual's experience. The continuum of experiences a person has from birth constitutes one's life–one's view of the world, one's story.

Narrative-making also reflects this continuum of experience. The stories an individual tells or writes throughout life stem from stories that were heard. These story transactions in turn become part of any future stories that may be told or written.

> In the broadest sense every story is a kind of retelling only comprehensible in the light of other texts or bits of them . . . We are all a plurality of other stories, including our own. We are our stories. (Rosen, 1986, p. 236)

Surely one underappreciated characteristic of older people is their ability to review, reflect, and generalize from past experience. They are able somehow to see the connections that exist among a multitude of experiences and learn from these connections. In this way they are able to better understand their own stories and life becomes more meaningful. Younger people, in their search for meaning, often wish they could be privy to this type of insight earlier in life. But hearing, reading, or writing stories affords a similar opportunity for the young. "Stories become a way in which the storyteller appraises his life experience" (Rosen, 1984, p. 10).

> . . . For we dream in narrative, daydream in narrative, remember, anticipate, hope, despair, believe, doubt, plan, revise, criticize, construct, gossip, learn, hate, and love by narrative. In order to really live, we make up stories about ourselves and others, about the personal as well as the social past and future. (Hardy, 1977, p. 13)

It is through continued experiences with story that individuals can learn to understand this process of reflection and appraisal and use it as a guide in everyday life, thinking and learning. "Through telling stories, humans build their experience of living. The representation of events in narrative discourse allows experiences to become internalized and owned" (Van Dongen, 1987, p. 81).

Mind (consciousness) and narrative (story-making) both exist in the continuum of human ability and desire to make meaning.

> To tell a story is to formulate an interlocking set of meanings: to listen to one is in its turn an active search for the teller's meaning via one's own: To retell a story is also to do just that because listening is a kind of retelling . . . Retelling [is] the ways in which we at one and the same time repeat the words and stories of others and also transform them. We even repeat our own words and stories as the context changes and new meaning potential asserts itself. (Rosen, 1986, pp. 231-35)

The more people involve themselves with stories—listening, telling, retelling—the more they come to understand the complexities and the benefits of the process the more accessible it becomes. There is much for the young and the old to learn from and through narrative.

Zavatsky, in "Journey Through the Feminine: The Life Review Poems of William Carlos Williams" (1984), emphasized the mutual benefits of the intergenerational experience with regard to the life review. Both participants contributed to an understanding of the cycle of generations and the continuity of human experience.

> It may not be the elderly person who initiates the life-review process at all . . . the child or grandchild (or a surrogate figure) coming with questions, at whatever age, has a significant role to play in it. Further, and on the assumption that one's own life and fate are inextricably bound to the lives and fates of one's parents, the life review may be just as crucial and instructive a *rite de passage* for the younger participant as it is for the aging or dying elder. . . . through the stories of our parents and grandparents we shape our own story, our own vision of ourselves. (Zavatsky, 1984, p. 176)

Life review has the potential to bridge the gap between classroom and social world and between spoken and written language. By asking questions of an elder, the interview experience can give a student access to a kind of information which is unavailable through more traditional means, namely: an experiential qualitative "feel" for past events; a sense of community and personal involvement in it; a knowledge and understanding of different generations; and insight into one person's story as a microcosm of the collective story of humanity.

Students who participate in the intergenerational interview process have opportunity to discover and identify the roots of their own values and to examine and reflect on the values of an individual more experienced at living. At the same time the process is illuminating for the older person who is given opportunity to talk to someone who was just beginning this lifelong discovery process.

To explore the processes of intergenerational interviewing and life review and their relationship to writing and reading, several projects were initiated by the author involving high school students and senior citizens. In these projects the students were paired with older members of the community and spent from two to four hour-long sessions talking with them.

To prepare for these meetings, the students read and discussed literature and other materials related to older people in society. They then developed questions that they felt were significant to ask their older partners. The questions were evaluated and categorized by the students for use during the interviews. The project director also met with the older people to prepare them for their experience with teenagers. The interviews were taped and loosely transcribed by the students, who were asked to develop several different types of writing based on the interviews. The writings were published in a booklet, a copy of which was given to all the participants.

The first long-term project was initiated in 1985 with fourteen students from the author's remedial reading class (grades 9-12). The return of Halley's Comet was used as a time marker to provide focus for interviews with twelve elders from a local senior center, all of whom could remember the comet's previous sighting in 1910. To prepare, the students spoke with an astronomer, with representatives of the Union County (New Jersey) Division on Aging and with members of the New Jersey Historical Commission. The project lasted about six months and yielded a small booklet and a slide show which detailed the experiences of the participants. The students learned much about the communication process and how it can break down stereotypes. Talking to the senior citizens and writing about them helped the students to view themselves as much more than their "remedial" labels would imply. (For further information about this project, see Lubarsky, Nancy, "A Glance at the Past, A Glimpse of the Future," *Journal of Reading,* March, 1987.)

The second project involved twenty high school juniors from a general English class taught by the author during the 1987-88 school year. Over a four-week period, the students interviewed thirteen members of the community who had resided in the town for at least fifty years. A booklet, produced at the end of the project, contained photographs and stories about the town and was partially funded by the New Jersey Historical Commission. Another important project outcome was a video which chronicled the project from beginning to end. This was placed in the school library and will be available to students and teachers who may wish to replicate the project. In addition to learning from and about senior citizens, the students gained a stronger sense of community and an appreciation for their hometown and its residents.

In a third project which took place in 1992, thirteen students each interviewed a family member to learn about an old family recipe and then developed questions which would help them get at "the story" which accompanied the recipe. Both stories and recipes were put together in a booklet entitled "Food for Thought" which was distributed to all the participants. A luncheon was then held to allow the participants to cook and sample the recipes. Through this project the students made connections on multiple levels–history, culture, family–and they learned how cuisine can serve as a window and a catalyst to deepening understanding of each of these.

In another project that lasted three years (beginning in 1990) the author examined the link between intergenerational interviews and the development of writing. Three students were asked to select a family member who was at least two generations older to interview about his or her life. The students conducted interviews over a four-month period, examined transcripts of the interviews, and wrote both informally (through the use of journals) and formally (through essays, stories, poems, and plays) about this process. The writing generated was influenced by the structure of the interviews. For example, one student focused her questions on how her life compared with her grandmother's and wrote poetry influenced by this comparison. Another student's questions yielded a chronology of the events of her uncle's life and in a short story she tried to link these events. A third student kept returning to the same issues in her pattern of questioning, much like a spiral. Her poems and essay also reflected this structure. In all instances the students wrote in a variety of genres and took risks in that they may have chosen genres with which they were unfamiliar.

Thematic links from the interviews to the writing were also examined in transcripts of the interviews and in writing samples. What the students identified as major themes in the interviews were found to have been incorporated into their writing. The author also noted that informal discussion of the themes along with written assignments resulted in improved capacity for abstract consideration and interpretation by the students. The students also felt the writing experiences enabled them to act as real researchers/ethnographers and to work on topics that were authentically connected to their lives.

A more recent project (1994), funded by a grant from the National Council of Teachers of English, was conducted with a tenth grade English class. The fifteen students interviewed fourteen community members in a local senior center about how life in their hometown had changed over the years. Student attitudes about writing both before and after the interview experience were measured and revealed that the students saw writing in this context as a much more natural, personal experience than the standard classroom exercises. A video was also produced which followed the participants in their discovery process.

Through the projects described above, the students created questions which helped to elicit the stories of elderly individuals. During this process the students not only listened to the stories, but in fact collaborated with the older people in their creations. The stories were eventually put into finished, printed story products that uniquely belonged to both the tellers and the listeners.

Initially, both the students and their elderly partners were shy and uncertain of what to say. Neither group felt that their thoughts and experiences were of any importance. But after several sessions, formal interviews became dialogues which ultimately became conversations about issues and ideas which concerned both young and old.

Through participation in the story-telling process, the students developed understanding, sensitivity and respect for the elders, the community, and for their shared history. Deeply involved in the review/creation of stories, the students also learned firsthand about the structure of storytelling and the special power it imparts to both the listener and the teller. The older people learned that what they had to say had value and significance for the young people and for themselves.

The manner of asking questions in these projects was based on the students' personal concerns and knowledge and also on what they heard and responded to during the interviews. As a result, the created "story" was the outcome of a dynamic process between the student and the older person.

By integrating the formal and informal processes described above the curriculum was self-generated and initiated through the students. They were not passive listeners, but took an active role in the creation of the narratives and in the development of themes they would eventually write about. Each interview yielded a unique and personalized narrative structure that mirrored a structuring or restructuring of the thinking taking place in the mind of the participant.

These projects helped both students and elders learn how to really listen to one another, and both groups learned to question stereotypes and assumptions about people and ideas. They learned to value their own voices and experiences. The students in particular gained a new understanding of story and how the creation of a story can impact on its creators. The sharing of stories bonds people and brings them into a common reality, an experience that is never lost.

Writing and talking about these experiences enabled the participants to reconstruct the past and discover how the stories of the people they were talking with somehow connected to them. It also allowed them to construct or reconstruct their present world in light of this new information. They saw how their lives were distinctly different, yet strikingly similar. But most importantly, the conversations and writing which emerged from these intergenerational experiences empowered the students and their older counterparts to envision the future as dynamic and ever-changing–a future based on integrated lives and experiences, on common goals and dreams, on respect and understanding–a future based on the sharing of stories.

AUTHOR NOTE

Nancy Lubarsky's work has appeared in the *Journal of Reading* and the *NJCTE Journal*. She is interested in exploring how the link between generations can serve as a catalyst for connecting literature and writing with students' lives.

REFERENCES

Dewey, J. (1938). *Experience in education*. New York: Collier Books.

Dobrof, Rose. (1984). Introduction: A time for reclaiming the past. In M. Kaminsky (Ed.), *The uses of reminiscence*. New York: The Haworth Press, Inc.

Hardy, B. (1977). Narrative as a primary act of mind. In M. Meek et al. (Eds.), *The cool web*. London: The Bodley Head.

Kaminsky, M. (1984). *The use of reminiscence: New ways of working with older adults*. New York: The Haworth Press, Inc.

Kaminsky, M. (1984). Transfiguring life: Images of continuity among the fragments. In M. Kaminsky (Ed.), *The uses of reminiscence*. New York: The Haworth Press, Inc.

Lubarsky, N. (1987). A glance at the past, a glimpse of the future. *Journal of Reading*, 30, 520-29.

Moody, H.R. (1984). Reminiscence and the recovery of the public world. In M. Kaminsky (Ed.), *The uses of reminiscence*. New York: The Haworth Press, Inc.

Rosen, H. (1984). *Stories and meanings*. Sheffield: The National Association for the Teaching of English.
Rosen, H. (1986). The importance of story. *Language Arts*, *63*, 226-37.
Van Dongen, R. (1987). Children's narrative thought, at home and at school. *Language Arts*, *64*, 79-87.
Zavatsky, B. (1984). Journey through the feminine: The life review poems of William Carlos Williams. In M. Kaminsky (Ed.), *The uses of reminiscence*. New York: The Haworth Press, Inc.

Sore Tongues and Stiff Necks– Problem Solving Through a Grandparent Discussion/Support Group

Helene Block Fields, MEd

SUMMARY. This article describes the creation and functioning of a grandparent discussion/support group which met monthly for eight years at a suburban community college in Illinois. This group was formed in response to requests from grandparents and dealt with multigenerational issues. Descriptions of the meeting format and examples of the problems and solutions that were discussed are given. Conclusions and recommendations resulting from the experience of leading this group are described. *[Article copies available for a fee from The Haworth Document Delivery Service: 1-800-342-9678. E-mail address: getinfo@haworth.com]*

INTRODUCTION

During recent decades the roles and responsibilities of modern grandparents have changed dramatically (Strom & Strom, 1991). Societal changes including divorce, mobility, working mothers, and new options for older people have forced grandparents to assess their positions and

Helene Block Fields is Professor Emeritus, Oakton Community College, Des Plaines, IL.

[Haworth co-indexing entry note]: "Sore Tongues and Stiff Necks–Problem Solving Through a Grandparent Discussion/Support Group." Fields, Helene Block. Co-published simultaneously in the *Journal of Gerontological Social Work* (The Haworth Press, Inc.) Vol. 28, No. 1/2, 1997, pp. 151-162; and: *Intergenerational Approaches in Aging: Implications for Education, Policy and Practice* (ed: Kevin Brabazon, and Robert Disch) The Haworth Press, Inc., 1997, pp. 151-162. Single or multiple copies of this article are available for a fee from The Haworth Document Delivery Service [1-800-342-9678, 9:00 a.m. - 5:00 p.m. (EST). E-mail address: getinfo@haworth.com].

151

influence in the family. Grandparents are often caught in conflicting wants and needs: to sit for grandchildren or take a trip . . . to include step-grand-children in gifts and/or wills . . . to speak up when they see unhealthy behavior in their grandchildren.

These new grandparent issues were documented in a few early books and articles, such as Kornhaber and Woodward's book (1981). Some stud-ies also showed that many grandparents chose not to be intimately in-volved with their grandchildren; they desired emotional detachment and occasional visits rather than intimate relationships. Mutual independence and autonomy was valued over interdependence and close family support (Cherlin and Furstenberg, 1986).

Such issues and problems became evident in 1985 in the question and answer session after my speech at Oakton Community College in Skokie, Illinois for the older adult lecture series on the topic of The Changing Role of Grandparents. As a grandmother, professor of early childhood educa-tion, and coordinator of the Center for Family Education at the college, I knew that this was a timely topic. The high level of community interest was evident when over seventy seniors braved 8° weather to discuss this topic. The intense feelings of joy, abandonment, and sorrow that emerged during the question session were unforgettable. Afterward a small group of grandparents requested some follow-up sessions and left their phone num-bers.

Because of the direct relevance of my experience in setting up intergen-erational and volunteer grandparent programs, I felt comfortable in con-ducting these sessions. In addition, I had previously taught courses in group dynamics for educators of young children and had recently com-pleted a self-imposed seven month internship working with older adults in an adult day care program once a week. I helped set up an intergeneration-al program there, and conducted group sessions with the seniors.

Initially I had no intention to facilitate an on-going discussion group at our college. However, when the enthusiastic grandparents met for the first time, I saw an immense potential for solving common grandparenting problems through sharing and group discussion of issues and feelings. The attendees had similar reactions, so we agreed to meet regularly, once per month, for 1 1/2 hours. These meetings were sponsored by the Center for Family Education and were free of charge.

I looked for published literature about this type of support group, in which none of the grandparents were raising their grandchildren, but did not find any.

DESCRIPTION OF THE GROUP

From the initial meeting attended by 7 grandparents, the group soon grew to about 25 members. Over the following years, attendance varied from about 13 to 35. The age of members ranged from 58 to 82. Most were from the suburban middle class and were comfortable in this college setting. About 80% were female, and about 20% were widowed. A total of half of the members listed their occupations as either housewife or retired. Some 80% of the members had attended college. Family members of the group members included about 60 adult children and 75 grandchildren. About half of these adult children and grandchildren were living in other parts of the United States.

There were a number of group members who seldom missed a meeting. Most of these "regulars" were not facing difficult grandparenting problems of their own. They often served as mentors for other attendees.

The group members and I soon realized that most of the issues raised in the group were direct outcomes of modern societal changes. Historically, grandparents' roles were clearly defined and structured. Grandparents used to be the revered (and often feared) elders of the clan. The relative decline of the nuclear family plus growing ageist attitudes have propelled modern grandparents into new and vulnerable positions.

Our group discussed these issues and the consensus was that, indeed, attitudes and expectations of adult children toward grandparents have changed radically. Every grandparent spoke of being raised by "strict" parents. Every grandparent was taught to be "good" (even the grandfathers in attendance) and every grandparent learned to respect elders, have good manners, and follow the rules of the house. Women, especially, were trained to acquiesce in order to gain acceptance and feel loved.

A few members felt that they were in grandparent limbo, that they were faced with being grandparents in an alien world . . . a world where adult children did not telephone or care . . . where grandchildren were rude, unresponsive, or simply not interested in being loved. Were their perceptions accurate or were they, too, a part of the problem?

Those grandparents, indeed, had sore tongues and stiff necks . . . sore tongues from biting back words and stiff necks from turning the other cheek.

TYPICAL MEETING FORMAT

The format of this group was based on group dynamics techniques described in a book by Jean Illsley Clarke (1984). Basic ground rules included: respect for one another's opinions, serious consideration of solutions suggested for problems, confidentiality, and adherence to specific brainstorming procedures when appropriate.

I made sure that everyone had a name tag and that all attendees (including latecomers) were seated in a semi-circle. We briefly introduced ourselves and enumerated our grandchildren. I then led a 10-15 minute discussion of a current issue in grandparenting, based perhaps upon a newspaper article or a specific prior request. Occasionally, I showed a short video. However, there was always time for problem solving.

As facilitator, I then asked who had an urgent or important issue to share with the group. If more than one person responded, each grandparent who wanted to talk gave a one or two sentence description of the issue. Each topic was then listed on the board. I then conducted a priority assessment with the group. Only two or three topics could be covered in the time available.

The grandparent with the most crucial or burning issue went first and the group heard the entire scenario from the person who was chosen. Everyone only listened at that time. I encouraged the speaker to be clear, gently interrupting if the grandparent went off the subject. I also helped with closure within the time frame of about three to five minutes. Then I summed up the situation for the group in a few sentences and verified my accuracy with the speaker.

At this point, the grandparent was asked if he or she was willing to hear all suggestions from the group and write all of them down on paper without comment. This process was not easy, since the grandparents often became defensive if someone suggested something they could not or would not do. It was my role to remind the grandparent of the agreement to not discuss or defend any of these ideas, but just to write them down. When all suggestions were presented and listed, the speaker could choose one or two suggestions for the group to discuss.

The purpose of this method was to provide the grandparent with a list of possible solutions to the problem. Then the grandparent could think about the ideas at home and perhaps try a new way to alleviate the difficulty.

Some grandparents needed more help in dealing with emotional problems than could be dealt with in a monthly discussion group. For them I suggested referrals for counseling or therapy, when appropriate.

PROBLEMS AND SOLUTIONS

Three major categories of problems that were brought up frequently were: communicating with adult children and grandchildren, long distance grandparenting, and grandparents of divorce. Examples of these and other problems and some solutions which were suggested are described in the following sections.

Communication Problems with Adult Children and Grandchildren

These complex issues are discussed in (Kornhaber, 1994) and (Strom & Strom, 1991). Surely, in over eight years I interacted with some grandparents who had "chronic" sore tongues and stiff necks. They had serious communication problems and could not comfortably discuss any concerns, feelings, or issues about grandchildren with their adult children. These grandparents were frustrated and confused. They didn't know how to confront or negotiate, so they agreed at all times or were silent. The bottom line was that their relationships with their children lacked authenticity. They said that if they were really open and honest, they feared their adult children would take offense and punish them by keeping the grandchildren away (McCarthy, 1993). After discussing this issue, the group agreed that in special instances (abuse, serious health issues, etc.), grandparents had to risk speaking up.

Other grandparents did not seem threatened by occasional disagreements. Communication with their adult children was comfortable. These grandparents tried to keep up with contemporary modes of parenting and were able to give and seek advice. They did not overreact when challenged (Strom & Strom, 1991). For them, grandparenting was a joy. They enjoyed the rewards of a lifetime of good communication with their adult children, although they recognized that occasionally they, too, had to bite their tongues.

The same issues were evident in communicating with grandchildren. Frustrated grandparents found no common topics to discuss with their grandchildren. Many were uneasy and couldn't have meaningful conversations with them other than "How is school, and how do you like your teacher?" They seemed incapable of joining their grandchildren in play, humor, or even joint activities (Elkind, 1990).

After much discussion of this problem, it became clear that the grandparents had forgotten or never knew what was developmentally appropriate for children at different ages and stages (Erikson, 1963; Crites, 1989). They needed ideas and information in order to form close relationships with their grandchildren.

Of course, much depended on the "style" of grandparent interactions. The "involved" grandparent saw, heard, and interacted with the grandchild on a regular basis . . . the "companionate" grandparent wanted to be a pal and was content with little involvement or responsibility . . . or the "remote" grandparent: kind, but disinterested, who was either too far away or too formal (Cherlin and Furstenberg, 1986). The younger grandparents in the group seemed to have more contact with their grandchildren (Johnson, 1985). However, one 75-year-old grandmother was regularly baby-sitting her great-grandchild!

The following example shows how an "involved" but uneasy grandmother solved her communications dilemma with the group's help:

The problem: "I have been picking up my grandson and taking him to the day care center for two years now. It's been difficult, because it's in the middle of the day right after he gets out of kindergarten, but I wanted to be helpful to my children. Now I've been offered a job in the afternoon and really want to take it. I don't know how to tell my son and daughter-in-law about this. I'm afraid they'll be mad."

Suggestions from the group: "Could you explain the situation to your son; perhaps he'll understand your predicament." "Why don't you just telephone your daughter-in-law and tell her how happy you are to find this job . . . then offer to help find a new driver?" "How come you're so nervous about disappointing your son and his wife?" "Are you worried about your grandson's feelings? He's used to seeing you every day." "How do you feel about not seeing your grandson every day?" "Be sure to use 'I' messages when you talk to them."

In the discussion that followed, the grandparent chose to discuss her own feelings and zero in on some of the suggestions. She admitted there had been some tension over old arguments and none of those involved were able to talk about them. She liked the telephone idea and the thought that she could help find someone new to pick up her grandson. She said she would try using the "I" messages learned in group and thanked everyone for the help and especially for listening.

Feedback from the grandparent one month later (not mandatory in this group): "I did it! It wasn't easy and my son sounded a bit mad, but I made myself sound cheerful and kept saying how I felt and what I needed. He relaxed a little when I offered to find a replacement . . . and I love my new job. I've offered to sit more often in the evening so my grandson and I can still have some alone time."

Long Distance Grandparent Problems

One of the most difficult challenges in our grandparent group was supporting long distance grandparents (Kornhaber, 1994; Strom & Strom, 1991). We knew it was hard for them to hear of the delightful interactions between grandchildren and grandparents who live close to one another. Far away grandparents often sadly described the pain of parting after visits or holidays. They told how much it hurt to say good-bye to beloved grandchildren. Some grandparents appeared to be in mourning over the loss of on-going relationships. Some were angry; they felt cheated by life. A distraught group member said that she did not want the grandmother role—the price was too high.

The group uncharacteristically responded with shock and dismay. I had to stop their outpouring and remind them that this was the place where any feelings could be expressed and accepted as real for that person. They settled down; I then asked the grandmother if she still wanted ideas that might make the separation more bearable. She agreed to write down all the suggestions and comments.

The group then gave her some excellent ideas on how to bond from afar. I suggested books and articles for long distance connections, such as ". . . the telephone, videotape, and lens and shutter connection" (Wasserman, 1996). Other long distance grandparents shared their feelings; many said they have adjusted to living apart, but none were happy about it. Best of all, they shared their own creative solutions.

An example follows:

One grandmother told how she sent her preschool grandchildren who live in Israel a monthly package . . . a scrapbook filled with pictures and descriptions of everyday events in the lives of their grandparents. She included menus, tickets to movies, and photos of grandpa fishing and shopping at the supermarket in the colorful album. The uniqueness of her idea was that she taped her own voice and at the end of each page she rang a bell and said, "Turn the page."

When the album arrived in Israel, then it was the delighted grandchildren's turn to send another one back. After the children collected pictures, homework pages, cartoons, and special lists of what they would do when grandma and grandpa came to visit this year, their mother helped them tape their own ideas and words. At the end of each page, mother would ring a bell and the children chimed in, "Turn the page!" Coupons redeemable for one visit to the library or circus were enclosed in the monthly package. Grandma even made a calendar to be used during the last month just before the visits . . . airplane stickers were placed on each day in anticipation of the month-long reunion.

This was truly a partnership; a labor of love. It took time, commitment, and energy. However, the grandmother said that by the time they arrived for their yearly visit, the children knew them better than any other relative, and vice-versa.

Grandparents of Divorce

During the first year of the grandparent group we conducted a survey of grandparents who were dealing with divorce. They wrote of their confused and sad feelings. They told how they handled the breakup of family connections.

"We had to work hard at developing cordial relations with our ex-son-in-law so we could have our grandson for visits when we're in the area." "I'm still sad; often wish they could have worked out the 'kinks' and stayed together." "We've kept close for the children's sake and we are still, after all these years, friends." "It doesn't feel good when my ex-daughter-in-law picks up my grandson at our house, but I must be civil to her . . . or else!" "During the divorce I tried not to take sides and just be there for the grandchildren; it hurt a lot. I missed the sense of family we use to have and I miss my daughter-in-law." "I've contacted my lawyer to see about grandparent's visitation rights. There is so much bitterness I'm afraid I'll be left out in the cold."

Generalizing about grandparents of divorce is difficult since there are so many variables to consider in each case. However, after a divorce, the mother's parents will usually continue to be a major source of emotional and often financial support. Sometimes the family moves into the maternal grandparent's home. Often, the paternal grandparents see less of the grandchildren (Johnson, 1985).

Today, all states have some statutes concerning grandparents' visitation rights. Interestingly, in the eight years our group was together, only two or three requests were made for information on petitioning the courts for visitation rights (Kornhaber, 1994; Robertson, Tice, & Loeb, 1985). It appeared that the other grandparents were capable of going through the difficult adjustments necessary to create workable relationships in their divorced families.

Since I was a participating member of this group as well as the facilitator, I decided, at one of the first meetings, to share my own experiences as a grandmother of divorce. This is what happened: my son and daughter-in-law divorced suddenly when my grandson was two years old. I thought the world had ended. Ultimately, with cooperation and love on all sides for the precious child in our midst, we bit our tongues and turned our other checks. That was fifteen years ago and happily, we have become what I call mended. The fabric of our family has remained intact. Even those who remarried have stayed connected and I have become a grandmother figure to all newcomers. The adults and grandchildren seem secure in the knowledge that they have been part of a new and important healing process.

Other Problems

Most of the other problems brought up for discussion by group members were of the following types: Jealousy between maternal and paternal grandparents; The supergrandparent syndrome: I can't do it all! Intermarriages and grandchildren connections; Frustration over poor manners and lax discipline; Handling holidays and excessive gift giving; Pros and cons of helping raise a grandchild; The media revolution's impact on grandchildren; Sharing bad news with grandchildren: coping with loss; Gender issues: the stereotyped roles of grandfathers; Coping alone: how intergenerational programs help.

COMMUNITY ACTIVITIES

At my invitation, a number of grandparents from this group participated in community programs involving families and children. Several such activities were carried out at various times over the eight years. These included:

Volunteer Grandparents (Grandparents Unlimited)

Six or seven grandparents volunteered in our college-based nursery program, local elementary schools, and day care centers. Some continued this service for many years, finding great pleasure in contributing to the growth of young children. Some volunteers have grandchildren living near as well as far, although most of them have older grandchildren.

Traveling Grandparents

Through the Center for Family Education, I responded to requests from a few principals and teachers to bring healthy involved older adults to schools to answer questions from junior and senior high school students about aging. The students were truly impressed by these grandparents. They were awed by the grandmother of 3 who, at age 72, bowled 140 in her league; they roared when an 84-year-old grandmother said (after being asked if she was afraid to die) that no, she wasn't . . . but she never buys green bananas. The 70-year-old grandfather amazed them when he described his hobby of deep sea fishing for shark's jaws.

Afterwards, the students wrote poignant letters of thanks: "My feelings toward old people changed after your visit–these people were active, warm, and friendly." "Getting old does not necessarily mean that you can't enjoy life." "I realized that not all seniors are like my grandmother who is sick in a nursing home with Alzheimer's disease . . . the seniors advised me wisely, to remember her good times with my family instead of being bitter about the bad times." "Now I understand my grandparents better and I realize they need love and attention, too. I don't fear death after this discussion. Now I look forward to my older years. From now on I'll give my attention and respect to senior citizens."

The high school teacher's views are worth mentioning: ". . . the students expressed how much they enjoyed talking to the seniors–something they did not admit about any other speaker . . . and more than that, they were able to ask them questions they had feared asking of parents or even the teacher."

Participation in College Activities

Some members of the group became active in setting up booths at Oakton College Family Day to share articles and views with other grandparents. Once they led a panel discussion on the challenges of modern grandparenting. A few were invited by professors in psychology, sociology, and intergenerational education to be guest lecturers.

CONCLUSIONS AND EVALUATIONS

As the years went by, it became apparent that many of the grandparents were absorbing new attitudes and using some new techniques to help solve problems in their daily lives. I observed actual changes in personality (a more relaxed and thoughtful way of interacting) as well as improved self-esteem in a number of grandparents.

Particular areas where the grandparents seemed to make good progress were:

- Accepting that adult children have the right to raise their own children as they wish;
- Realizing that grandchildren's behavior, although sometimes hard to understand, is often age and stage appropriate;
- Using appropriate communication and listening techniques when interacting with adult children and grandchildren;
- Reaching out to family members for advice and support when needed;

- Accepting that grandparents are important and necessary in the lives of their grandchildren and that connections are possible, whether living near or far;
- Volunteering in intergenerational programs in their communities.

This discussion/support group ended with my retirement in 1993, so the above conclusions are ones which I have had time to reflect upon. In May 1995, we held a reunion of the grandparent group at Oakton College. This provided a good opportunity for retrospective evaluation by the seventeen returning group members.

To that end, I asked for feedback on why they attended this group for so long, which ideas or suggestions helped them, and what they learned. I provided them with a list of topics that we covered and asked which of these met their needs.

The following quotes were in response to the question, *What did you learn?* "To learn from other people on how to deal with grandchildren . . ."; "to know what to expect at different ages . . ."; "to see that I was not alone in trying to be a good grandparent . . ."; "to learn from other people's successes and failures . . ."; "to be able to rely on my own judgment now that I've heard it before . . ."; "to be a presence in my family and not a judgmental ogre . . ."; "I developed more self-confidence by listening; I could filter my thoughts through others' comments."

What brought you back? "Leadership, discussion quality, and problem solving ideas . . ."; "because they helped me when I was in trouble . . ."; "I knew I could drop in whenever I could and always be welcome . . ."; "all of us have a personal inner need to be reassured that we are O.K."

The majority of respondents said that feelings of joy and happiness predominated when they shared their positive interchanges with grandchildren. Anger, sadness, and depression predominated when they spoke of deep pain and problems.

They agreed that because of the changes in society, grandparents truly need a safe place to share feelings and learn from one another. They favored social service agencies, colleges and religious institutions as appropriate places for such groups to meet.

I was especially delighted when one grandparent wrote, "Who needs Ann Landers when we have each other?!"

FUTURE DIRECTIONS

It is evident that grandparents face new and perplexing challenges in today's world (Newman, 1989). Many can benefit greatly from support and encouragement. Thus, the need is clear for grandparent discussion/ support groups to become an integral part of the offerings in social service and educational facilities. In an aging society, it becomes crucial to pursue this goal in a serious way.

Professionals in the field of gerontological social work are well qualified to encourage and organize grandparent discussion/support groups in their communities. The growth of these groups would help build stronger relationships and alleviate misunderstandings in multigenerational family systems. It's time to fill this unmet need in our society.

REFERENCES

Cherlin, Andrew J. and Furstenburg, Frank (1986). *The New American Grandparent*. New York: Basic Books.

Clarke, Jean Illsley (1984). *Who, Me Lead a Group?* Minneapolis: Winston Press.

Crites, Marsha (1989). Child Development and Intergenerational Programming. In Newman & Brummel (Eds.) *Intergenerational Programs: Imperatives, Strategies, Impacts, Trends*. Binghamton, NY: The Haworth Press, Inc. p. 33.

Elkind, David (1990). *Grandparenting*. Glenview, Illinois: Scott, Foresman, and Co.

Erikson, Erik (1963). *Childhood and Society*. New York: W.W. Norton.

Johnson, Colleen (1985). Grandparenting Options in Divorcing Families: An Anthropological Perspective. In Bengston & Robertson (Eds.) *Grandparenthood*. Beverly Hills, California: Sage Publications. p. 81.

Kornhaber, Arthur (1994). *Grandparent Power!* New York: Crown Publishers.

Kornhaber, Arthur and Woodward, Kenneth (1981). *Grandparents-Grandchildren: The Vital Connection*. New York: Archer Press/Doubleday.

McCarthy, Michael (1993). Yes, Mother, That Really Is How We Plan To Raise Zoe. *Wall Street Journal*: October 26.

Newman, Sally (1989). The Intergenerational Movement and Its Relationship to Children and Families: Interview with Margaret McFarland. In Newman & Brummel (Eds.) *Intergenerational Programs: Imperatives, Strategies, Impacts, Trends*. Binghamton, NY: The Haworth Press, Inc.

Robertson, Joan F., Tice, Carol H. and Loeb, Leonard L. (1985). Grandparenthood–From Knowledge to Programs and Policy. In Bengston & Robertson (Eds.) *Grandparenthood*. Beverly Hills, California: Sage Publications.

Strom, Robert D. and Strom, Shirley K. (1991). *Becoming a Better Grandparent*. Newbury Park, California: Sage Publications.

Wasserman, Selma (1996). 3rd edition. *The Long Distance Grandmother: How to Stay Close to Distant Grandchildren*. Washington: Hartly and Marks.

Why a Geriatric Center?

Dee Baecher-Brown, MA

SUMMARY. The nurturing environment of a geriatric center is uniquely suited to the needs of young people and thus to intergenerational relationships and programming. Because a nursing home has a relatively stable and accessible population of elderly residents, rich relationships between students and residents have time to develop. A geriatric facility also provides an atmosphere for staff that, for the most part, is not crisis-oriented. For these reasons the geriatric center is an ideal place to link the generations.

This paper discusses programs developed at the Isabella Geriatric Center in New York City which link generations, create a sense of family, strengthen the community, and make the skills and experience of different generations available to one another. Selected programs are proposed as ones which could be developed by any geriatric center which has resources similar to those at Isabella. *[Article copies available for a fee from The Haworth Document Delivery Service: 1-800-342-9678. E-mail address: getinfo@haworth.com]*

GERIATRIC CENTERS

In 1995, there were 1.5 million elderly and disabled persons living in sixteen thousand non-profit and federal, state and local government nursing homes and geriatric centers in the United States. Many homes are part of a continuing care retirement community. There are 1,200 such communities in 42 states serving 350,000 older adults. They offer independent

---

Dee Baecher-Brown is presently Executive Director of the Community Foundation of the Virgin Islands.

[Haworth co-indexing entry note]: "Why a Geriatric Center?" Baecher-Brown, Dee. Co-published simultaneously in the *Journal of Gerontological Social Work* (The Haworth Press, Inc.) Vol. 28, No. 1/2, 1997, pp. 163-170; and: *Intergenerational Approaches in Aging: Implications for Education, Policy and Practice* (ed: Kevin Brabazon, and Robert Disch) The Haworth Press, Inc., 1997, pp. 163-170. Single or multiple copies of this article are available for a fee from The Haworth Document Delivery Service [1-800-342-9678, 9:00 a.m. - 5:00 p.m. (EST). E-mail address: getinfo@haworth.com].

living, assisted living and nursing care. Most facilities are designed to provide a complete range of services. They become not only the home, but the world of their clients. Geriatric centers are staffed round-the-clock, 365 days a year.

STAFFING AND THE WORK ENVIRONMENT

Comprehensive, direct services for residents of a geriatric center include medical, nursing, social work, rehabilitation, dietary, pharmacy, housekeeping, laundry, facilities maintenance, security and recreation. Support for the activities and staff of the facility include administration, finance, development, quality assurance, medical records, human resources, public affairs, community services and volunteers. The staff of such a facility includes representatives from most "worlds of work," a valuable characteristic when training young people in employment skills. A unifying element for all, whether administrator, housekeeper, nurse, computer specialist, pharmacist, engineer, security officer, etc., should be an understanding of the residents they serve and the role that each staff person plays in maintaining a high quality of care in their facility.

THE NURTURING ENVIRONMENT

The general awareness of the needs of the elderly and disabled leads to a *nurturing environment* at a geriatric center. This atmosphere is uniquely suited to the needs of young people, especially those who are considered "at-risk." In meeting and visiting elderly residents, students realize that they add to the quality of life of the residents, which provides them with a purpose and a feeling of accomplishment. The students' success with the residents strengthens feelings of self worth (Faer, 1995).

A geriatric center is also able to provide a secure and stimulating learning environment for young adults. The students are exposed to staff from many different fields and follow various career paths. At the geriatric center students are able to learn and develop new skills, and gain self-confidence. They can receive special training and learn about a wide range of careers in health. While building on the natural instincts of adolescents to make the world a better place, a geriatric facility can offer a supportive atmosphere that integrates community involvement with academic excellence.

Because a nursing home has a relatively stable and accessible population of elderly residents, it can provide the necessary time for relationships to develop between students and residents. The residents benefit from the on-going special attention given to them by the young people; and they are able to pass on to another generation their own learning and life experiences. For these reasons, both the elderly residents and the young people experience a sense of accomplishment.

A geriatric center also provides an atmosphere for staff which, for the most part, is not crisis-oriented. Most of the staff have reasonably predictable work days in which they can schedule time for training and support for the young adults. They often welcome the diversity in their jobs that working with young people offers.

In order for young people to succeed in an organizational setting, it is important for staff to "invest" in them. *Mentoring* is an important service that is often available in a nursing home because of the presence of a wide range of service-oriented professionals. Much of the success in the Isabella intergenerational programs is attributable to the fact that the Center is committed to providing orientation and ongoing support for young participants (Henkin & Sweeney, 1989).

Evidence for the intergenerational "viability" and social relevance of the geriatric center is indicated in the *Five Fundamental Resources for Children and Youth* proposed by President Clinton in the preparations for "The President's Summit for America's Future," held in Philadelphia in April, 1997 (Corporation for National Service, 1997). The five resources listed are: *an ongoing relationship with a caring adult; safe places to learn and grow; marketable skills through effective education; a healthy start; and an opportunity to give back.* Of these, four are identified above as resources available in a geriatric center.

ISABELLA'S INTERGENERATIONAL HISTORY

The founding of the Isabella Home in 1875 was based on the ideals of one young woman, Isabella Uhl, and her concern for aged women and a compassion for those in need. She envisioned a world where the elderly would be cared for with dignity and respect. Today, 120 years after its creation, the Isabella Geriatric Center continues to expand that vision by incorporating intergenerational programming.

The Isabella Geriatric Center has a long history of involving young people with our residents. Years ago, Isabella staff had observed intergenerational "magic" with college and graduate students doing field work in psychology, sociology and public health. It was clear that these students were learning and enjoying their work with the elderly. Field work was teaching them that working in geriatrics was important and that it was something they could do–and wanted to do. Staff recognized that this same process could occur with high school students and younger children (Angelis, 1992).

In the past two decades close to 2,000 individuals from more than 20 high schools, colleges and youth programs have been involved in work training, intergenerational, and volunteer activities at Isabella. In 1975 Isabella initiated efforts to bridge the gap between the generations and to dispel stereotypes by joining the New York City School Volunteers Program. Over time, this program involved 60 elderly Isabella residents as tutors to Latino third-graders from "slow reading classes."

At the time, the success of the program provided proof for something that we now take for granted: that the very young and the very old have a great deal to offer to each other. Moreover, it showed that the geriatric center was an appropriate arena for this to take place.

Building on the success of the award winning tutoring program, Isabella was able to help institute another first–a Montessori learning-intervention preschool on-site at Isabella, adding another intergenerational component (Seefeldt, 1987a). Isabella was also the first to welcome a team of teenagers from the New York City Volunteer Corps into a geriatric center.

The Brookdale Center on Aging of Hunter College collaborated in developing an oral history project for teens and elderly residents. Teenagers studied the theory and practice of "life-history" and interviewed residents (Disch, 1988). There was some concern about matching "at-risk" teens with sophisticated and generally well-educated Europeans, who were then the dominant Isabella population. However, believing that it could make a difference in the lives of both populations, staff at Isabella went ahead with the project. The outcome was an anthology of life histories and some wonderful intergenerational relationships (Seefeldt, 1987).

THREE "STANDARD" PROGRAMS
FOR A GERIATRIC CENTER

The following three programs can be established in a geriatric center or nursing home as long as the essential resources are available, i.e., space; staff with an interest in youth and who recognize the value of intergenerational relationships; and proximity to educational institutions.

1. On-Site Child Day Care Services

In April 1991, Isabella opened an on-site day care center for infants and toddlers of employees and the families in the community–an intergenerational sharing of space and facilities. The children visit with the residents, spending several hours a week on the nursing home floors. Residents and children take trips together, participate in music programs and have parties to celebrate milestones in their lives. This on-site child care center provides our elderly residents with some of the basic pleasures of family life.

2. Middle School Programs

Isabella's programs with Middle Schools are designed to facilitate the interaction of sixth and seventh grade children with disoriented/confused residents. To prepare students for their visits, Isabella staff meet with teachers to help them prepare and implement course materials about aging. The curriculum is then integrated into the students' academic program at school.

On a weekly basis, the children have one-to-one friendly visits with the residents, and also plan and participate in recreational events. At the end of the school year, students compile booklets with some photographs and creative writing about "their residents" (Aday, Rice & Evans, 1991).

3. Health Careers Partnership

Based on Isabella's intergenerational history, it was natural for staff to reach out to their next door neighbor, George Washington High School, to establish a health careers program for 150 students from the school (Baecher, 1995).

The *Health Careers Partnership* is a comprehensive, three-year program to motivate students to complete high school and to consider a career in health care by using a specialized health-careers curriculum and providing work experience in a health care setting. Through the Partnership, Isabella provides support for an urban school whose students are considered "at risk" of dropping out. Mentoring, Training and Education, and Replication are crucial aspects of the Partnership Program.

Mentoring

More than 50 staff members of the Isabella Geriatric Center serve as mentors to Health Careers Partnership students. Students are matched with an Isabella staff member in a program of at least a year of one-to-one mentoring. Mentors receive 4 hours orientation and training and commit to spending an hour and a half each week with their young "Partner." The mentors, including top administrators, health care deliverers and all levels of support staff, share their skills and experience in weekly sessions with the students.

Isabella's mentors are responding to a national call for action to reach out to the children who are growing up in poverty and community violence, who all too often are alone, exposed and forgotten. In "Turning Points," a report by the *Carnegie Council on Adolescent Development* (1989) there is a strong recommendation that "Every student . . . be well known by at least one adult. Students should be able to rely on that adult . . . to marshal every school and community resource needed for the student to succeed, and help to fashion a promising vision of the future." At Isabella, the mentors play this important role in the lives of our students.

According to one of the Isabella residents, the young people in the program are "better than medicine."

Training and Education

For third-year students in the Health Careers Partnership, Isabella staff provide the 100-hour Nursing Assistant training course and the 60-hour internship required to take the New York State certification examination. To date, twenty-nine students have successfully completed the training course and internship and have been certified as New York State Nursing Assistants. A number of these young people are currently employed at Isabella. The positive reactions of residents and staff to the empathy and hard work of these young people again reinforces our commitment to providing intergenerational experience.

In addition to the Nursing Assistant Training program, training and supervision are also provided for graduate students completing field work assignments for degrees in Public Health and Social Work. Isabella staff also work with undergraduates from many different colleges and universities who are completing course internships in areas such as Social Service, Administration, Rehabilitation, and Recreation Therapy.

Replication of Successful Programs

On March 13, 1996, administrators and staff from eleven New York State geriatric centers gathered at Isabella to learn about replicating Isabella's successful intergenerational initiative, the Health Careers Partnership. With one geriatric center in New Jersey having successfully replicated the Partnership, the Isabella staff are confident that replication is a worthwhile and achievable goal. A 100-page Program Guidebook is available to assist geriatric centers in replicating the award-winning Health Careers Partnership. The Guidebook includes information about the Mentoring and the

Training and Education components of Isabella's intergenerational programming.

CONCLUSION

Intergenerational programming is seen at Isabella as a key ingredient in the mission of the geriatric center to deliver the highest quality of care to elderly clients (Roundtable Discussion, U.S. Senate, 1992).

The administration and staff at Isabella have devoted much of the last 20 years to assuring that interaction between young and old would happen while simultaneously playing an important role in the community outside the institution as well. Building on strengths that are inherent in nursing homes, programs have been developed that impact the lives of elders, youth and the adults, such as parents and teachers, who interact with at-risk youth. *These programs are replicable and can be developed at any geriatric center that has the same basic resources available as Isabella.*

AUTHOR NOTE

As Director of Volunteer Services at the Isabella Geriatric Center in New York City, Dee Baecher-Brown was responsible for the development and administration of the Health Careers Partnership, an award-winning intergenerational health-careers mentoring program.

REFERENCES

Aday, H.A., Rice, C. & Evans, E. (1991). Intergenerational Partners Project: A Model Linking Elementary Students with Senior Center Volunteers. *The Gerontologist*, Vol. 31, No. 2, 263-266.

Angelis, J. (1992). The Genesis of an Intergenerational Program. *Educational Gerontology*, 18: 317-327.

Armengol, R. (1992). Getting Older and Getting Better. *Phi Delta Kappan*, February, 467-470.

Baecher, D. (1995). *A Program Guidebook: Isabella Geriatric Center's Health Careers Partnership*. Isabella Geriatric Center, New York, NY.

Carnegie Council on Adolescent Development (1989). *Turning Points: Preparing American Youth for the 21st Century*. Carnegie Corporation, New York, NY.

Corporation for National Service (1997). *The President's Summit for America's Future*. Corporation for National Service, Washington, DC.

Disch, Robert (1988). The Young, the Old and the Life Review. *Journal of Gerontological Social Work*, 12 (3/4), 125-135.

Faer, M. (1995). *The Intergenerational Life History Project: Promoting Health and Reducing Disease in Adolescents and Elders*. Public Health Reports, March, 194-198.

Henkin, N.Z. & Sweeney, S.W. (1989). Linking Systems: A Systems Approach to Intergenerational Programming. *Intergenerational Programs Part II: Strategies*. The Haworth Press, Inc. 165-172.

Roundtable Discussion, Special Committee on Aging, United States Senate (1993). *Intergenerational Mentoring*. November 12, 1992, Serial No. 102-26.

Seefeldt, C. (1987). The Effects of Preschoolers' Visits to a Nursing Home. *The Gerontologist*, Vol. 27, No. 2, 228-232.

Seefeldt, C. (1987). Intergenerational Programs: Making Them Work. *Childhood Education*, October, 14-18.

SECTION V:
APPROACHES TO EVALUATION

Program effectiveness has always been of concern to funders and interest in this area is growing in the intergenerational field. From a management control perspective, performance measures should be established during the planning phase to provide a basis for measuring operations and evaluating outcomes. Since intergenerational programs contain a mix of at least two generically different types of program goals, it is natural that evaluation methods have been developed to address both.

In the first paper in this section, Ward suggests that funders are often more interested in program impact on critical social issues than on outcomes related to the older/younger relationship. He discusses how evaluation in different types of organizations can be strengthened to accomplish this goal.

In the second paper in this section, Kuehne and Collins argue that observational research is particularly appropriate for studying and evaluating intergenerational programs in which the relationships between participants are of particular importance. The authors describe their methodologies in detail.

Intergenerational Program Evaluation for the 1990s and Beyond

Christopher R. Ward, PhD

During the 1990s, evaluation has become an increasingly important component of intergenerational programs. Compared to a decade ago, funders more frequently ask for evidence that programs achieve their goals and objectives, intergenerational professionals seek more substantial information about program processes, and policy makers wish to understand the impact of intergenerational programs in more depth.

Given the increasing importance of evaluation, how should the intergenerational field approach evaluation as we move toward the year 2000? In this article, I argue that the approach should be two-fold: first, intergenerational programs of all types must emphasize the thoughtful, comprehensive planning of evaluation. Given the changing political and funding environment, professionals at all levels must plan their evaluation proactively, weighing carefully what they wish to learn, considering the audience to which they will address their evaluation, and assigning clear roles and responsibilities.

Second, the intergenerational field needs to strengthen evaluation in three specific areas:

- The rapidly growing number of small, community-based programs need to design evaluations that describe in detail who they are and what they do focus on measuring the outcomes of one or two key

Christopher R. Ward is Assistant Director of Generations Together at the University of Pittsburgh.

[Haworth co-indexing entry note]: "Intergenerational Program Evaluation for the 1990s and Beyond." Ward, Christopher R. Co-published simultaneously in the *Journal of Gerontological Social Work* (The Haworth Press, Inc.) Vol. 28, No. 3, 1997, pp. 173-181; and: *Intergenerational Approaches in Aging: Implications for Education, Policy and Practice* (ed: Kevin Brabazon, and Robert Disch) The Haworth Press, Inc., 1997, pp. 173-181. Single or multiple copies of this article are available for a fee from The Haworth Document Delivery Service [1-800-342-9678, 9:00 a.m. - 5:00 p.m. (EST). E-mail address: getinfo@haworth.com].

objectives, and take advantage of previously developed instruments, including the attitude measures popular in the 1970s and 1980s.

- Larger regional or national intergenerational programs developed to demonstrate solutions to social problems must focus on evaluating their impact based on clearly defined objectives related to these problems.
- The intergenerational field must strengthen its overall evaluation capacity by increasing the evaluation skills of intergenerational professionals through the articulation of competencies and the provision of appropriate training.

This two-fold approach builds from the rationale and basic components of evaluation of intergenerational programs suggested in the 1980s (Bocian & Newman, 1989).

THE CONTEXT

Several factors are now shaping the context for evaluation of intergenerational programs. The rapid growth of the intergenerational field means that literally thousands of individuals, agencies, and organizations are currently conducting intergenerational programs. These programs vary in complexity, sophistication, and size. This growth means that many programmers are evaluating intergenerational efforts for the first time. Moreover, many intergenerational efforts are conducted by persons not regularly associated with the traditional intergenerational networks, organizations, and leadership. The broadening of the field means new challenges to disseminating previously developed evaluation techniques, strategies, and materials.

Second, during the last decade intergenerational programs have been increasingly put forward as a means to address the nation's social problems. This new role adds to these programs' more conventional functions such as changing attitudes (old to young and young to old), increasing self esteem and life satisfaction, and providing fulfilling social roles for older adults and nurturing for children and youth. Intergenerational programs are being used to help at-risk students achieve better grades, aid families in coping with illness, reduce neighborhood violence, increase retention of minority students in colleges and universities, fight drug and alcohol abuse in elementary and middle schools, and provide skilled workers in child care (see, for example, Freedman, 1988; *Family Friends*, 1993; Smith, T., Mack, C., & Tittnich, E., 1993).

Two beliefs drive the emphasis on intergenerational programs as solutions to social problems: (1) that older adults and youth offer unique,

untapped resources to each other, and (2) that government and foundatiᵤ
are more likely to fund intergenerational problems that help to solve critical social problems than they are to support less targeted programs. For
evaluators, the growing emphasis on intergenerational programs as solutions to social problems has meant that funders and other stakeholders are
often interested in outcomes that are not directly related to the older-youn-
ger relationship. Likewise, funders are often interested in only one of the
two age-group constituencies. For example, state and federal education
agencies who fund intergenerational programs typically want to know the
impact of the program on students, but have little or no formal interest in
its impact on older adults.

A third and more recent development important to evaluation of intergenerational programs has been the reshaping of the American political
landscape. Funding for many programs that address the kinds of social
problems listed above is being reduced. At the same time, discussion of
entitlements has given new opportunity to the intergenerational conflict
proponents to picture Americans as divided by age and age-related economic issues. In this context of leaner times and more scrutiny, intergenerational programs need to describe what they do with passion and accuracy, and demonstrate their positive impacts to a degree they have not had to
in earlier eras. Overall, quality evaluation has become much more important to the well-being and future of the intergenerational field.

Given this context, the need for the intergenerational field to develop
well-planned evaluation is clear. That planning should include the following steps.

EVALUATION PLANNING

The development of an intergenerational program evaluation should
parallel and interact with the planning and development of the program
activities. Those responsible for programs of all kinds should step through
a series of questions similar to the following.

What do you want to know about your program? Staff should list what
they need to know to improve the program, to make it more effective, and
to better understand its processes or impact. They should assume that the
evaluation's primary purpose is to provide information that is useful to
them and that meets their needs. They do not need to concern themselves
at this initial point with what they "should" do or what others have done
in other programs.

*Who is the audience(s) for the evaluation? How will they use the in-
formation you provide to them?* Most evaluations will have an audience

beyond the immediate program staff. Among possible audiences are funders, boards of directors, supervisors, other groups interested in implementing intergenerational programs, the public, and program participants. Funders and other decision-makers may use the evaluation to judge whether or not the program continues, to recommend changes, or to increase or decrease funding. Before the program starts, staff should determine the primary audience for the evaluation and try to determine how the evaluation will be used and what information is most valued by the audience.

How do the requirements of the audience modify what you want to know? In some cases the audience for the evaluation may have the same interests as the staff. In other cases, their interests may differ. For example, staff may want a great deal of information on a program's processes in order to modify what they do. A board or funder may be more interested in the impact of the program on one or more constituencies. A crucial–although sometimes difficult–function of the planning process is to prioritize what various groups wish to learn.

What specific kinds of information do you need to tell you what you want to know? Evaluations can gather a wide variety of information, in many forms. For some audiences, anecdotal or case history information may best summarize the program. For a public agency mandated to reduce teenage drug abuse, the information will likely be statistics on change in the level of drug usage. For many intergenerational programs, the community or the youth serving or elderly serving agencies may be most interested in changes in attitudes about the other group.

How will you gather the information? It is only at this point in the planning that those responsible for the evaluation should decide how to gather the information they need: questionnaires, interviews, existing statistics (standardized test scores, for example), observations, and so forth. Among the options at this point are various existing instruments such as life satisfaction, self-esteem, or attitudes on aging scales. However, all too often, persons developing programs put this as the first step before considering what they want to learn, what their audience wants, and what kind of information is most important.

How will you report information? During the planning process some attention should be given to how the evaluation will be conveyed to the audience and when it must be complete. Some audiences may prefer a simple oral presentation. In many cases, graphs, tables, and other illustrative material may be needed.

What must you do with the information you gather so it can be reported clearly? The information gathered in questionnaires, interviews, existing records, and so forth must be converted into a meaningful form. In soı. cases, special expertise may be required for statistical analysis. However, most audiences will prefer a clear, brief presentation to one that is highly complex or technical.

What are the resources and constraints on the evaluation? As the staff plans, they will need to consider what the program and its budget can devote to the evaluation. For example, how much staff time can be given over to the evaluation? What human resources are available–does someone on the program or agency staff have experience in setting up a database to track participants? Does the agency or a partnering agency have someone skilled in interviewing who can help with the evaluation?

Several constraints relate to the participants in intergenerational programs. For example, if the program includes very small children or very frail elderly, will they be able to complete certain kinds of instruments? If they will not be able to complete the instruments, what other options are available to gather needed data? Answers to these questions may modify the types of information gathered or the way in which information is gathered.

Who is responsible for _ ? Finally, the staff planning the evaluation need to be just as precise about roles and responsibilities for the evaluation as they are about those for program activities. Before the intergenerational program begins, planners should state clearly who is responsible for overall planning and management; for selection or construction of instruments; for data gathering; for data coding, entry, and analysis; and for writing the evaluation report.

Conscious attention to the planning of intergenerational program evaluations is an important advance for the field. However, the complexity of the intergenerational field also means that specific directions are called for in several areas.

PROPOSED DIRECTIONS

Community-Based Programs

At Generations Together's National Intergenerational Training Institute, in training sessions at conferences, and through telephone calls from the field, practitioners from community-based programs have indicated increasing interest in evaluation of their own programs. At the same time, these program professionals frequently explain the constraints they face in developing and implementing evaluations and voice their frustration at evaluation designs more appropriate for larger institutions. From these conversations have emerged several possible directions for small intergenerational programs.

Programs should be sure to gather detailed descriptive information. Programmers often overlook the usefulness to the evaluation process of descriptive data. How many older adults/youth participate? Who are they (age, ethnicity, economic status)? How are they recruited? What activities do the young and old do together? How many hours per week do interactions occur? Answers to these specific questions can be supplemented with a running log or other qualitative methods to gather program highlights, problems and successes, and anecdotes. For many audiences, a detailed, focused description of the program, its activities, and its participants will suffice as an evaluation.

Programs should gather one or two vital measures of the program's impact on younger and older participants. Many programs attempt to gather too much information. Staff and volunteers get overwhelmed in choosing and administering instruments or become discouraged as they face entering and analyzing huge amounts of data. In the end, little evaluation is accomplished. In a program's critical moments–such as when a school superintendent wants evidence that demonstrates why an intergenerational program's funding should not be cut–most programs need only a few key items of information. For example, in such a critical moment, participants' change in grades in several basic subjects may be all that is needed. The answers to a few open-ended questions about older adults' experience in a program which get read, summarized, and presented are worth far more than lengthy questionnaires or interviews that do not get transcribed or that produce information that does not get presented to an audience.

Finally, small, community-based programs should make use of existing instruments or questions from those instruments. For many programs, existing instruments can be an important component of an evaluation. Scales that measure attitudes toward aging, the self esteem of older adults, or other standardized instruments can provide convenient ways to measure change in participants (see for example, Neugarten, Havighurst, & Tobin, 1961; Rosenberg, 1969; Seefeldt, 1989). Questionnaires constructed by other programs can also be adapted and modified for use by similar programs.

Programs Addressing Social Problems

Larger regional or national intergenerational programs developed as possible solutions to social problems face different evaluation issues than do smaller programs. In part, in this time of political change these larger programs bear the burden of demonstrating that intergenerational programs can provide efficient, humane solutions to pressing social problems.

Neugarten, B., Havighurst, R., & Tobin, S. (1961). The measurement of life satisfaction. *Journal of Gerontology,* 16, 134-143.

Rosenberg, M. (1969). Self-esteem scale. In Rosenberg, M. *Society and the adolescent self-image* (pp. 305-307). Princeton, NJ: Princeton University Press.

Seefeldt, C. (1989). Intergenerational programs–Impact on Attitudes. In S. Newman & S. Brummel (Eds.), *Intergenerational programs: Imperatives, strategies, impacts, trends* (pp. 185-194). New York: The Haworth Press, Inc.

Smith, T., Mack, C., & Tittnich, E. (1993). *Generations together: A job-training curriculum for older workers in child care.* Syracuse, NY: Syracuse University Press and Generations Together.

Observational Research in Intergenerational Programming: Need and Opportunity

Valerie S. Kuehne, PhD
Caroline L. Collins, PhD

SUMMARY. Research in the field of intergenerational programming is rapidly growing in both quantity and quality. Both those who plan and work directly with intergenerational program participants in the human services and those who hold positions as researchers and evaluators need to be encouraged to research and evaluate their programs. We argue that observational research, though not without its shortcomings, should be more widely used to study and evaluate intergenerational program effectiveness and the relationships among people within them. We also provide some examples of observational strategies useful in practice-based research. We conclude that by recording details of the actual program interactions and relationships and examining them carefully or preserving them for later scrutiny, intergenerational program planners can learn to make relationship-based interventions successful and rewarding for their clients and themselves. *[Article copies available for a fee from The Haworth Document Delivery Service: 1-800-342-9678. E-mail address: getinfo@haworth.com]*

Valerie S. Kuehne is Associate Professor and Director, School of Child and Youth Care, University of Victoria, British Columbia. Caroline L. Collins received her doctorate from Stanford in psychology and is now working on a master's degree in the Interactive Telecommunications Program at New York University.

[Haworth co-indexing entry note]: "Observational Research in Intergenerational Programming: Need and Opportunity." Kuehne, Valerie S., and Caroline L. Collins. Co-published simultaneously in the *Journal of Gerontological Social Work* (The Haworth Press, Inc.) Vol. 28, No. 3, 1997, pp. 183-193; and: *Intergenerational Approaches in Aging: Implications for Education, Policy and Practice* (ed: Kevin Brabazon, and Robert Disch) The Haworth Press, Inc., 1997, pp. 183-193. Single or multiple copies of this article are available for a fee from The Haworth Document Delivery Service [1-800-342-9678, 9:00 a.m. - 5:00 p.m. (EST). E-mail address: getinfo@haworth.com].

183

INTRODUCTION

The idea of organized, community-based intergenerational programs is, by now, perhaps two decades old. The model for such programs emerged in the 1970s and, since then, thousands of programs linking the old and the young have been started all over North America (e.g., Ontario Ministry of Community and Social Services, 1987; Tice, 1985). These programs have emerged because human service practitioners, including child and youth care workers, social workers, nurses, activity therapists, educators, community development workers, and others working with children, youth, older adults, and their families have realized the richness of knowledge and experience that can be shared in the interactions and relationships between persons of sometimes vastly different ages. For example, where education or skill building is the goal, older adults can be real-life educators, imparting experience-based knowledge to preschool or school-age children that may be based in times past, or helping youth and young adults to develop skills for healthy lifestyles or jobs. Alternatively, older adults can enter into short- and long-term caring relationships with children, youth and families who have special physical, emotional, or social needs. These relationships take place in homes, schools, child and adult day care centers, religious institutions, hospitals, and various community agencies. And while these relationships may sometimes be created to benefit primarily the children, youth and families involved, researchers have documented that older adults participating in intergenerational programs, who typically range in age from 50 to 75 and beyond, can also benefit from relating to community members much younger than they (Kuehne & Sears, 1993; Stewart, Franz & Layton, 1988).

There have been a number of concerted efforts in the professional practice literature to convince a wide variety of human service workers that research and evaluation do not belong solely in the ivory tower of the university, but also in their worlds of practice with children, youth, families, and older adults (e.g., Bullock, 1989; Kreuger, 1982; Pence, 1990; Wells & Whittaker, 1989). Nevertheless, while the growth of intergenerational programs in communities around North America might be described as an explosion, our knowledge of program effectiveness lags far behind (Kuehne, 1990). Essentially, there are four reasons for this lack of program-based knowledge.

First, intergenerational programs are simply not studied or evaluated adequately. In fact, many intergenerational initiatives come and go undocumented and unmeasured, so that when personnel change or memories wane, programs cannot be replicated, and learning must begin again! Reasons for this lack of documentation range from views that intergenerational relationships contain some "magic" and therefore need not be subjected to the scrutiny of science, to simple ignorance about the value of evaluation and research, to unfamiliarity with applied research and evaluation methods.

Second, inappropriate measures are sometimes used to determine whether programs have "worked" or not, so that knowledge generated by the evaluation is severely limited in its usefulness to others. For example, a program may have been very effective in decreasing feelings of social isolation—a success in no uncertain terms. But if the only measures employed were those that measured the children's attitudes toward the elderly before and after the program, this grand success will have gone undetected. Observational studies of intergenerational programs can enhance the implementers' sense of what has been accomplished during the intervention, prompting the use of appropriate before and after measures in subsequent programs.

Third, some programs may simply be ineffective, so its seems that there are no "results" to document. Documenting a "failure" often proves less than appealing to program developers, and so often remains undone. This reason, like the first, can facilitate mistakes being repeated.

Fourth, the perception that research is just too difficult, or that it must be conducted in a scientific laboratory to be important, prevents many adequately-credentialed professionals from contributing to the intergenerational knowledge base.

The research that does exist on intergenerational programs primarily focuses on program effects on the children and youth who participate in them; for example, studies have focused on young people's attitudes toward the elderly (e.g., Seefeldt, 1984; Sparling & Roberts, 1985), self esteem (e.g., Kuehne, 1990), coping skills and resilience (e.g., Styles & Morrow, 1992; Werner & Smith, 1982) and school attendance (e.g., Freedman, 1992). However, given that programs do not always affect the outcomes mentioned above, the effect is not what was expected, or the resources for outcome-oriented research and evaluation are limited, we propose that more practitioners should consider studying the face-to-face dynamics of the intergenerational relationships they are facilitating. Where programs are "successful" in bringing about their intended results, such observational research will provide process- or relationship-oriented information to practitioners that can be extremely helpful in replicating program success. In fact, if more careful attention were paid to the intergenerational interactions and relationships that comprise intergenerational programs, we would be better prepared to fully understand the successes and the failures of a variety of intergenerational program models, and better able to design effective program experiences.

In sum, we argue that observational research is greatly underused as a method of studying and evaluating intergenerational programs and the relationships among the people within them. There exists a real need and opportunity in the field of intergenerational programming to enhance our understanding of intergenerational relationships and intergenerational program effectiveness. What should practitioners consider when planning an observational study of their intergenerational program?

FACTORS AFFECTING INTERGENERATIONAL INTERACTIONS AND RELATIONSHIPS

Researchers from a number of disciplines have been studying interactions and relationships between two or more persons for a number of years and in a number of different settings. For example, psychologists have studied small group and one-to-one (or dyadic) interactions in laboratories (e.g., Collins & Gould, 1994; Ickes, Robertson, Tooke, & Teng, 1986; Sabatelli, Buck, & Kenny, 1986), sociologists have examined group relationships from a number of different perspectives (e.g., Durkheim, 1933; Hare, Borgatta & Bales, 1955), educators have developed sophisticated methods of interaction analysis for the classroom (e.g., Flanders & Amidon, 1981), and family therapists have developed models explaining family interaction patterns (e.g., Minuchin, 1974). However, interactions between intergenerational program participants have not been extensively examined using these or other methods (Kuehne, 1989; Newman & Ward, 1992-3). Therefore, it is not entirely clear that findings from such research are applicable to intergenerational relationships as they occur in the programs that human service practitioners often facilitate. What is unique about intergenerational relationships that warrants special consideration, and how will an observational approach enable this consideration?

Our understanding of the multidisciplinary interaction literature and our experiences in researching intergenerational interactions and relationships in both the university laboratory and programs in the field suggest that what we know in general about interactions and relationships between persons may not apply directly to those in which one person is significantly younger and the other significantly older. Why might this be so?

First, persons from other age group may be stigmatized, the older adults perhaps for oldness, the children or youth perhaps for behavioral difficulties or whatever characteristic may have led to their participation in the program initially, and this stigmatization may have a great deal to do with the interactions and relationships that occur between them. Many of us are keenly aware that it is not as simple as putting two people in a room to "relate."

Second, interaction patterns between these persons of (vastly) different age may be due to a host of factors that are less related to the persons involved, and more related to the hero groups' socialization about one another. For example, older adults with hearing or speech impairments may not be able to respond appropriately to young children in conversation, especially if the children are inexperienced in communicating with such persons (e.g., Ryan, Giles, Bartolucci & Henwood, 1986). Or, due to children's early negativity toward older persons (e.g., Seefeldt, Jantz, Galper & Serock, 1977; Kuehne, 1988), fear or negative attitudes about older adults may prohibit relationship development between children and older persons at all.

Alternatively, perhaps persons of different ages view the purposes and forms of social interactions differently, and it is this perspective that is responsible for the relationships they develop (e.g., Carstensen, 1991).

A third reason that both "common" and "scientific" knowledge about interactions and relationships may not apply to those found in community-based intergenerational programs is related to the characteristics of these relationships. For example, it may be that the length of time over which younger and older persons relate in community-based programs is potentially shorter than other "real world" relationships children and youth form with peers or neighbors, yet longer than the relationships studied by researchers in university laboratories. These relationships are also voluntary and often egalitarian, making them unlike those found in most families, schools and agencies (Kuehne, 1989; Sussman & Pfeifer, 1988), where adults usually hold power over children.

These three major factors potentially influence the interactions and relationships occurring in intergenerational programs in such fundamental ways that research approaches and theories from other disciplines are of questionable value to understanding intergenerational relationships. As a result, if we are really going to understand the dynamics and benefits of intergenerational program relationships for the children and youth involved, observation-based methods are needed that make few assumptions about the meaning of behaviors. Fox and Giles (1993) make a call for observational research in intergenerational programs, indicating that it is clearly important to determine how both younger and older persons are communicating in intergenerational programs.

OBSERVATION-BASED MODELS
FOR EXAMINING INTERGENERATIONAL PROGRAM
INTERACTIONS AND RELATIONSHIPS

There are two major types of observation-based models developed specifically for examining intergenerational interactions and relationships. In one model, observers record interactions using a checklist of verbal and nonverbal behaviors (Cicirell, 1986; Kuehne, 1989, 1992; Onawola & Newman, 1985). Over a specified period of time, dyads and groups of children and older adults can be observed and their interactions coded on a number of preselected verbal and nonverbal variables. Such variables might include touching, demonstrating, agreeing, complimenting, encouraging, and so on. It is important to note that the variables used on the checklist of all three models are relevant to the intergenerational programs for which they were designed. This is an important point, for observational methods that "fit" the interactions and relationships being observed will provide the most useful information.

The second type of observation-based model for examining the interactions and relationships in intergenerational programs involves videotaping (Newman & Ward, 1992-3). Using this method, a video camera focuses on small groups of older adults and children, recording their behaviors for a predefined period of time. Newman and Ward chose to code their videotaped behaviors by randomly selecting ten-second segments from the tape of each small group. Then, independent coders scored each segment, compared their scoring, and reconciled differences where they occurred.

Both of these observation-based models have helped not only those who work directly with children, youth and the older adults, but those who research or evaluate what occurs between children or youth and older adults in various intergenerational programs as well. The specific type of observational method chosen by researchers is influenced by a host of factors (Weick, 1985). What researchers have found in their studies also varies somewhat by the program type, setting and authors; however, each of the investigations reveals potentially important program characteristics that would be useful in evaluation and research. For example, Cicirelli (1986) found that interactions between preschool children and older adult day care clients in one intergenerational program were primarily task-oriented and emotionally neutral. One of his recommendations to agency staff was that they consider revising their intergenerational program activities so that those relationships between participants could be better fostered—one of the program's goals. In another study, Kuehne (1990) found that the interactions between school age children and older adults were much more "positive" than those between preschool children and older persons. She recommended that if older adult participants were to continue with a weekly intergenerational program over the course of one year and not drop out due to frustration, child day care center staff should carefully plan activities and select child participants old and independent enough to require relatively little direct staff supervision. This program change would likely help to foster the friendships staff had envisioned between program participants by reducing the negative verbalizations of older adults toward children (e.g., scolding), and the uncooperative and ignoring behaviors demonstrated by young children toward the older adults.

RECOMMENDATIONS FOR PROGRAM-BASED RESEARCH

Observational research can be very helpful in understanding the dynamics of intergenerational relationships and programs. But how should human service professionals approach this research and evaluation task? There are a number of recommendations we would make that are as applicable to observations of intergenerational programs as they are to other programs in which relationships are at the core.

First, build observation and an observer into your program. If you are developing a group program and you are the group facilitator, develop a checklist of behaviors and interaction patterns that are relevant to your program. Do not forget to include both positive and negative, verbal and nonverbal behaviors so that your observations can be broad-ranging and useful in explaining both positive and negative outcomes. Look at the kinds of interaction checklists others have developed; for example, examine these referenced in this paper or consult Weick (1985) or Ickes, Bissonnette, Garcia, and Stinson (1990). Examining the documented work of others will help you to avoid the pitfalls described earlier from research of other relationship types, and ensure that you remember to, for example, pilot test your checklist before you actually use it, develop a consistent system for collecting the observations, and interpret the results of your work appropriately. Using the work of others, where appropriate, helps to build the research and evaluation knowledge base in the intergenerational programming field, can reduce the resources required to plan and carry out program research and evaluation, and may make your observation checklist a more reliable and valid tool.

Second, if you have videotaping equipment available in your agency, consider using it in your observations (see Weick, 1985, for a decision tree that helps in determining whether video recording is likely to be useful). While the process of gathering and coding videotaped observations can be more complex than using a checklist, reviewing the tapes at a later date can reveal behaviors that you might miss in checklist-type observational techniques. Videotape gives the opportunity for multiple observers of the interactions and allows you to establish reliability of judgment among observers. Be sure that you have the written permission of all persons who will be videotaped, and that they understand all the contexts in which the videotape will later be viewed.

Third, consider following the intergenerational interactions and relationships over time. In one study, Kuehne (1990) followed the interaction patterns of intergenerational pairs over the course of one school year and found remarkable improvements in interaction quality over time. The program recommendations she was able to make following the entire observation period were much more insightful and accurate than those she would have been able to make after a short period of observation.

Fourth, consider additional ways of examining your program relationships, such as interviews with participants. If you really want to know what is occurring between group members, ask them! Kuehne (1990) did this in an intergenerational program study and determined the extent to which the information gathered through interviews was similar to that of observations. Although there was considerable congruence, the interviews were valuable in that they gave the participants an opportunity to explain some of the behaviors and interactions researchers observed in more objective, checklist fashion. Their input was then used to make recommendations for modifications to the program.

Fifth, to understand just how your program worked, consider relating the observation and interview information you have collected to objective measures of relevant program outcomes, such as changes in older adults' self esteem, or children's school attendance or performance. Did older adults who received more affection from children experience higher increases in "self esteem" than did older adults who received less affection from their young companions? Did children who ended up liking older adults more than before have more "positive interactions" than did children whose liking of older adults remained unchanged, or worsened? Of course, you should be sure that you define all important concepts carefully, particularly outcomes such as "self esteem" and "positive interactions;" where possible employ valid outcome measures whose usefulness have already been determined by other researchers.

Finally, consider making your findings public by presenting at a local, regional or national conference. You may also wish to design a press release for your local media to attract more community members to your program, as volunteers or participants, and advertise your success to potential funders. Other human service professionals may also be very interested in what you have discovered, may have helpful feedback about your findings or your program, and may be encouraged themselves. This builds the research base of the field and supports the notion that research and evaluation can and should occur in the everyday world of intergenerational programming.

CONCLUSION

Clearly, human service work is demanding enough that practitioners are not searching for additional activities to occupy their time. And while research and evaluation may appear on the surface to be far removed from what goes on in every day practice with children, youth, older adults and their families, this is not the case. The skills of observation, recording, and analysis are frequently taught and developed in professional education and training programs, placing observation-based research within the repertoire of many intergenerational programmers. The need for and value of such observations are critical to understanding clients' experience and developing better programs. The efforts of those who design and implement programs with children, youth, older adults and their families should never be wasted, even when a program may seem like a "failure." By taking up the opportunity to record details of the actual program interactions and relationships and examine them carefully or preserve them for later scrutiny, we can learn to make more of our relationship-based, intergenerational interventions successful and rewarding.

AUTHOR NOTE

Valerie S. Kuehne has spent much of the past decade focusing her research on intergenerational relationships in the contexts of family and community. She is currently editing a book on intergenerational program research that will be published in late 1997 to 1998.

Caroline L. Collins' research interests are the social applications of Internet technology.

REFERENCES

Bullock, R. (1989). Social Research. In B. Kahan (Ed.), *Child Care policy and Practice* (pp. 14-29). Toronto: Hodder & Stoughton.

Carstensen, L.L. (1991). Selectivity theory: Social activity in a life-span context. In K.W. Schaie & M.P. Lawton (Eds.), *Annual Review of Gerontology and Geriatrics*. vol. 11 (pp. 195-217). New York: Springer.

Cicirelli, V. (1986). *Intergenerational interactions in the adult day care setting: An evaluation study.* Unpublished manuscript, Purdue University.

Collins, C.L. & Gould, O.M. (1994) Getting to know you: How our own age and other's age influence self-disclosures. *International Journal of Aging and Human Development, 39*(1), 55-66.

Durkheim, E. (1933). *The Division of Labor in Society* (G. Simpson, Trans.). New York: Macmillan.

Flanders, N. & Amidon, E. (1981). *A Case Study of Educational Innovation: The History of Flander's Interaction Analysis System.* Oakland, CA: Amidon Associates.

Fox, S. & Giles, H. (1993). Accommodating intergenerational contact: A critique and theoretical model. *Journal of Aging Studies, 7*(43), 423-451.

Freedman, M. (1992). *The Kindness of Strangers: Reflections on the Mentoring Movement.* Philadelphia, PA: Public/Private Ventures.

Hare, A.P., Borgatta, B., & Bales, R. (Eds.) (1955). *Small Groups: Studies in Social Interaction.* New York: Knopf.

Ickes, W., Bissonette, V., Garcia, S, & Stinson, L.L. (1990). Implementing and using the dyadic interaction paradigm. In C. Hendrick & M.S. Clark (Eds.), *Research Methods in Personality and Social Psychology* (pp. 16-44). Newbury Park, CA: Sage.

Ickes, W., Robertson, E., Tooke, W. & Teng, G. (1986). Naturalistic social cognition: Methodology, assessment, and validation. *Journal of Personality and Social Psychology, 51*(1), 66-82.

Krueger, M. (1982). Child care worker involvement in research. *Journal of Child and Youth Care, 1*(1), 59-65.

Kuehne, V.S. (1988). Intergenerational relations: How do they affect children's attitudes toward the elderly? Unpublished Master's thesis, Northwestern University, Evanston, IL.

Kuehne, V.S. (1989). Younger friends/older friends: A study of intergenerational interactions. *Journal of Classroom Interaction, 24*(1), 14-21.

Kuehne, V.S. (1990). A comparative study of children's extra-familial intergenerational relations. Unpublished doctoral dissertation, Northwestern University, Evanston, IL.

Kuehne, V.S. (1992). Older adults in intergenerational programs; What are their experiences really like? *Activities, Adaptation, & Aging, 16*(4), 49-67.

Kuehne, V.S. & Sears, H. (1993). Beyond the call of duty: Older volunteers committed to children and families. *Journal of Applied Gerontology. 12*(4), 425-438.

Minuchin, S. (1974). *Families and Family Therapy.* Cambridge, MA: Harvard University Press.

Newman, S. & Ward, C. (1992-3). An Observational study of intergenerational activities and behavior change in dementing elders at adult day care centers. *Intergenerational Journal of Aging Human Development. 36*(3), 333-345.

Onawola, R. & Newman, S. (1985). Elders' Classroom Interaction Analysis Project. Pittsburgh, PA: University of Pittsburgh Center for Social and Urban Research. Unpublished manuscript.

Ontario Ministry of Community and Social Services (1987). *Young and Old Together: A Resource Manual for Developing Intergenerational Relationships.* Toronto: Ontario Ministry of Community and Social Services.

Pence, A. (1990). Worlds apart? Integrating research and practice in professional child and youth care training. *Child and Youth Services,* 13(2), 235-241.

Ryan, E.B., Giles, H., Bartolucci G. & Henwood, K. (1986). Psycholinguistic and social psychological components of communication by and with the elderly. *Language and Communication,* 6(1/2), 1-24.

Sabatelli, R.M., Buck, R. & Kenny, D.A. (1986). A social relations analysis of nonverbal communication accuracy in married couples. *Journal of Personality,* 53, 513-527.

Seefeldt, C. (1984). Children's attitudes toward the elderly: A cross-cultural comparison. *International Journal of Aging and Human Development,* 19(4), 319-328.

Seefeldt, C., Jantz, R., Galper, A. & Serock, K. (1977). Children's attitudes toward the elderly: Educational implications. *Educational Gerontology.* 2, 301-310.

Sparling, J. & Rogers, J. (1985). Intergenerational intervention: A reciprocal service delivery system for preschoolers, adolescents, and older persons. *Educational Gerontology.* 11, 41-55.

Stewart, A., Franz, C. & Layton, L. (1988). The changing self: Using personal documents to study lives. In D. McAdams & R. Ochberg (Eds.), *Psychobiography and Life Narratives* (pp. 41-74). Durham, NC: Duke University Press.

Styles, M. & Morrow, M. (1992). *Understanding How Youth and Elders Form Relationships: A Study of Four Linking Lifetime Programs.* Philadelphia, PA: Public/Private Ventures.

Sussman, M. & Pfeifer, S. (1988). Kin and kin-kin intergenerational connecting. *Gerontology Review,* 1(1), 75-84.

Tice, C. (1985). Perspectives on intergenerational initiatives: Past, present, and future. *Children Today,* 14(5), 6-10.

Weick, K.E. (1985). Systematic observational methods. In G. Lindzey & E. Aronson (Eds.), *The Handbook of Social Psychology: Vol. 1, Theory and Method* (3rd. ed.) (pp. 567-634). New York: Random House.

Wells, K. & Whittaker, J. (1989). Integrating research and agency-based practice: Approaches, Problems, and possibilities. In E. Balcerzak (Ed.), *Group Care of Children: Transitions Towards the Year 2000* (pp. 351-366). Washington, DC: Child Welfare League of America.

Werner, E. & Smith, R. (1982). *Vulnerable But Invincible: A Longitudinal Study of Resilient Children and Youth.* New York: McGraw-Hill.

SECTION VI:
COMMUNITY BUILDING

Several approaches to community building are tackled in this section, each one underscoring the important contribution made by the intergenerational "dynamic."

Henkin, Santiago, Sonkowsky and Tunick propose intergenerational programming as a significant approach to addressing one of the major challenges to building community: the need to develop cross-cultural understanding. This approach has self-evident value for a multicultural society such as the U.S.

In the second paper, Kaplan suggests that three community-building factors emerge from intergenerational community service projects: cross-generational unity, which is important for social stability; community activism, which creates community change and growth; and cultural continuity, which captures community "memory" for future development.

The various networks that provide services to communities in towns and cities around each state, e.g., aging, education, youth, family, child care, health, housing, etc., are usually distinct with different funding sources and regulations that govern them. Often these networks have little interaction with one another yet they may be providing services to the same or related individuals. The impact at the community level can be seen in resources that are only partially used, yet may be unavailable for other potential users. Typical examples are: school buses that are unused for a significant portion of the day, but which could be employed to transport senior citizens; or senior centers that are sometimes empty by late afternoon and are suitable for after-school programs.

The third paper (Callison and Kirk-Swaffar) discusses the development of local and statewide intergenerational networks, which is one approach to linking service delivery systems. The authors offer analysis of "best practices" based on their own experiences, in addition to surveys conducted with intergenerational networks nationwide.

Intergenerational Programming: A Vehicle for Promoting Intra- and Cross-Cultural Understanding

Nancy Z. Henkin, PhD
Nancy Santiago, MEd
Michael Sonkowsky, MA
Steven Tunick, MEd

Like a quilt rich in colors, textures and patterns, the United States is a nation comprised of many ethnic, racial, religious and cultural groups. It is estimated that by the year 2050, fifty percent of the United States population will be non-white (Louw, 1995). For some, this increased diversity is frightening, as evidenced by attempts to eliminate bilingual education programs and services to legal immigrants. Fortunately, however, there is also a growing recognition that diversity lends strength and uniqueness to the fabric of our society. Particularly in the educational and human services fields, "cultural diversity" and "cultural sensitivity" are being promoted as positive values. Corporate America, too, is beginning to see creating and managing a diverse workforce that can compete in the global

Nancy Z. Henkin is Founder and Executive Director of Temple University's *Center for Intergenerational Learning* and is a leading authority in the field. Nancy Santiago was Project Coordinator for *"Our Elders, Our Roots": A Multi-Cultural Intergenerational Community Service Project* at Temple University's Center for Intergenerational Learning. Michael Sonkowsky is a staff member at Temple University's Center for Intergenerational Learning. Steven Tunick died in 1996 at age 39; he was an inspiring leader in the intergenerational field.

[Haworth co-indexing entry note]: "Intergenerational Programming: A Vehicle for Promoting Intra- and Cross-Cultural Understanding." Henkin, Nancy Z. et al. Co-published simultaneously in the *Journal of Gerontological Social Work* (The Haworth Press, Inc.) Vol. 28, No. 3, 1997, pp. 197-209; and: *Intergenerational Approaches in Aging: Implications for Education, Policy and Practice* (ed: Kevin Brabazon, and Robert Disch) The Haworth Press, Inc., 1997, pp. 197-209. Single or multiple copies of this article are available for a fee from The Haworth Document Delivery Service [1-800-342-9678, 9:00 a.m. - 5:00 p.m. (EST). E-mail address: getinfo@haworth.com].

197

market as one of its major challenges. Yet despite this increased attention to diversity, there are no clear guidelines for moving us from a society that "tolerates" differences to one that "honors" them.

The intergenerational movement has always viewed differences between people as assets not stumbling blocks and sought to promote cooperation between diverse segments of our population. It grew out of a desire to combat ageism and age segregation–often as intractable in our society as racism and racial segregation–by creating programs that foster understanding across generations. Intergenerational programmers have recognized that age, like race and gender, is a cultural determinant. Today's young people are growing up in a different world from the one in which today's elders came of age. Young people have their own language, norms and values, which in many cases seem utterly foreign to older adults in their own families. Moreover, the separate cultures of young and old in America are pitted against one another in countless media images, divisive campaign strategies of political leaders, and rigidly segregated residential patterns. The pervasive age segregation in our society has a deleterious effect on the transmission of cultural heritage, particularly in many ethnic communities where "official" records of the group's legacy often do not exist in places like museums or in school textbooks. Without meaningful contact with older people, children are denied crucial opportunities to learn about the history of their own communities and to get to know individuals who can vividly demonstrate the significance of the past in the present. Older people, too, feel disconnected from the mainstream of society and lack opportunities to learn about new developments in cultural life.

Intergenerational programmers have worked hard to restore ties between old and young and create opportunities for the transmission of cultural heritage. Through oral history projects, cross-age arts activities and service programs, memories and traditions have been rediscovered and support systems strengthened in many communities. There is a need to expand these efforts to include a greater number of ethnic communities which are experiencing growing tensions between generations and difficulty accessing services (e.g., Latino/Hispanic, Asian/Pacific Islander, Native American and African-American). Intergenerational programming can be a powerful tool for restoring a "sense of community" and meeting individual and community needs. Most importantly, perhaps, cross-age approaches can also diffuse tensions between different ethnic/cultural groups and open up new possibilities for intergroup dialogue/exchange as well. Intergenerational programming is a way of tapping into the resources of people of all ages, mobilizing the wisdom of our elders and the energy of youth to meet new challenges of our increasingly diverse society.

INTERGENERATIONAL RELATIONS
IN ETHNIC COMMUNITIES

One of the reasons that formal intergenerational programs have not been as prevalent in many ethnic communities in America is that historically ties between generations have been strong, and informal cross-age interactions a part of every day life. Research attests to the importance of family cohesiveness and the prominent role of older people in many communities. Among African-Americans, for example, older adults have long been viewed as the family stabilizers who provide mental and spiritual support for kin, transmit folklore and family history, and serve as family advisors and mediators (Burton, 1991). Similarly, in many Asian societies, respect for the aged and "filial piety"–the obligation felt by children to support their parents as they age–have been highly valued and are reinforced by principals of ancestor worship (Gozdziak, 1988). Traditionally, the elderly were cared for in multi-generational households where roles were clearly defined (Lum, 1983). Multi-generational families have also been an integral part of many Latino/Hispanic communities, where elderly family members have fulfilled vital roles ranging from caretaker to counselor to disciplinarian (Sotomayor, 1989). In traditional Native American cultures, too, elders have always been afforded a very high degree of respect and the extended family has functioned as "a social unit with the welfare of each individual being shared by all" (Slaughter, 1976).

Unfortunately, an array of social, economic and cultural forces put stress on these traditional family ties. Changing family values, financial pressures, geographic mobility and increasing needs of young and old have led to a rise in intergenerational conflict in many of America's ethnic communities, particularly where English is a second language. For many older immigrants and refugees, life satisfaction revolves around the degree to which they can continue to occupy positions of respect and power within their families (Gelfand, 1982). However, a major discrepancy exists between traditional roles elders held in their homelands and those available to them in the United States. Many are no longer able to provide their children with financial support, land or other material goods. Difficulties in speaking English and understanding "mainstream" American culture often limit their ability to advise their families on important decisions. Without a basic knowledge of English, many have difficulty banking, shopping, accessing health and social services, and using public transportation on their own. The frequent lack of bilingual staff to assist in these tasks increases the isolation and feelings of helplessness experienced by limited-English elderly. Younger family members often displace elders in their roles as mediators with institutions such as schools and health/welfare agencies. As the contributions and assistance that elders can offer the family diminish, the elderly are put in an unfavorable exchange position and often feel alienated and depressed (Gozdziak, 1988).

While many limited-English elders struggle to maintain their roles as transmitters of traditional values and customs, their children and grandchildren tend to distance themselves from that cultural heritage. Daily interaction with other children in school and in their neighborhoods enables younger family members to improve their English language skills and imitate Western behaviors. The faster pace at which children tend to acculturate exacerbates family conflict (Alley, 1980). Whereas in their homelands showing deferential treatment to the elderly was accepted as the norm, this is usually not the case in the United States. Adult children, too, are pulled in different directions as they face life in a society in which "the emphasis on individualism, nuclear family autonomy and economic/racial discrimination create serious pressure" (Lum, 1983). The demands of work often make them unavailable to provide the levels of attention and ongoing assistance that their parents and other older family members expect.

Although it is true that "family" continues to be an important value in ethnic communities, some researchers suggest that there has been an idealization of the ethnic family, both on the part of the service network and ethnic communities themselves. Studies show that the growing levels of alienation and low life satisfaction among elders in these communities is partially a result of unmet expectations of family interaction (Weeks & Cuellar, 1981). Older minority women, in particular, are subject to psychological distress when their needs are not met by the kinship network (Markides, 1986). It is important for policy-makers and programmers not to assume that "families" are able to meet all the needs of their members. Culturally sensitive, formal interventions are needed to restore elders' sense of self-esteem, strengthen relationships between generations and provide specific health and social services.

CROSS-AGE PROGRAMS: BRINGING GENERATIONS AND CULTURES TOGETHER

In a number of places around the country, agencies are piloting intergenerational programs that address specific needs of particular ethnic groups and promote understanding of cultural issues both within and/or between different communities. An impressive variety of programs have been developed. For example, an organization called Interages in Montgomery County, Maryland, has been operating its Intergenerational Bridges

Project since 1990. The program pairs well-trained, supportive senior adult volunteer mentors with newly-arrived immigrant children identified by their ESOL (English for Speakers of Other Languages) teachers as needing additional support during their transition to a new culture. The program has involved around 100 children from over 20 different countries in Africa, Asia, Europe and the America; many coming from war-torn countries have had poor quality or interrupted education prior to their involvement in the program. Their mentors help them build communication, academic and social skills and ease some of the pain of getting to know a new school, a new language and new country. Since 1985, the Center for Intergenerational Learning at Temple University in Philadelphia, Pennsylvania, has been recruiting college student volunteers to help ease the transition to a new land for older immigrants and refugees through "Project LEIF" (Learning English Through Intergenerational Friendship). The young volunteers provide tutoring in English language skills for their new older friends at a variety of locations–in ethnic senior centers, at a Buddhist Temple, in community centers, and in their homes. Whether young are giving support to their elders or vice versa, these kinds of programs not only meet important service needs, but also provide opportunities for deeper cultural understanding and exchange for all participants.

Other intergenerational programs target specific ethnic communities and are designed to involve participants in a broad range of activities. For the past two years in Philadelphia, Pennsylvania, Temple University's Center for Intergenerational Learning has been involving groups of primarily immigrant students in community service activities that benefit non-English speaking elders through a program called "Our Elders, Our Roots." The students receive either academic credit or Work/Study stipends for their participation. The Work/Study students spend ten hours a week at senior centers or community-based organizations that serve specific ethnic groups. Students in the academic course attend class, volunteer three hours a week at the same sites, and write a final paper about their experience. Service activities have included: language skills tutoring; organizing traditional holiday celebrations; teaching citizenship, exercise and English classes; translating forms and letters; and visiting homebound elderly. The goal is for all the students in the program to gain a greater appreciation of their own and others' cultures, as well as a better understanding of the aging process. This project is now being replicated at San Francisco State, the University of New Mexico, and Northeastern University. In Boston, Massachusetts, an organization called "Arts-In-Progress" has been working to integrate the arts into the lives of that city's immigrant elders through "Project ECHO" (Elders, Culture, History, Ourselves). In weekly workshops with bilingual artists/instructors, these mostly non-English speaking elders have an opportunity to share and celebrate their life histories, talents and cultural heritage. Working together they develop original presentations of music, storytelling and theater which they perform for school children and other elders. Past projects undertaken by ECHO participants have included a booklet of Cape Verdean recipes, an oral history project pairing teens and elders from the Haitian community, an elder arts festival and "Nosotros Mismos," an educational theater piece exploring the cultures of the Dominican Republic, Puerto Rico and Colombia. In this way, participating elders build self-confidence and a sense of pride in their cultural backgrounds and life experiences.

Perhaps some of the most exciting and ambitious work now being done in the intergenerational field are *multi*-cultural intergenerational programs-designed to foster understanding and collaboration among culturally diverse groups. The presence of both old and young often breaks down barriers and stereotypes when culturally diverse groups are brought together. Participants assume the familiar roles of grandparent and grandchild with another, even though they may be meeting for the first time. The lifelong perspective of the elderly can help youth explore similarities as well as differences across racial and ethnic lines. The openness and energy of the young can inspire older people to take new risks and overcome cultural barriers they may have long assumed to be insurmountable. Through Elders Share The Arts (ESTA) in New York City, for example, young and old learn to celebrate their cultural heritages as they collaborate on community presentations. ESTA artists bring together older adults from senior centers and youth from neighborhood schools to explore history, values, and life experiences. The artists have the ability to elicit stories, songs and vivid memories from the participants and to help them express these things through a variety of artistic media. Every year, ESTA brings together the best performances from these workshops and puts on a Living History Festival involving the many ethnically diverse neighborhoods of New York. In Philadelphia, a Jewish Community Center offered a class entitled "New Branches, Distant Roots" which brought together a group of well-educated Jewish older adults, many of whom were refugees from the Holocaust, with a group of Southeast Asian teenagers from a low-income neighborhood. After being trained in oral history interviewing skills, the two groups met weekly for discussions on four simple topics: greeting, eating, dating and touching. As the weeks progressed, participants found that they were learning a great deal about each other's personal attitudes and cultural traditions. All of these programs enable participants to overcome initial mistrust and fears about other groups and gain a greater appreciation of experiences they have in common with those who seem so different.

DEVELOPING CULTURALLY APPROPRIATE INTERGENERATIONAL PROGRAMS

In order to plan and implement culturally appropriate intergenerational programs, it is important to find out more about the families and communities with whom you'll be working as well as your own level of cultural awareness. The following guidelines will help you frame your planning process.

Examine Our Own and Your Agency's Level of Cultural Sensitivity

Understanding how your cultural values and beliefs influence your attitudes and behavior will help you develop programs that are appropriate for the groups with whom you will be working. Examining your experiences with people from other ethnic groups and exploring your own assumptions and feelings will better prepare you to bring different age or cultural groups together. This self-exploration process must be ongoing, for often it is not until you are confronted with a different set of cultural experiences or values that you recognize some of your own prejudices. It is also important to assess the level of cultural awareness within your agency. How diverse is your agency's staff? Your clientele? What language is used to describe different populations? What kinds of outreach efforts have been tried in the past to include various groups?

Learn About the Structure and Characteristics of the Groups or Communities with Whom You Want to Work

It is important to remember that no cultural group is homogeneous; each is characterized by great diversity based on differences in socioeconomic level, age, gender, education, language, length of time in United States, urban/rural residence, immigration status, country of origin, or degree of assimilation/acculturation. The Pacific/Asian population, for example, represents over 24 countries. They do not share a common language, religion, or cultural background. When and why they immigrated, their educational levels, income, and occupation further differentiate this group. For example, while many Korean and Chinese immigrants came to the United States out of choice and with sufficient time to prepare for their move, many Cambodian and Vietnamese were abruptly torn from their homelands and told they could not return. In some Latino groups, migration is seen as a way of life. A pattern of "circular migration" (repeated migration to land of origin) is commonplace for many Puerto Ricans and Mexicans. This continuously revitalizes and renews cultural patterns and minimizes the degree of loneliness and isolation experienced by other groups (Sotomayor, 1989).

In order to learn about a specific ethnic group, it is necessary to get assistance from both informal and formal leaders as well as from others who have successfully worked with this group. Key individuals may be in visible positions such as heads of community-based organizations, or may be unofficial but well-known to community members. Individuals who link community members to mainstream institutions are particularly important to identify. Having the right individual(s) conduct a thorough community assessment and developing trusting relationships with key leaders are essential. In-depth interviews and informal conversations with a variety of people, survey research, observations, and/or case studies are all effective strategies for getting information. Learning when to ask questions and what questions to ask is the key to the success of any community assessment. The following are some sample questions you may want to ask:

- In what ways are members of this group diverse?
- What subgroups exist within this community? What role do kinship groups and/or social networks play in the community?
- Who are the key leaders/How can you enlist their help?
- What are the roles and responsibilities that "respected" persons hold?
- Who are the decision-makers within the community? Who has the power? Is this based on age, status, language proficiency?
- How is information disseminated? Word-of-mouth? Community publications?
- What other organizations have a history of working with this group?
- How does the group view "outsiders"?
- To what extent do families rely on outside services to meet health and social service needs?
- Is greater value placed on the "individual" or the "group"? What implications does that have for the types of activities that would be most appropriate?

Explore How Cultural Values and Attitudes Can Affect the Way an Intergenerational Program Is Developed

As you learn about the structure of the community in which you are working, begin to explore some of the values and attitudes prevalent among the people who will be participating in your program. Becoming familiar with another group's values and way of life can be a difficult challenge, but unless this exploration is done carefully, the likelihood of success is minimal. The following are some of the areas that should be examined.

Expectations of Filial Support–In some communities, "outsiders" are not welcomed to assist in the care of the elderly. Cultural norms regarding filial support often have a major impact on utilization of services. In most Asian and Latino communities, caring for the elderly is considered a "family matter" not a social issue (Gelfand, 1994). This norm must be taken into account if one is considering starting a friendly visiting or respite care program involving nonfamilial young people. Careful planning and an understanding of initial familial resistance are needed in order to design a program that has a high likelihood of success.

Questions to Ask:

- Who makes decisions in families?
- What expectations do family members have of each other?
- Would having a young person provide services be perceived as inappropriate?
- How comfortable would older family members feel relating to someone outside their group?

Child Rearing–Varieties of attitudes toward child rearing exist both within and between ethnic groups. Views on issues such as discipline, roles and responsibilities, degree to which children can question authority, and norms for adult-child interactions should be understood before planning an intergenerational program. If you were planning a program that involves older adults mentoring youth or supporting parents of different ethnic backgrounds, it is essential to sensitize them to cultural differences. This will minimize the chances for judgmental behavior and misunderstandings.

Questions to Ask:

- How are children viewed and what is their role in the family? (Are children the center of attention, given decision-making roles or are they to be "seen and not heard"?)

- Can a child address an adult directly or must this be done via a parent or grandparent?
- What kinds of rules exist regarding participation in after-school, evening, weekend or overnight activities?
- What are the norms of interaction between adults and children?

Respect for Authority and Hierarchy—Awareness of the hierarchial structure within a community, family, and/or ethnic-based organization is extremely important. Everyone involved in a program must understand the need to acknowledge both formal and informal community leaders as well as those who are most respected within the family. Programs that promote "reciprocity" are more acceptable to both elders and youth than those that are one-directional. For example, if you're designing a literacy project that involves older adults as the learners, you can also build in an oral history component that utilizes the older adults as teachers. This will enable elders to maintain their role as respected persons in the community.

Questions to Ask:

- How does one show respect for authority figures (e.g., gifts, gestures)?
- Are group members likely to challenge an authority figure?
- What skills/resources do elders have that can be shared with youth?

Attitudes Toward Health and Illness—If you are planning to develop an intergenerational program related to health issues, it is important to understand how each community defines "wellness." In some Latino communities, for example, physical and emotional illness are intertwined. There are a variety of spiritual healers in the Latino community, including: Curandero [person who helps through prayer], Yerbero [herbalistic healer], Espiritistas [practices Espiritism, a religious sect that communicates with spirits], and Santero [practices Santeria, a sect that teaches people to placate the supernatural] (Randall-David, 1989). Traditional Native Americans, too, may see disease as "a phenomenon of the supernatural" (Atkinson, Morten, & Sue, 1979). In some African American communities, religious beliefs affect individuals' conceptions about illness. The church plays a major role in the lives of many older adults. In many Asian cultures, individuals feel personally responsible for their illness, believing it may be a result of bad conduct by a family member (Randall-David, 1989). Older adults, in particular, are reluctant to seek outside help in health matters and want to die at home, not in a hospital.

Questions to Ask:

- What are people's beliefs/attitudes concerning the prevention, diagnosis, and treatment of disease (both physical and mental)?
- What types of practitioners or other individuals are best able to diagnose and treat mental illness?
- What are attitudes toward "outsiders" providing help?

Time Perception—Cultures vary in their orientation toward time. Some Latinos, for example, tend to be more concerned with the present than the future and have a "polychronic" (engaging in several things at the same time) rather than "monochronic" or linear time orientation. Many Native Americans have a "spacial" view of time; events, for example, may take place at a location rather than at a certain time. "Natural phenomena, the occurrence of events, and the location in space of these events, as well as an internal feeling of synchronicity, are the determinants of the passage of time for a traditional Native American" (Deloria, 1973). Differing views of temporal concepts have given rise to the stereotypical notions of "Latin" or "Indian time." It is important not to assume that "lateness" implies resistance, rudeness or laziness.

Attitudes Toward Volunteerism—Although structured volunteer programs are not commonplace in many ethnic communities, the idea of "helping others" is often an essential part of community life. Older adults, for example, are major contributors to their families and religious groups, yet their activities often go uncounted in volunteer data (Maldonado, 1975).

Questions to Ask:

- Do cultural norms prohibit volunteering outside the community?
- Is "helping others" expected of certain age groups?
- What kind of helping activities occur naturally within this community (e.g., caring for grandchildren)?

Recognize Differences in Verbal and Non-Verbal Communication Patterns

Whether you are interviewing community leaders or conducting a specific group activity, it is important to be aware of cultural differences in communication styles. For example, in some communities individuals feel more comfortable openly expressing their emotions than in others. Level of formality and comfort with self-disclosure are other issues that vary across cultures.

Questions to Ask:

- What is the significance of looking someone straight in the eye? (Honesty, shame or disrespect, challenging authority?)
- How important is "small talk" at the beginning of a conversation?
- What are the norms related to touching while conversing? Does this vary by gender?
- What are the norms related to social distance and body space?
- How comfortable are people expressing their emotions in public? Does this vary by gender and age?
- How comfortable are people with self-disclosure?
- What topics are taboo or inappropriate to discuss with a stranger?
- How is silence viewed and/or used in this community?
- Is direct questioning of leaders appropriate?
- Are there specific titles or gestures that connote respect and should be used when addressing the elders or leaders of the community?

CONCLUSION

It is clear that multicultural intergenerational programs can play an important role in strengthening familial ties, providing needed services to young and old and fostering a sense of connectedness in our communities. In this era of limited government resources and services, intergenerational programming represents a cost-effective model for supporting individuals and families throughout the life cycle. The challenge facing us now is to form linkages between institutions which serve youth and older adults, which may also be ethnic-based. Through these partnerships, not only will culturally appropriate programs be developed and sustained, but an expanded definition of "community" will emerge.

AUTHOR NOTE

A faculty member with the School of Education at Temple, Nancy Z. Henkin has developed a wide variety of cross-age programs and has consulted with numerous local and national organizations in the aging, youth and education fields.

Nancy Santiago is currently working with the School District of Philadelphia where she develops culturally oriented service learning programs at schools in a predominantly Latino section of the city.

Michael Sonkowsky edits the Center's nationally disseminated newsletter,

Interchange, and helps in the production of written intergenerational program development materials used across the country.

An outstanding trainer and program developer, Steven Tunick helped create innovative cross-age programs at hundreds of schools, religious/cultural institutions, community-based agencies and national organizations. Mr. Tunick was also involved in Jewish education and served on the Board of "Operation Understanding," a program which brings together Jewish and African-American youth in an effort to repair the rift that divides these communities.

BIBLIOGRAPHY

Alley, J. (1980). Better Understanding of the Indochinese Student. *Education*, 101, 111-114.

Atkinson, D.R., Morten, G., and Sue, D.W. (1979) *Counseling American Minorities: A Cross-Cultural Perspective*. Dubuque: William C. Brown Co. Publishing.

Burton, Linda M. and Dilworth-Anderson, Peggy (1991) Intergenerational Family Roles of Aged. *Marriage and Family Review*, 16, 311-330.

Deloria, V., Jr. (1973). *God is Red*. New York: Grosset and Dunlap.

Gelfand, D. (1994). *Aging and Ethnicity: Knowledge and Services*. New York: Springer.

Gelfand, D. (1982). *Aging: The Ethnic Factor*. Boston: Little Brown.

Gozdziak, E. (1989). *Older Refugees in the United States: From Dignity to Despair*. Washington, DC: Refugee Policy Group.

Louw, Lente-Louise (1995). No Potential Lost The Valuing Diversity Journey–An Integrated Approach to Systematic Change. *Valuing Diversity: New Tools For a New Reality*. New York, NY. McGraw Hill, Inc. pp. 15-58.

Lum, Doman (1983). Asian-Americans and Their Aged. In R. McNeeley and J. Colen (Eds.). *Aging in Minority Groups*. Beverly Hills: SAGE Publications.

Randall-David, E. (1989). *Strategies for Working with Culturally Diverse Communities and Clients*. Bethesda, Maryland: The Association for the Care of Children's Health.

Maldonado, D. (1975). *The Chicano aged*. Social Work, 20, 213-16.

Markides, K.S. (1986). *Aging and Ethnicity*. Beverly Hills, CA: SAGE Publications.

Slaughter, E.L. (1976). *Indian Child Welfare: A Review of Literature*. Center for Social Research and Development. Denver, Colorado: Denver Research Institute.

Sotomayor, Marta (1989). The Hispanic Elderly and the Intergenerational Family. *Journal of Children in Contemporary Society*, 20, 55-77.

Weeks, J. & Cuellar, J. (1981). The Role of Family Members in Helping Networks of Older People. *The Gerontologist*, 21, 338-94.

The Benefits of Intergenerational Community Service Projects: Implications for Promoting Intergenerational Unity, Community Activism, and Cultural Continuity

Matt Kaplan, PhD

INTRODUCTION

Whether "intergenerational programming" stands the test of time as an integrative human services "field" rather than another fad or catchphrase will likely be linked with the effectiveness of efforts to document the value and significance of intergenerational initiatives. Certainly, there is an underlying conceptual framework which identifies parameters of human development relevance and social policy-related significance (Kingson, Hirshorn, & Cornman, 1986; Moody & Disch, 1989; and Newman & Brummel, 1989); this is useful for conceptually linking evidence about the psychosocial and community impact of various intergenerational program approaches.

The focus of this paper is on the benefits associated with one type of

Matt Kaplan is Associate Professor at the Department of Psychology, Hawaii Pacific University.

[Haworth co-indexing entry note]: "The Benefits of Intergenerational Community Service Projects: Implications for Promoting Intergenerational Unity, Community Activism, and Cultural Continuity." Kaplan, Matt. Co-published simultaneously in the *Journal of Gerontological Social Work* (The Haworth Press, Inc.) Vol. 28, No. 3, 1997, pp. 211-228; and: *Intergenerational Approaches in Aging: Implications for Education, Policy and Practice* (ed: Kevin Brabazon, and Robert Disch) The Haworth Press, Inc., 1997, pp. 211-228. Single or multiple copies of this article are available for a fee from The Haworth Document Delivery Service [1-800-342-9678, 9:00 a.m. - 5:00 p.m. (EST). E-mail address: getinfo@ haworth.com].

intergenerational program. "Intergenerational community service programs" are designed to "engage citizens in activities and projects to benefit the community and to meet unmet safety, human, education or environmental needs" (Generations United, 1994, p. xii).

The aim is to provide additional case study data indicating that intergenerational community service programs, when developed along sound program planning principles, invoke powerful communication and social support dynamics that not only have a significant impact on the lives of the participants but also generate community improvements and help establish a sense of cultural identity and continuity (e.g., see Generations United, 1994).

The program evaluation data presented in this paper is of a case study format, consisting primarily of testimony from the project staff and participants involved in an intergenerational community service program called "Neighborhoods 2000," which was implemented in seven American neighborhoods over a seven year period (1987-1994).

In order to put program evaluation results into perspective, the following section will review some other intergenerational community service program approaches and indicate how they influence individuals and communities and have cultural implications.

INTERGENERATIONAL COMMUNITY SERVICE PROGRAMS

Historically, the focus of most intergenerational program initiatives has been on developing activities and experiences that bring together people under 21 and over 60, with a clear goal of promoting relationships that will help either the young, the elderly, or both groups of participants. Accordingly, many program models were conceived in a manner in which one age group is the provider of a service and the other age group is the recipient of the service. However, in recent years, there is growing interest in developing intergenerational programming initiatives which have relevance beyond the anticipated impact on the lives of the participants. "Intergenerational community service projects" represent one such category of programs; they are designed to create community service opportunities, where participating youth and older adults work together to study community issues, improve local conditions, and help people in need.

There are several outcomes that most intergenerational community service programs have in common. First, the youth and senior adult participants often accomplish their community improvement goals, and this has quality of life implications for both generations. Furthermore, as they work together to investigate and improve community conditions, they help expand each other's understanding of real societal problems and reconceptualize how they view their own role as "citizens." It is this promotion of the "ideal of common citizenship" that Moody and Disch (1989) refer to as the most powerful legitimation strategy supporting intergenerational programs.

Many intergenerational community service programs are driven by the same spirit of service that fuels the national youth service movement (Noah, 1986), which is also evident in the elderly services arena as reflected in the motto of the American Association of Retired Persons (AARP)–"To Serve, Not to be Served" (Strunz & Reville, 1985).

Accordingly, older adults have been incorporated into an array of service-learning projects, which simultaneously serve an experiential education function and provide a public service. The "Self-Esteem Through Service" (SETS) program, for example, engages elders residing in senior housing facilities and at-risk middle school students in collaborative service projects; they work together to help the homeless, hospital bound individuals, and others in need of assistance (AARP, 1993). Such projects have profound impacts on the young and older adult service providers; they develop communication and leadership skills and, in many cases, a heightened sense of community and citizenship responsibility (Generations United, 1994; Kaplan, 1991).

Some intergenerational programs, such as "Hidden Treasure," are designed to preserve local heritage. This program, originally funded by the National Endowment for the Humanities and developed by the Community Education Center at Oklahoma State University, uses tapes, videos, essays, slide-tape presentations and live demonstrations to accomplish its community education goals (AARP, 1993).

Another example of an intergenerational program designed to preserve local culture is "Language Link" created by the Seneca Nation in 1992, with funds from the Commission on National and Community Service. Youth and tribal elders of the Seneca Tribal Nation are united in language study and other activities in a joint quest to revive and preserve the Seneca language (Generations United, 1994). The older adult participants of such programs "convey cultural information to a new generation . . . and youth learn about and develop an appreciation for rich cultural heritages, traditions, and histories" (Generations United, 1994, p. 5).

The collaborative process, which takes place within a non-judgmental atmosphere of mutual support, teaches the youth and the senior adults that they have something to give to society and that their views and contributions are valued by others. Both gain new insights into community development issues as they learn to understand and better tolerate differences in the community.

DESCRIPTION OF "NEIGHBORHOODS 2000" AND ITS EVOLUTION: INTRODUCTION TO RESEARCH

The remainder of this paper describes the evolution of one intergenerational community service program model called "Neighborhoods 2000," and the nature of its impact on program participants, their communities, and their sense of culture.

The Neighborhoods 2000 model was originally developed at the Center for Human Environments, City University of New York Graduate School and University Center, as a strategy for helping youth and elderly people to understand the human side of neighborhoods: to engender an awareness that there are people of other age groups who have valuable insights into community life.

The demonstration project began as a community organizing and research project in Long Island City, New York, in 1987. After working to assess the degree to which community residents knew about the large-scale development plans for the neighborhood,[1] it became evident that the development process was proceeding in a non-participatory manner and that most residents were ill-informed and anxious about local urban planning procedures and proposals.

In a series of preliminary interviews with community residents, community organization administrators and members, and human service professionals, a rift was detected between local youth and older adults in terms of their perceptions of each other's community needs. Local youth felt that senior adults wanted only passive recreational opportunities (which was not corroborated by the seniors). Seniors, on the other hand, were not sure what the youth wanted and expressed a concern that there were not enough constructive activities to keep neighborhood youth occupied.

Concern over this initial finding led to the decision to develop the project in a manner which would simultaneously promote intergenerational communication and participatory community planning and development. The project was ultimately entitled "Long Island City 2000" (LIC 2000) to represent the project's goal of having Long Island City residents of all ages work together to create the future of their neighborhood.

The initiative meetings were followed by two intergenerational community planning events, entitled "Community Mural Day" and "Futures Festival." The planning and implementation of the events brought residents of all ages together to present and discuss their neighborhood development ideas with the aid of various media. (See Kaplan, 1990, for a review of this intergenerational special events approach.)

The next phase of the project involved working with the local school district and staff at civic and senior citizen organizations to establish a school-based curriculum and recruit senior adult volunteers. Basically, the Neighborhoods 2000 curriculum represents an approach for bringing young adolescents and senior adults from the same neighborhoods together in a school setting to work on a series of communication and neighborhood exploration activities designed to introduce them to the lives and perceptions of people in other age groups, and to the world of community activism.

The final curricular format consisted of a series of eight activities conducted in 22 lessons, from January to June 1988. Activities included: land-use mapping, photographic neighborhood surveys, reminiscence interviews where seniors recounted their community memories and experiences, autobiographical walking tours, model building of the "ideal" neighborhood, and presentations (including the end-of-year "Display Day" event) in which project participants communicated their local development concerns to community planners and human service professionals. Each project activity lasted between one and four weeks depending upon the activity, the skill and interest level of the project participants, and time constraints.

In total, over a seven-year period (1987-1994), projects have been implemented in seven neighborhoods: Long Island City, NY (1987-88); Mount Vernon, NY (1988-1994); East Harlem, NY (1989-90); Downtown Honolulu, HI (1991-94); Ala Wai, HI (1992-94); Ewa, HI (1992-94); and Waikiki, HI (1993-94).

Each of the subsequent Neighborhoods 2000 projects involved a similar set of activities, with participants consisting of as many as 48 senior adults and a class of fourth, fifth, or sixth grade students. (For a detailed description of the curriculum, refer to Kaplan, 1994.) Each project differed in some aspect or other. They varied in line with: the problems, resources, and local improvement strategies pursued in each neighborhood; opportunities for community research and participation; and the perceptions and creativity of senior adult volunteers, students, project staff members, and school personnel.

The impact of the seven Neighborhoods 2000 projects on the participants was determined primarily by self-reported data (pre- and post-project questionnaires, interviews, and journals) and observations of project staff which usually included college student interns and teachers.

Program impact on the participants was found to occur in the following ways:

- The need to be understood: Eradicating age-related stereotypes;
- Perceptions of intergenerational continuity: The emergence of a sense of camaraderie;
- Building a sense of "citizenship responsibility" and a community activism orientation;
- Community improvement themes; and
- Conveyance of a sense of cultural continuity.

THE NEED TO BE UNDERSTOOD:
ERADICATING AGE-RELATED STEREOTYPES

At the beginning of the projects, children expressed many negative age-related stereotypical views, such as:

> I think it would be sad to be an elderly person because then I would have to live in an old folks' home and I would be with other old people and my body would feel like hell. I would have arthritis and lots of pain. I think I would spend my time just watching T.V. in my wheelchair or rocking chair and reading the newspaper or a book.

The majority of youth made statements about how life after 60 years old is unidimensional and uninteresting. For example, comments like, "they just take care of their pets," and "they like being old because they get a free bus pass" were prevalent.

The senior adult participants were distressed at the negative age-related stereotypes held by youth. One senior adult volunteer, a three-year veteran of the Downtown 2000 project (Honolulu, Hawaii), wrote in her journal about an 11-year-old student pretending to be 62 years old:

> He hunched his shoulders and pretended to walk with a cane and said in a creaky-cracky voice that he wanted to be retired. That was an A-plus performance but his version of a 62-year-old was nix! Where did he see such a person? In a nursing home? A neighborhood? Or does he have such a relative? He wasn't even aware that three of us seniors are over 62, and don't even slightly resemble the character he portrayed, not bent over and not talking in a creaky-cracky voice. We seniors need to show the children that we can really work side by side

with them, communicate and understand them, give or take on the many ideas we all have and tell them life stories of our experiences as well as listen to their life stories. We also need to tell them about the other activities we're involved in, such as helping less fortunate seniors and entertaining them, learning new crafts and skills, and even going back to school to further our education. Hardly any bent over or creaky-cracky 62-year-olds here.

As the students got to know the senior adults on a personal level, they began to question and see past the unidimensional, stereotypical views of passivity and illness, and realize that it is an error to equate physical limitations with mental disability. The following student journal entries and post-project comments about senior adults illustrate the development of positive views toward senior adults:

Grandma S. showed a picture of herself. She was the only one to remember to bring pictures in our group. And I thought senior citizens forgot.

(After seeing one of the senior adults dance during Display Day practice) So this is how you keep young?

We went to the Community Center. We saw seniors, they could walk and move without help. The seniors were exercising and we saw some of the gardens they had planted.

By the way the seniors acted, you'd think differently about them because most people think all seniors walk so very slow and they don't like to do anything but sleep. But that's not the way these seniors act. They are so full of energy and they are fun to be with.

I always knew that some of them (senior adults) liked kids . . . I didn't know that they had parties.

In similar fashion, many of the senior adult volunteers learned to re-evaluate some of their own negative views of children. Senior adult volunteers expressed surprise at the students creativity and competence as learners and community planners:

At the beginning of the project, I was very dubious just what contributions 10-11 year olds could make to a study of the neighborhood. During the first session, I was convinced that they were too young, too disinterested, too unaware of what was going on around them for this project. During the second session, I began to respect them for their awareness of their surroundings . . .

The issues, ideas, and concerns expressed by the students were relevant and realistic. The dilapidated conditions of the community, the lack of playground space and activities, and the need to improve and change our villages are certainly evident through the students' eyes and the senior members' realizations.

One of the college student interns wrote in her journal:

The seniors found out through the interviews how much social pressure the children face and especially how much more responsibilities they have as compared to when they were the children's age. The seniors were surprised by how many of the children come from broken homes, how many of them are from single parent households, and are 'latchkey' kids. One senior had a shock when he was talking to his group of eight and found seven of them came from single-parent households.

To be responsible for providing people with such stereotype-breaking experiences has self-affirmation value–the value of being understood as you are, rather than how the media presents you.

PERCEPTIONS OF INTERGENERATIONAL CONTINUITY: THE EMERGENCE OF A SENSE OF CAMARADERIE

The students and elders shared their life experiences and how certain events helped shape their views. Through this type of sharing, project participants learned about similarities and differences in their lives. In fact, many participants made comments that indicated an emerging awareness of how their own aging process fits into the continuum of human life. Closely tied to this intergenerational continuity theme was evidence of a growing sense of camaraderie between the generations.

In reflecting upon how the project experience fit into their lives, many of the senior adults emphasized the importance, for them and for the students, of connecting with today's youth:

The children are the future, and will inherit our country. We seniors hope to teach them that, even though lifestyles of different generations change rapidly, we must not have our moral values disrupted.

Yes, the years are many that exist between us, but the basics—the foundations of love, respect, sacrifices and caring for one another—must always be carried on, without change.

They don't 'high hat' us and we don't 'high-hat' them . . . We just enjoyed speaking with each other. It was important that we let the young people know that we were once young ourselves.

Also, as students reevaluated their negative attitudes about senior adults, some were also rethinking their own aging process. One student wrote:

If I were old and a senior citizen, I would be living in a nice house and still be working as a volunteer at some good project. I would exercise every day by walking or jogging around the block. I would also be visiting my grandchildren and my other relatives. I would visit the library, visit some exhibit museums, even travel to new places and learn new things. I hope to also maybe be one of the senior citizens of Downtown 2000. I think I would do a lot of things when I am a senior citizen.

In many cases, project participants learned that they have much in common with each other, including some neighborhood-related concerns, despite age differences. This sentiment is evident in the following comments made by senior adult volunteers:

In the small groups of three or four, we had the freedom to express ourselves and our lifestyles, and to talk about our neighborhood. Two wished there were children their ages in the neighborhood to play with and one feared going out after dark because of being physically hurt. I shared an almost similar experience . . . I also don't feel safe going out after dark so I plan my activities for the daylight hours.

The young want a world that is drug-free. So do we! They resent the graffiti around them. We do too! They are anxious to recycle, and clean up the air and the land. We certainly agree with them on this! So obviously, we can help each other make this a better world if we put our heads together and try to make it so.

One of the interns noted:

They discussed how the problems faced by the children of the past have evolved into the societal problems faced by the youth of today. Together they bring forth new ideas and plans to change the future . . .

BUILDING A SENSE OF "CITIZENSHIP RESPONSIBILITY" AND A COMMUNITY ACTIVISM ORIENTATION

Part of the agenda of many educators is to create "responsible citizens" who respect the rights and needs of others and who are ready and able to work for community improvement. However, it is far easier to agree on the definition of "responsible citizens" than to figure out how to create them.

The Neighborhoods 2000 approach represents one strategy for instilling in youth and senior adults a sense of active citizenship. The goal is to dynamically involve project participants in collaborative community research and improvement endeavors of their choosing. Through such involvement, project participants realize that they have the potential and even the responsibility to make things better.

As a result of their project experiences, many participants became noticeably less passive about accepting the neighborhood as is. After the land-use mapping exercise, for example, one student stated:

> In my block there are only apartment buildings. I think there should be stores and malls so I would go there every day. There should be a park with a swing and a pool. I want parks, malls, and stores because my block is so boring and plain. I would want to do more things after school.

A senior adult participant commented:

> (The project) breaks down the four walls of the classroom and encourages us to look beyond and see how the actions of others in our community affect us and how we have the power to affect others positively.

Similarly, a teacher observed:

> After brainstorming and selecting issues they are interested in, the children feel empowered to make others aware of such issues and to do something positive to help or teach others.

The Neighborhoods 2000 curriculum is based on the premise that activism doesn't just happen; it requires communication skills development, exposure to the issues and people with expertise in community development procedures, and opportunities to assume realistic responsibilities. Accordingly, participants are exposed to classroom and fieldwork activities designed to help instill a range of communication and problem solving skills. One teacher commented:

> Each week's experiences teaches them the most important life skills of learning to give and take, accepting and valuing the opinion of others, making compromises, practicing critical and creative thinking skills to solve problems, and having fun and getting along with people of any age.

When asked what the project taught them about how they could improve their neighborhoods, students responded that they were more likely to be aware of how changes in their own actions could lead to neighborhood improvement.

> It's important to take the initiative to communicate with those in charge like we did (during the 'Display Day' event).

> You could make suggestions to the community board, or maybe even approach your senator. You have a right to speak up when you see things going wrong.

> (I learned) the importance of telling people about what you want in your neighborhood . . . and asking them what they want . . . and telling what you don't want.

> I learned not to litter and to try to keep things clean in your neighborhood . . . Also to help stop people from destroying it (the neighborhood).

Some of the senior adult participants perceived their project-related efforts to be an outgrowth of, and contributor to, their own sense of citizenship responsibilities:

> Unlike other projects with which I volunteer, I have expanded my life by becoming more aware of the current issues facing our community. Like with most seniors, I keep up with the news. However, becoming actively involved and getting to know the children makes

the many problems facing the children and their parents personal issues for me as well.

Another senior stated:

> If the students shared their experiences of issues and concerns with their parents—it was worth it. If their parents shared this information with relatives and friends—it made it worth it. And if the community at large got to positively thinking about the issues and concerns— that's even better. Changes for the better can only happen through the concerted efforts of the community.

Project experiences taught participants about the operations of local government and this influenced their conceptualizations about citizen involvement and neighborhood change. By the end of the projects, many participants displayed increased knowledge about how to work with local government. Some became more competent in utilizing letter writing campaigns, petitions, and surveys and interviews as intervention strategies aimed at improving neighborhood conditions. Participants displayed more awareness of local development issues and less hesitancy in sharing their concerns with local agency representatives, community organizers, and other residents.

At the end-of-year Display Day presentations of participants' ideas for neighborhood improvement, public officials and community residents made many comments about participants' skills and inclination related to community activism, and noted that their viewpoints on community development issues were both intelligent and incisive.

However, it should be kept in mind that development of community research skills and an orientation toward activism are a gradual process. In the beginning of the projects, for example, it was usually apparent that many participants had difficulties expressing their community hopes and concerns in written or oral form. Many were better able to express their neighborhood improvement ideas through sketches, songs, dance, poetry, drama, maps, models, photographs and videotapes.

A contributing factor in encouraging participants to develop and share community development ideas was the assurance that their projects were not "empty" exercises, irrelevant to their lives. The use of the local media served not only to publicize the project and participants' plans and concerns, but also to attribute legitimacy to their views which, in some cases, led to dialogue with public officials and community organization administrators.

COMMUNITY IMPROVEMENT THEMES

In all of the projects participants learned how investigating their neighborhoods' past has significance for figuring out desired future directions. In the Ewa (Hawaii) projects, for example, participants learned about quality of life discontinuities associated with the economic void created when the sugar industry left Ewa. One senior adult participant noted:

> Ewa is a nice place to live, but it was a better place. It had many features that made it an ideal community. It had places of learning, worship, recreation, and socialization. There was gainful employment for all, health services for the sick, safety and security in the villages and a sense of community and belonging. The steady decline of the sugar industry and the eventual closing of the sugar mill brought about a gradual decline and deterioration, and the loss of many things that contributed a great deal to the quality of life in the community.

The 1992-93 participants of the Downtown 2000 project focused on the following issues in Honolulu: environmental concerns, safety, the need for more recreational facilities (especially a bike track), the need for an overpass on Punchbowl Street, and the needs of homeless children. One of the groups organized a school wide collection of donations for children of homeless families; 23 boxes of toys and clothing donations were received and distributed to local relief agencies. Another group created a petition campaign aimed at prompting the city to build an overpass on the Diamond Head (mountain) side of Royal Elementary School.

In the Ala Wai project (1992-93), participants were concerned about obsolete playground equipment and the dumping of hazardous wastes into storm drains. They worked with the Interagency Water Quality Action Program (Department of Health) to organize and implement a public outreach information campaign, which involved stenciling "Kokua (Hawaiian word for please) Dump No Waste/Goes to Beach" signs around local storm drains. They also developed a playground equipment enhancement plan which they presented to Parks Department officials.

In the 1990-91 Mount Vernon project, participants were concerned about drugs and drug-related violence, litter, and the lack of recreational facilities for children (such as ice skating rinks). However, after finding out from the Mount Vernon Recreation Department that there was an extensive network of youth clubs, leagues and programs, project participants determined that the problem was not one of limited recreational opportunities but, rather, one of an inadequate publicity mechanism to notify local families about the various activities.

In this instance there was marked agreement regarding community issues and problems of concern to the youth and senior adult participants. Drug abuse, violence, and recreational program limitations were examples of shared concern. However, there were occasional exceptions to this pattern of intergenerational unity on the issues. One such instance was with the Ala Wai 2000 project (1993-94), when a small intergenerational group of program participants explored the feasibility of building a walking bridge over the Ala Wai Canal. The two seniors in the group had mixed feelings about the bridge and the four students were strongly in favor of it. They conducted a community survey and the results indicated a broad intergenerational conflict about the bridges. In response to the question, "Do you want a bridge?" only seven of the 16 senior adults who were interviewed favored the bridge, whereas 33 of the 35 youth (under 18 years of age) and 25 of 28 young and middle-aged adults (under 60 years of age) favored the bridge. The senior adults, who were more likely to be homeowners, wanted to maintain the quiet residential nature of the Ala Wai community, whereas the younger adults and youth were more likely to note the advantages of "opening up" the neighborhood to the stores and nightlife of Waikiki.

Problems such as the local drug trade of East Harlem and the underutilization of recreational facilities in Mount Vernon are complex issues requiring long-term study and ongoing intervention. Accordingly, insofar as the projects last for less than one school year, there is never enough time to engage public officials and local planning professionals in dialogue about community problems or to begin the long process of working collaboratively in promoting participants' neighborhood improvement suggestions. Nevertheless, at least progress was always made in helping participants better understand, concretize, and develop their own opinions about community development-related issues.

CONVEYANCE OF A SENSE OF CULTURAL CONTINUITY

Through learning about life experience and values of the older adult volunteers, students were exposed to empirical data about the temporal component of community life, a benchmark upon which to frame their own emerging community and societal perceptions. Mount Vernon students, for example, wrote in their journals:

> In the past, it was peaceful in Mount Vernon. People would go to the store, leave their keys with their neighbors, and nothing would happen to their houses. There was not a lot of crime around. It was nice and very peaceful.

Long ago they didn't have TV, Nintendo, cars or CD players. For fun they listened to victrolas, radio, and played outside and rode their bikes. They had skates, but they had to have a key to skate. But now they have roller blades. The girls played jump rope, and some girls jumped "double dutch." The boys played with marbles, and they built wooden wagons. Now they have dirt bikes.

I think life was much better then, than now. Life was better, because there was not a lot of killing. People were friendlier and didn't have to worry about going out without being hurt. I think life everywhere was good.

The senior adults also learned about the temporal component of community life. For instance, one senior observed:

As the senior adults share their past experiences with our young people, they provide an insight to simpler times, family ties and caring communities. Meanwhile young people aid the senior adults to adjust and understand their fast-paced time of technology. By utilizing the knowledge and experience of both worlds we can build better citizens today while showing our young people the path to becoming better leaders in the future.

When project participants focused on the past, present and the future of their neighborhoods, they were at the same time talking about values, about how to live. This type of dialogue was more of a dialectic than a linear disposition of changing values. As a result, some project participants learned to reassess their definitions of "progress"; children learned that newer is not necessarily better, and older adults became more familiar with current issues related to sexual equality, technological development, and youth self-expression.

In multicultural neighborhoods, respect for the various cultures was promoted through walking tours, songs, and interviews. During a walking tour in Downtown Honolulu, for example, one senior adult of Chinese descent stopped the group in front of a statue of Confucius, at the Young's Noodle Factory, and in front of a traditional herb shop to discuss aspects of Chinese culture. One of the college interns commented about the Chinatown part of the tour:

It felt like another country. I had never seen so many different goods. (They) had to call me to leave one of the stores.

In the Hawaii projects, Hawaiian songs and dance (hula) served as a unifying force which crossed intercultural and intergenerational boundaries.

At the end of the Display Day events, for example, everyone joined hands and sang "Aloha Oe."[2] Also, the visit to Iolani Palace (a historical site which served as the official state residence of Hawaiian royalty) enriched everyone's knowledge and appreciation of the Hawaiian culture. Through the singing and the hula performances (some conducted by senior adults, some by the students, and some together), and visits to culturally significant sites, respect for the Hawaiian cultural heritage was strengthened.

As noted above, intergenerational programming is a broad field, often associated with a wide range of benefits for the participants. Neighborhoods 2000 represents one intergenerational community service program approach, which is based upon the concept of utilizing the communal concerns of youth and senior adults as a focal point for stimulating intergenerational collaboration and joint involvement in community affairs.

SUMMARY AND CONCLUSIONS

As the youth and older adult participants joined each other as neighborhood researchers and service providers, they were forced to clarify their own value assumptions about each other, their community, and their own roles in community development. In terms of promoting intergenerational understanding and unity, members of both age groups learned to question negative age-related stereotypes. They also learned that the generations are interdependent, and that they have shared concerns about the quality of life in their communities (e.g., security, trash removal, recreational opportunities, etc.).

Through their project experiences, participants learned critical thinking, communication and decision-making skills, including learning to listen, how and when to initiate dialogue, how to use clarity and use persuasion in presenting one's points, and the art of negotiation. These skills are invaluable in terms of preparing people to function in a world of changing social, political, economic, and environmental conditions.

When it came to identifying neighborhood needs, particularly those in relation to settings used by children, the students were very perceptive. Where the Neighborhoods 2000 model falls short, however, is in providing an ongoing mechanism for incorporating children's feedback into the local development decision-making process. The value of the projects is more in terms of "planting the seeds" of community activism. As a result of their involvement in what they viewed as a successful community participation experience, many participants were clearly influenced to be more civic-minded and to view their own "citizenship" in action oriented as well as educational terms.

Intergenerational community service projects such as Neighborhoods 2000 also have "cultural continuity" significance in terms of helping people look forward as well as backward. In the context of community development, this is translated into the goal of building communities that are strengthened by the roots of the past but, at the same time, focused on the challenges of the future.

IMPLICATIONS

One measure of a culture's survival is how its traditions are passed on from one generation to the next. While the family unit has traditionally been the natural venue for establishing intergenerational understanding and cultural continuity, in these times of rapidly changing demographics (including a declining incidence of co-residing multigenerational families) and changing social values, there is concern that people in the younger generations are increasingly losing awareness of, and respect for, the experiences of people in the older generations, and vice versa. In such cases, the potential for senior adults to fulfill their unique role as conveyers of culture is diminished.

However, intergenerational programs, in which participants exchange information and discuss their cultural and social values, function as an important bridge between the experiential realities of different generations.

If there is continued growth in the number and scope of intergenerational community service projects. It is possible that this will have implications for revitalizing popular conceptions of intergenerational respect and support, citizenship responsibility, experiential education, and political activism.

NOTES

1. The Hunters Point Waterfront Redevelopment Plan, developed by the Port Authority of New York and New Jersey with support from the Department of City Planning, was a megaplan for a $ 1.5 billion renovation of a previously under-utilized waterfront site area (Grusen et al., 1986).

2. "Aloha Oe," literally translated as "Farewell To Thee," is a Hawaiian song that invokes emotional feelings of unity.

AUTHOR NOTE

Matt Kaplan has written widely in the intergenerational field and will soon publish *The Role of Intergenerational Programs for Supporting Children, Youth and Elders in Japan*, SUNY Press (late 1997) co-authored with three Japanese scholars.

REFERENCES

American Association of Retired Persons (AARP) (1993). *Intergenerational Projects Idea Book.* Washington, DC: AARP.

Generations United (1994). *Young and old serving together: Meeting community needs through intergenerational partnership.* Washington DC: CWIA.

Grusen Partnership/Beyer Blinder Belle Associated Planners & Architects (1986). The Hunter's Point Waterfront development draft master plan alternative. NY: Port Authority of New York & New Jersey.

Kaplan, M. (1994). Side-by-side: *Exploring your neighborhood through intergenerational activities.* MIG Communications: San Francisco.

Kaplan, M. (1991). *An intergenerational approach to community education and action.* Unpublished Ph.D. dissertation. City University of New York Graduate School and University Center.

Kaplan, M. (1990). "Designing community participation special events that cross generational boundaries." In R. Selby, K. Anthony, J. Choi, & B. Orland. (Eds.) *Proceedings of the 21st Annual Conference of the Environmental Design Research Association.* Champaign, IL.

Kingson, Hirshorn, & Cornman (1986). *Ties that bind: The interdependence of generations.* The Gerontological Society of America, York, PA: Maple Press Company.

Moody, H.R., & Disch R. (1989). Intergenerational programming between young and old. *The Generational Journal, 1*(3). 25-27.

Newman, S., & Brummel, S.W. (Eds.) (1989). *Intergenerational programs: Imperatives, strategies, impacts, trends.* Binghamton, NY: The Haworth Press, Inc.

Noah, T. (1986, November). We need you: National service, An idea whose time has come. *The Washington Monthly.*

Strunz, K., & Reville, S. (1985). *Growing together: An intergenerational sourcebook.* Jointly published by the American Association of Retired Persons and The Elvirita Lewis Foundation.

Forming Intergenerational Program Networks

Herbert Callison, MS
Donna Kirk-Swaffar, MA

INTRODUCTION

In the spring of 1991, funding was provided by Mainstream, Inc., to coordinate a conference of representatives of intergenerational networks from throughout the United States and Canada for the purpose of discussing the formation and maintenance of intergenerational networks. Thirty-three people attended the conference in Kansas City, Missouri. Goals for the meeting were exchanging ideas about techniques for starting and continuing networks and identifying barriers to intergenerational network building.

Four years later, in November 1995, Mainstream, Inc. received a grant from the H.W. Durham Foundation to conduct a follow-up survey of those meeting participants and others who had joined state or local intergenerational networks during the intervening years. The survey would attempt to confirm or deny concluding statements from the 1991 meeting delibera-

Herbert Callison is Executive Director at Mainstream, Inc. and is also Adjunct Assistant Professor at Washburn University in Topeka, and author of numerous books and articles on community issues. Donna Kirk-Swaffar is Communications Director and a Project Director at Mainstream, Inc., where she develops and presents training sessions on quality management and organizational communications topics.

[Haworth co-indexing entry note]: "Forming Intergenerational Program Networks." Callison, Herbert, and Donna Kirk-Swaffar. Co-published simultaneously in the *Journal of Gerontological Social Work* (The Haworth Press, Inc.) Vol. 28, No. 3, 1997, pp. 229-241; and: *Intergenerational Approaches in Aging: Implications for Education, Policy and Practice* (ed: Kevin Brabazon, and Robert Disch) The Haworth Press, Inc., 1997, pp. 229-241. Single or multiple copies of this article are available for a fee from The Haworth Document Delivery Service [1-800-342-9678, 9:00 a.m. - 5:00 p.m. (EST). E-mail address: getinfo@haworth.com].

229

tions. Factors that were deemed critical to intergenerational network success (which were phrased in question form for the survey) are listed in Table 1.[1]

Thirty-four potential respondents were mailed the survey. Twenty-two responses were received. Nineteen of the respondents completed surveys, five responses indicate no network existed in their state, and one potential respondent refused to participate. Of the 19 completed surveys, 17 revealed an existing network, while two surveys indicated a network had failed. Of the 17 existing networks, 12 were state networks, four were regional networks, and one network was local. The following article is a summation of the results of the 1991 meeting of representatives of intergenerational networks and the Durham survey.

TABLE 1. Necessary Elements for Successful Intergenerational Network Formation

Agency Involvement
- Community support for "intergenerational cooperation" among agencies representing both elder and children's groups.
- Broad-based membership representing both public and private agencies.
- Active participation by elected officials and administrators of state and local aging and children's departments.

Volunteer Participation and Cooperation
- Dynamic steering committee, ad hoc committee, board of directors, and other leaders, i.e., they possessed the energy, commitment, knowledge, skills, and charisma to recruit others to join the network.
- Sustained enthusiasm from the original core of volunteers through the network's developmental stage.
- Consensus reached by original core of volunteers on the basic tasks of the network.
- Willingness by members to advocate for issues determined by the network.

Network Structure
- Creation of a formal structure such as an executive committee, board of directors, bylaws.
- Evidence of strategic planning that resulted in well-defined goals and objectives.

Generation of Program Resources (personnel and fiscal)
- Establishment of a funding base.
- Creation of a marketing plan for the promotion of the network and its activities.

COMMUNITY SUPPORT

The development of community support is a prerequisite to the successful creation and maintenance of an intergenerational network. The nucleus of the network includes representatives of state agencies, local public and private intergenerational programs, elected bodies, and volunteer groups such as the American Association of Retired Persons (AARP), children and aging coalitions, and silver-haired legislatures. Recruitment targets individuals who have been identified as having a vested interest in forming the network.

The potential of an intergenerational network as an advocacy group is a key motivator for the initial core group to form. In most states the promise of addressing local, state, and federal legislative and/or conducting forums for citizens to express their views is a key ingredient in the stimulation of the initial volunteer interest. However, advocacy alone will not sustain interest in the group, and the proposed network remains more of an association if advocacy is the only cohesive force.

Subsequent meetings of the ad hoc or steering committee that began the network focus on forming goals, objectives, and the structure of the network. Co-chairs are selected, often representing key organizations such as the state council on aging or children's coalition. Each person who attends these planning meetings is asked to commit time, funds, credibility, or gifts-in-kind as a way of ensuring commitment to the network. Tasks are assigned to members, and no one is considered an advisory or honorary member.

A roster of members is created and expanded by requesting mailing lists from member organizations. The roster also identifies organizations or agencies that are willing to provide assistance such as printing, mailing, and/or staffing the network. Meetings of the ad hoc or steering committee as well as membership meetings are held throughout the state to increase the network's visibility. If local networks form on a state, county, or regional level, they are encouraged to join together to represent a more widespread geographical area.

STRATEGIC PLANNING

Strategic planning by the core group and/or full membership is vital to the maintenance of an intergenerational network. It is especially important to expand the network's leadership pool during the development and implementation of the strategic plan. A danger exists of excluding the general membership and weakening the ultimate success of the plan. This danger could be exaggerated if the core group has a difficult time sharing control of the organization. The strategic plan includes goals and objectives, assigned tasks, and identification of resources. The mechanism for developing a strategic plan varies: Development by subcommittee, all-member retreat or regional planning followed by state planning.

The more difficult tasks during strategic planning are prioritizing issues and the development of a consensus of the selection of issues. Dividing a list of potential issues into administrative (or external) issues and organizational (or internal issues) and determining a set of standards for prioritizing and consensus building is helpful.

Prioritizing and consensus building is a deductive process, with the consensus being formed around terminology acceptable to a majority of network members. After members select and prioritize the issues, they develop a work plan.

Some standards are applied during the deductive process:

- deal with issues not being addressed by other coalitions or networks;
- look at issues representing a timely public need;
- adopt issues that will attract in-kind and financial resources;
- consider issues currently occupying media time and space;
- establish priorities that represent concerns of participating organizations; and
- support issues that will merge different interests of participating organizations.

Issues are divided into two categories: non-programmatic and programmatic. Non-programmatic issues are concerns that transcend direct services offered by organizations represented in the network membership. Programmatic issues are concerns that enhance or hinder the direct services offered by organizations represented in the network membership.

Examples of non-programmatic issues include care of elders and/or children; health care reform; effective use of environmental issues; bias, such as ageism, sexism, racism, and anti-youth culture; grandparents' and grandchildren's rights; and the sandwich generation. Programmatic issues include recruitment and management of volunteers, staff and volunteer training, program development and management, and program evaluation.

THE NETWORK STRUCTURE

The indispensable element in the maintenance of an intergenerational network is the establishment of a solid structural base. The structural base is composed of a conceptual framework, a formal structure, strategic planning, ongoing community education, productive activities, a host sponsor, and multiple funding sources.

The conceptual framework is the development of a consensus regarding a conceptual framework among founding members that can be perpetuated even though the membership may change. The conceptual framework becomes the basis for strategic planning, the creation of an infrastructure, and the development of productive activities.

The formal structure is comprised of a corporate entity, non-profit status, bylaws, a board of directors, an executive committee, working subcommittees, and a supportive membership. An ad hoc or steering committee assumes responsibility for the development of the formal structure. The skeleton of the intergenerational network, created during the meetings of this committee, evolves into a formal network structure. Ad hoc or steering committee members assume leadership of the formal network subcommittees.

Once the formal network structure is established, membership is viewed by the public as stable and long-term. Establishing the formal network structure may take as long as 18 months.

The successful network has members who are invested in the network's philosophy, policy, and programs. The network's power base is spread widely among the membership, with individual members operating on an equal plane with each other. Every effort is made to minimize the danger of one constituency (aging or youth) being over-identified with the network and ensure that network activities do not increase competition between members. By this time the successful network has solicited participation from agency directors or state department heads.

Fortunately, network members are usually chosen for their considerable communication skills and access to resources. As a result, intergenerational networks offer technical assistance, conduct research, identify and share resources, assist with fund-raising, develop and coordinate programs, advocate for constituents, initiate and change policies, identify issues, and inform the public about intergenerational interdependence and cooperation.

Possible functions that intergenerational networks assume include coordinating training, conferences, events, and technical assistance; conducting surveys of direct service providers and using the information to publish resource directories or solicit support for network members; assisting memberships with local problems such as obtaining liability insurance and recruiting volunteers; and maintaining a resource bank of printed materials and audiovisuals that can be used for training and public relations.

PUBLIC RELATIONS AND MARKETING

Efforts to educate the community about the network begins as soon as the conceptual framework is established and continues throughout the life of the network. Community education is carried out as part of a marketing plan that includes: printed materials (brochures, newsletters); audio-visuals (videos, public service announcements, radio spots); and community outreach (speaker's bureau, workshops, technical assistance, and conferences). Initial marketing can begin by merely identifying and contacting intergenerational programs within the geographic area targeted for membership in the network and/or conducting an awards banquet.

The purpose of the public relations effort is to expand awareness of the value of intergenerational cooperation. The marketing plan builds on the goals and objectives of the network and on the results of evaluations regarding successes and failures of previous intergenerational efforts. Some intergenerational networks wait until the network has established credibility with a few key public and private agencies before beginning a public relations and marketing campaign.

The first step in marketing is the use of network members to educate other members and potential members. The information transferred among members includes the philosophy and policy of the network, issues to be addressed by network members, tasks and functions of the network, and the successes and failures of individual intergenerational programs. For example, members of intergenerational programs are educated regarding prerequisites to program success, such as recruiting seniors, orienting and preparing volunteers, building program flexibility, creating an ongoing array of services for seniors and children, and meeting expectations of both elders and children.

The second step in marketing is the preparation of network members for the successful use of the media. Workshops are conducted for network members. Reporters are invited to present sessions on writing press releases, contacting media representatives, gaining access to the media, and the differences in the various forms of the media (television, radio, and newspapers). A directory of contact persons, dates of publication and acceptance of information, and addresses and telephone numbers of media outlets is prepared and distributed to network members.

The third step in marketing is the creation and distribution of print, audiovisual, and other educational materials. Developing educational materials serves a dual purpose: educating the media regarding intergenerational programs, and providing information to the media that can be transmitted to the general public. The printed materials are designed to educate people about the purpose and operation of intergenerational programs in a concise, clear manner. Educational materials may include brochures, fact sheets, posters, videos, public service announcements, radio spots, and promotional items such as refrigerator magnets.

Involving the media in the intergenerational network is one way of planning and carrying out the marketing plan. Representations from the media or public relations firms can be invited to become members, or advisors to, the network and/or to attend intergenerational network meetings, conferences, and other activities.

Media representatives can be invited to cover stories or to print press releases. Press releases can include packets of information with an invitation to attend meetings, visit intergenerational programs, or print articles about intergenerational activities. Good, clear visuals (photos and videos) can be sent with the printed material. Each media release should also include the purpose of intergenerational programs and their method of operation. It is especially important to highlight programs that operate in the geographic area receiving the media release.

Retired journalists and photographers can be recruited to write stories and take pictures to enhance the stories. Celebrities can be used in public service announcements, videos, and pictures, or as key figures at events. Members of intergenerational networks can speak at conferences of organizations or associations whose members work with elders or children.

FUNDING

Adequate funding is crucial to successful intergenerational network maintenance. However, before fund-raising can begin, the network must: (1) develop a clear statement of purpose for the fund, (2) approve a budget, and (3) launch a public relations or marketing campaign.

The goals, objectives, and philosophy of the network form the basis for the stated use of the funds. In fact, information provided to the Internal Revenue Service when applying for tax exempt status is similar to the data that should be used when approaching potential funders.

Funds are budgeted for the following purposes: network staff support; office space; supplies (postage, paper); utilities (telephone, electricity); equipment (computer, FAX, copier); stationary, brochure, and newsletter printing; travel costs, including subsistence; development or purchase of audio-visual materials; sponsorship of workshops and conferences; costs of public relations activities; fund-raising; and other costs related to network activities such as providing technical assistance and training to members. By using volunteers and in-kind contributions of printing, mailing, and staff time, many networks operate effectively with less income.

Prior to a fund-raising campaign, network members must select a fund-raising committee or finance committee to direct it. The committee comprises network members from business, the media, the public, and intergenerational programs. Each committee member is selected based on expertise in budgeting and/or fund-raising. Committee chairs should have name recognition and agree to work on behalf of the network.

Multiple funding sources are necessary. Funding is received from local, state, and federal agencies; foundations; corporations; membership dues; fees for services; special events; and sales of goods. An annual budget is established based on the funds committed. Recruiting for-profit members such as companies with kinship care programs can enhance fund-raising efforts.

Strategies for obtaining the funds are established; for example, requesting funds from a foundation or corporation for network support staff, seeking technical assistance and training money from state departments, and finding in-kind donors for office space and printing. Mailing lists of individuals, foundations, and corporations are compiled in cooperation with network members. Current information is accumulated regarding potential funding sources from network members and visits to the nearest grantsmanship center. The preferable budget divides the income among as many sources as possible so that individual requests are lower and a donor's withdrawal of funds at a future date will not undermine the network's funding base.

Grant proposals are submitted to foundations and corporations. Contact persons at foundations and corporations are identified and approached personally to ascertain their interest in intergenerational programs prior to the submission of a proposal. Most foundations and corporations establish and publish guidelines of program interests for grants and application procedures. Network members are cognizant of foundations and corporations that are funding individual intergenerational programs to avoid accusations of stealing funds by individual network members or double-dipping by foundations or corporations.

State agencies (state departments of aging, children's services, and education) are approached for funds to assist agencies providing services to their clients to initiate or to continue intergenerational programs. The funds are requested in conjunction with the state's budget development process. Seeking funds from state agencies for specific purposes such as technical assistance, training, and conferences is sometimes easier than seeking money for general operating costs.

Respondents to the Durham survey noted the positive aspects of having a host sponsor, an agency or organization that will serve as the host to the state network. Host sponsors are varied but generally are direct service providers in the aging or children's field; government agencies (Area Agency on Aging); and universities or colleges. Host sponsors provide valuable in-kind support (printing, telephones, office space, etc.).

Productive activities for host sponsors are direct service projects (foster grandparents, mentoring, adopt-a-grandparent, Ameri-serve fix-up campaigns), training and technical assistance, and/or maintenance of an advocacy camp (publications, lobbyists, collaboration facilitation).

Network members identify national sources of funds for direct services that can be accessed at the state level. For example, the Center for Substance Abuse Prevention has funds that can be requested through state offices to assist with school drug abuse prevention programs. Foundations or corporations that give grants to the AARP may also give grants to intergenerational networks.

Other sources of funding include in-kind contributions of space, materials, and personal time. A directory is maintained with lists of corporations and individuals who offer in-kind assistance and the type of assistance available. Elder and youth volunteers are used to supplement staff. Local foundations, corporations, and governments are asked to help with network activities that will benefit the local community. Dues from members and fees from workshop or conference participants are collected.

Potential donors receive information regarding network activities before, during, and after the fund-raising campaign, whether or not they are active donors. Information about network activities presents potential donors with a continual affirmation of the benefits from supporting the network. Reference to specific programs is essential, with honest information about successes, problems, and failures. An accounting of the use of funds previously obtained is presented.

UTILIZING ELECTED OFFICIALS
AND STATE ADMINISTRATORS

Elected officials and top administrators of state and local departments of aging or children's services are asked to assist with the formation and maintenance of the intergenerational network. The specific targets are officials or administrators who will benefit from the successful formation of an intergenerational network or who demonstrate an interest in supporting programs for either elders or the young. As part of the recruitment process, elected officials and state administrators are informed about the potential for the members of the intergenerational network to advocate for legislation favorable to the cause of intergenerational and other volunteer efforts.

A brochure, newsletter, or other printed piece is mailed first-class to the homes of local representatives of the U.S. Congress and local and state elected officials. In addition, a carefully selected spokesperson can personally visit with elected officials and state administrators about issues related to intergenerational programs.

The information provided to elected officials and state administrators during personal visits is agreed upon by network members. Policy or issue priorities and information about them is requested from national organizations such as Generations United, AARP, and Americorp. Local representatives of members of these national organizations also assist in contacting elected officials and administrators.

IDENTIFYING AND OVERCOMING BARRIERS

As previously mentioned, an established leadership core (steering committee or executive committee) is a prerequisite to overcoming barriers to intergenerational networking. The leadership core comprises network members who are credible, hard-working, capable planners, committed and/or skilled fund-raisers. Nine additional barriers are most likely to challenge the efforts of the network and its leadership.

Scarce Resources

Scarce resources refers to inadequate money and insufficient time. Two strategies can overcome the paucity of resources: the securing of commitments for ongoing funding and in-kind contributions of resources and people, and the development of a fund-raising plan that will minimize dependence upon a single source or few sources for support.

Ill-Defined Goals and Objectives

Ill-defined goals and objectives mean a lack of clearly identified purpose for the network and/or assignment of responsibilities for carrying out these purposes. The lack of well-defined goals and objectives is countered by initiating strategic planning designed to answer the following questions: What is the network's mission? What benefits will network members receive from participation? An outside facilitator is often asked to assist in the development of the network's goals and objectives.

Imbalanced Representation

The failure to achieve a balance of representation among network members can be overcome by broadening the leadership and membership base to include representatives from programs serving both elders and children, consumers associated with these programs, and supporters of these programs.

Lack of Identified Networking Benefits

A failure to identify the benefits of networking for members is also a possible barrier. One way to counter this barrier is for members to assume responsibility for meeting the network's established purposes. Evaluations of network activities aid in the determination of future purposes.

Unfavorable Perception of Network Purpose

This barrier often occurs when members fail to develop an accurate and timely description of network activities. A well-planned marketing campaign with strong visuals (videos and pictures) can overcome this barrier. Inviting the public to participate in and/or view the activities of the network is another countermeasure.

Network Member Competition

Another barrier develops when network members begin competing for the adoption of their favorite issues as the priority for the network at the expense of other issues. The danger from this barrier is minimized by keeping the network's purpose, goals, objectives, and issues general and overarching.

Turfism

Turfism is protecting an agency's delivery of service territory, i.e., funding, client territory, or political positioning. Although respondents to the Durham survey did not identify turfism as an existing problem, it is an issue to be aware of. Network members must establish a common purpose in which all agencies can concur prior to distributing power and/or authority among network members. A second tactic is encouraging friendly collaboration between network members and member agencies when addressing issues.

Lack of Volunteer Commitment

To keep volunteers enthusiastic and committed, the network must promote intrinsic gratification and reward volunteers through recognition events. Participants need to be reassured that they are making a significant impact from the inception of the network onward. Some of the same methods employers use to motivate employees are used with volunteers.

Rural/Urban Differences

The differences in agency problems between rural and urban members are sometimes considered problems. The forming of city, county, and/or regional networks can compensate for the geographical and rural/urban differences.

Geographic Obstacles

Geographic obstacles also may prevent the successful maintenance of an intergenerational network. Mini-networking through the formation of city-wide, county-wide, or regional networks is also seen as a solution to this problem. A second remedy is the rotation of meeting locations around the state to attract new members and showcase intergenerational programs. Exploration of computer-based communication, i.e., e-mail and the World Wide Web, may bring additional solutions to light in this area.

CONCLUSION

It is not difficult to initiate intergenerational networks. Volunteers, especially volunteers representing elder groups, become enthusiastic about the network idea. A committed core group is formed and, in most cases, remains active for an extended period of time. The problem is maintenance of the intergenerational network.

Developing community support for intergenerational cooperation is the first step in maintaining an intergenerational network. Strong community support requires recruiting dynamic, enthusiastic, and energetic leaders; including private and public agencies as members; and ensuring participation of elected officials and administrators of state and local departments of aging and children's services (or their representatives).

After the membership is established, members forge a formal structure that includes an executive committee, a board of directors, and bylaws. At the same time, strategic planning is initiated to define goals and objectives for the network. Network members formed a consensus on the basic priorities for network support.

When the network structure has been formalized, network members develop and carry out a marketing plan designed to continue the recruitment of members and encourage general public interest in intergenerational cooperation. The marketing plan includes prioritized issues for advocacy. The marketing plan also helps establish a funding base to ensure the continued survival and growth of the network.

Without exception, respondents to the Durham survey believed their efforts on behalf of intergenerational networks were worth the time and energy expended. The camaraderie that was created and the mutual support received from intergenerational program representatives surpassed any problems or issues that emerged.

Intergenerational program representatives who join intergenerational networks share a common belief in the value of intergenerational cooperation and the promise of intergenerational volunteerism at a time when government entitlement programs are being reduced and more extended families are assuming responsibility for family parenting. The formation and maintenance of intergenerational networks at a state, regional, and local level are viewed as a way of addressing these concerns both through advocacy and direct service delivery.

NOTE

1. Mainstream, Inc. is a non-profit corporation that provides assistance to human service agencies. This article is drawn from the experience of the author as project administrator during the development of the Kansas Intergenerational Network, the conclusions of the participants during the original meeting of representatives of intergenerational networks, and the results of the Durham survey. The April 1991 conference was funded by the Charles Mott Foundation, the H.W. Durham Foundation, and the United Methodist Health Ministry Fund.

SECTION VII:
THE ROAD AHEAD

Towards Civic Renewal:
How Senior Citizens
Could Save Civil Society

Marc Freedman

> I am of the opinion that my life belongs to the whole community and as long as I live it is my privilege to do for it whatever I can. . . . Life is no "brief candle" to me. It is a sort of splendid torch, which I have got hold of for the moment and I want to make it burn as brightly as possible before handing it on to future generations.
>
> —George Bernard Shaw, *Man and Superman*

THE EROSION OF CIVIL SOCIETY

When the French sociologist Alexis de Tocqueville visited this country in 1840, he was moved by the pervasiveness of civic and volunteer activ-

---

Marc Freedman is Vice President of Public/Private Ventures and Visiting Fellow of Kings College, University of London.

[Haworth co-indexing entry note]: "Towards Civic Renewal: How Senior Citizens Could Save Civil Society." Freedman, Marc. Co-published simultaneously in the *Journal of Gerontological Social Work* (The Haworth Press, Inc.) Vol. 28, No. 3, 1997, pp. 243-263; and: *Intergenerational Approaches in Aging: Implications for Education, Policy and Practice* (ed: Kevin Brabazon, and Robert Disch) The Haworth Press, Inc., 1997, pp. 243-263. Single or multiple copies of this article are available for a fee from The Haworth Document Delivery Service [1-800-342-9678, 9:00 a.m. - 5:00 p.m. (EST). E-mail address: getinfo@haworth.com].

243

ity, pronouncing that the American "heart readily leans to the side of kindness" (Tocqueville, 1863). In particular, he was taken by the vast web of civic organizations and the propensity of Americans to voluntarily assist those less fortunate.

A century and a half later, there is grave concern that the connections that so impressed Tocqueville (he called them the *social integuments*) are unravelling. Whether contemporary observers use the term community, or civil society, or social capital, an increasing number of social critics across the political spectrum have come to worry that the bonds that connect us at the local level and serve as an essential counterbalance to American individualism and our competitive economy have fallen into grave disrepair.

Senator Bill Bradley observes that our social ecology has become as fragile and threatened as its natural counterpart: "Like fish floating on the surface of a polluted river," he warns, "the network of voluntary associations in America seems to be dying." Bradley is joined in his urgency by conservative commentator George Will, who cautions that "there is nothing trivial about the cumulative weight . . . of declining civic engagement and social connectedness" (Bradley, 1996).

The concerns voiced by Bradley and Will are supported by a range of scholars including Alan Wolfe, Amitai Etzioni, Jean Bethke Elshtain, Robert Bellah, and, most recently, Harvard political scientist Robert Putnam. In "Bowling Alone: America's Declining Social Capital," Putnam (1995) uses the decline of bowling leagues in this country as a whimsical but telling indicator of the overall deterioration of civil society. Agreeing with Tocqueville that voluntarism and civic activity are hallmarks of American life, he goes on to present a wide variety of evidence coming from surveys and other research showing that we are losing an essential aspect of the national character. Not only have we seen sharp declines in voting, churchgoing, and labor union membership, but groups like the Red Cross, League of Women Voters, and Scouts are sustaining a sharp loss of membership.

One of the most disturbing trends Putnam relates is in Parent-Teacher Association membership. Over the past generation, participation in PTAs has declined from 12 million (1964) to 7 million (1982), after dropping as low as 5 million. Research by the late University of Chicago sociologist James Coleman shows that this type of parental participation is a particularly effective form of social capital, and accounts for much of the difference in performance between public and parochial school students (Putnam, 1995).

Overall, voluntarism continues to drop. The most recent Gallup Survey on giving and volunteering in the United States, commissioned by Independent Sector, shows a 6 percent loss between 1989 and 1993. In 1989, 54% of Americans volunteered. By 1991, that number had dropped to 51%, dipping to 49% in 1995. In addition, the Gallup survey showed that three-quarters of these volunteers give fewer than 5 hours per week, and that the percentage of volunteers giving fewer hours than the previous year had jumped substantially. One of the most interesting findings was that informal voluntarism had decreased, in particular a 15% decrease since 1991. During the same four-year period, overall household charitable giving declined by 11% (Independent Sector, 1996).

The overall consequence of these trends remains to be determined; however, their implications are ominous. Not only are we in danger of losing what has been a defining feature of American life, but face a decline in organizational and human resources dedicated to strengthening the social fabric at precisely the juncture when government support for a wide variety of social, educational, and environmental concerns is drying up. Furthermore, there is considerable evidence that this decline in the civic infrastructure may undermine our society's ability to pass on essential attitudes and behaviors. The institutions of civil society play an important educational role, through developing young people and bringing individuals together in ways that reveal their interdependence, thereby serving to inculcate the values of sociability, cooperation, and community.

NO TIME TO CARE

The causes of any change of this magnitude are complex and difficult to identify with much precision. Among the influences are undoubtedly changes in family life, geographic mobility, television, and the rise of new information technology. However, one change stands out in particular: the time crunch faced by so many American adults attempting to simultaneously raise children and make a living. Quite simply, too few middle-age Americans have the time to care, not only for their children and parents, but for the wider community.

As Harvard economist Juliet Schor documents, since 1970 alone, the average American works an additional 164 hours of paid work a year–the equivalent of an extra month's labor. The result, occurring just as the two-income household was becoming the middle-class standard, is "a profound structural crisis of time." This time crisis has squeezed out informal caring for the young and old, as well as wider civic participation in volunteer causes. Surveys show a dramatic increase in those who answer affirmatively to the question "I never have enough time to get things done" (Schor, 1991).

When not working or childrearing, few middle-aged parents have the energy for more than flicking on the television or engaging in passive pursuits (the daily hours of television watching has doubled over the past generation). Even involvement in civic organizations is often confined to writing out a check. There has been huge growth in groups such as AARP, which require little face-to-face interaction as a condition of membership. But as Putnam (1996) points out, there is a great difference between this type of involvement and that associated with civil society: "From the point of view of social connectedness, the Environmental Defense Fund and a bowling league are just not in the same category."

The landscape is not entirely bleak. Some causes, such as AIDS volunteering, have emerged to address new crises. However, the new forms of voluntarism themselves have encountered obstacles related to the time squeeze. A telling example is the mentoring movement that has sprung up in cities across the United States. Motivated by the realization that adults in our society are not spending enough time with the younger generation, the mentoring movement focuses on recruiting adult role models to work one-on-one with young people from single-parent and disadvantaged families. Volunteers in mentoring programs come forward out of the recognition that isolation is a real problem in the daily life of kids, yet these role models are the same individuals who themselves are working 50, 60, even 70 hours a week–who are struggling to spend time with their own kids. The result is that they are, on the whole, much better at signing up than showing up, and mentoring programs have been struggling to find volunteers who can provide the reliable and persistent contact so important for helping young people navigate the transition to adulthood (Freedman, 1993).

The structural crisis in time that Schor describes must be seen particularly in the context of the changing role of women. Women have been hit hardest by the time squeeze, primarily because they continue to shoulder the majority of childrearing duties while adding on the second shift of paid employment. Women have always worked, but primarily before and after raising children. However, since the 1970s this pattern has changed. Today, 60 percent of mothers with preschoolers (and 50 percent of mothers with infants) work in the paid labor force, up from 19 percent in 1960. And two-thirds of the mothers who work have full-time jobs (Moen, 1994).

Sociologist Arlie Hochschild of the University of California, Berkeley has shown that women work an extra 15 hours a week than men, when childrearing, housework, and paid employment in the labor force are combined. That adds up to an additional month of *twenty-four-hour* days each year (Hochschild, 1989).

Hochschild and others have documented the pressures created by the "time famine" women face, and much debate surrounds the parenting deficit in our society. Less attention is paid to the impact of increased working hours and women's migration to the labor market on civic life extending beyond the home. However, the consequences have been dramatic. For most of this century, women have been the glue in communities, holding the social fabric together through an array of unpaid, undervalued, often unnoticed caring and volunteer work. Women still volunteer more than men (51 percent in comparison to 44 percent). However, after putting in a 70 or 80 or 100 hour week raising kids and bringing home a salary, few women have the energy left to devote more hours to nurturing the greater good.

Given these trends, it is no surprise that women's voluntarism is also on the decline. As one businesswoman—who was not even raising children—explained to the *Boston Globe*: "You have to give up something to be a success in business. There's not time for everything. Me . . . I have very little time for my spiritual life. I don't have a civic life. And I do very little with friendships" (Sirianni & Walsh, 1991).

NO TURNING BACK

As communities begin to feel the effects of the time squeeze, and as women withdraw from their previous roles as bastions of social connection, a backlash has emerged. Reactionaries have argued that women leave their jobs and return to previous roles at home and in the community. Of course, this perspective is unfair. While women tended to the critical, unpaid tasks of society, others were liberated to concentrate entirely on remunerated work in a country where this work is valued much more highly. Fairness aside, economic pressures and the intrinsic rewards of careers will continue to propel women to work.

More promising are two other approaches to the current dilemma. One is to reform work to reduce weekly hours, provide more flexibility, extend parental leave, and incorporate other interventions that are more family and community friendly. Another is to ensure that men assume their fair share of domestic duties, with the hope that more equal roles at home will enable both men and women to be more civic.

These positions offer a partial long-term solution. However, dramatic cutbacks in public funding for education, child care, social services, and other essential areas, coupled with burgeoning needs on the part of vulnerable citizens and the environment, demands more substantial assistance than most people who are simultaneously working and raising kids can commit. And over the short-term, there is little likelihood that a generation of overworked Americans can compensate for the millions of hours of formal and informal community-keeping women long rendered.

Does this mean that our crisis will continue with only partial relief in sight? In his essay "Building Community," John Gardner offers both consolation and wisdom about the historical process of community erosion and renewal. Writing at the age of 80 and from the vantage of many decades developing new strategies for strengthening these bonds, Gardner observes that the "disintegration of human communities is as old as human history." However, he adds, so are the opportunities for renewal: "We can't know all the forms community will take, but we know the values and the kinds of supporting structures we want to preserve. We are a community building species. We might become remarkably ingenious at creating new forms of community for a swiftly changing world" (Gardner, 1991).

One of the principal challenges confronting Americans today is to identify and develop those emerging trends with the potential to fill the vacuum that has opened up in our communities and bring about substantial social renewal. Of all the available options, none is more promising than the aging of our society that will transform the social landscape over the next half century.

THE AGE REVOLUTION

The argument set out in the balance of this paper is that America's vast and growing older population could come to be the new trustees of community—provided we create institutions and opportunities for service that enable seniors to make a genuine contribution while benefitting themselves in the process.

America is in the midst of a demographic revolution as profound as the one in women's roles. The population of Americans over 65 has doubled over the past thirty years, and will double again over the next thirty. From 2010 to 2030 this group will grow by 75%, while the rest of the population declines by 3%. Soon nearly one in five Americans will be over 65 (U.S. Bureau of the Census, 1996).

For the most part, however, this transformation is portrayed as a source of impending strife: of new strains on families, human services, and the economy, and of a dramatic increase in age-related dependence and decay. We hear often about coming generational conflict, that a vast cohort of "greedy geezers" unconcerned about the fate of children is bankrupting our future.

While the aging of American society will undoubtedly bring with it many difficult challenges, lost amid the barrage of concerns is the fact that America today possesses, and will soon possess to an even greater degree, the healthiest, best-educated, most vigorous, longest-living–and largest–population of retirees in our nation's history. Only 5 percent of these seniors reside in nursing homes; fewer than 20 percent encounter substantial disability, while 60 percent report no disability whatsoever.

These elders may well constitute our only *increasing* natural resource. In fact, the aging of our society is every bit as much an opportunity to be seized as a problem to be solved.

The argument for harnessing the vast productive and humanitarian potential in the senior population–particularly through national service and voluntarism–begins with the demographics; however, it extends much further. There is evidence to suggest that these older adults may well be available to help. In 1948, for example, 90 percent of men between 55 and 64 were working; nearly a half century later, only 67 percent of that population works. In general, retirement frees a substantial amount of new time: on the average, 25 hours a week for men and 18 for women. Furthermore, many economists believe that the trends in technology and internationalization of the economy may produce even more dramatic reductions in labor-market participation (Robinson, 1991).

At the same time, Americans are living substantially longer. Life expectancy has increased by 50 percent since the turn of the century, from 48 to 75 years, a jump bigger than the increase over the previous millennium. And even the most conservative demographers project further increases in the coming century. The net result is that Americans are already spending a significant proportion–for many, more than one-third–of their lives after retirement.

While some seniors undoubtedly prefer to spend their later years on the golf course or the tour bus, there is evidence that many older adults are searching for options that enable them to remain productively engaged in their communities. As one recent U.S. Administration on Aging-sponsored survey reveals, a full 37.4 percent of older Americans say they would volunteer if asked, while an additional 25.6 percent already volunteering indicate that they would like to devote more time to service. When seniors are polled about preferences for volunteer and service assignments, helping the younger generation is the most frequent response (Marriott, etc., 1991).

Interest among seniors in volunteer and service participation likely reflects self-interest as much as altruism. For many, retirement means a jarring transition from engagement to disengagement, from productivity to idleness. Fifty-five percent of elder respondents to a Louis Harris Poll lament the loss of usefulness after retirement. The average older American watches a staggering 43 hours of television each week. (Along with watching television, performing housework is the other major activity absorbing the time liberated after retirement.)

Researchers consider isolation and loss of purpose to be key factors increasing seniors' risk of premature physical deterioration, depression and untimely death. Conversely, they see productive engagement and strong social networks as contributing to prolonged mental and physical health. A 25-year National Institute of Mental Health study finds, for example, that "highly organized activity is the single strongest predictor, other than not smoking, of longevity and vitality" (*Newsweek*, 1986; Friedan, 1995).

Productive activity, particularly through voluntarism and community service, provides opportunities for engagement, activity, acquaintanceship and growth. According to Erik Erikson, these opportunities can meet a deeper need as well, satisfying the impulse toward generativity, which Erikson defines as the instinctual drive to pass on to the next generation what an individual has learned from life. The principal challenge of later life, he writes, is coming to terms with the notion, "I am what survives of me" (Erikson, 1968).

While predictions of coming generational conflict are often overstated, there can be no doubt that in a society divided by class, race and gender, tensions between the generations exist as well. In the absence of cross-generational contact and engagement, these tensions might worsen as the demographic composition of society continues to shift.

Projects engaging seniors to help young people provide a particularly appealing potential antidote to these strains. Indeed, there is evidence suggesting just such an effect. In the early 1980s, for example, Miami began vigorously recruiting elder school volunteers, who in turn became linchpins in a successful campaign to pass a highly contested billion-dollar school bond issue (Louv, 1994a).

More generally, engaging seniors can also contribute to preserving essential features of our civil society. In this context, the ideal of senior service is compelling, in the words of Margaret Mead, "as a way to restore a sense of community, a knowledge of the past, and a sense of the future" (Mead, 1970).

INSTITUTIONAL LAG

While the gender revolution first, and now the demographic revolution in age, have dramatically shifted the social landscape, we have yet to develop the appropriate institutions that accompany this new reality. We face what former National Institute on Aging director Mathilda White Riley terms a "structural lag" (Riley, Kahn & Foner, 1994). She points out that this mismatch between realities and roles is not simply a matter of institutions and organizations, but has a cultural dimension as well, involving outdated expectations, mores, and laws.

A few years ago American historian and former Librarian of Congress Daniel Boorstin offered similar observations and a possible explanation for the existence of the structural lag. One reason, he suggests, is that America has always been a young nation, one that split off from the old world of Europe and that has traditionally valued the independence, spirit, and vigor of youth. He adds that we have been particularly ingenious in inventing institutions for youth, among them the GI Bill and the system of land grant colleges, aimed at making full use of our youth resources. This has been true in the arena of national and community service as well, where the CCC and the Peace Corps–two institutions that have long focused on engaging young people–are the best known examples of the service enterprise.

Our orientation to youth has not served us well, however, as we have matured as a nation, and Boorstin points out that we have not evidenced any comparable genius in developing mechanisms to tap the productive and humanitarian potential residing in the older population:

> The most conspicuous American institution directed to senior citizens is the so-called Leisure City, a place not of creation but of recreation and vegetation. Our concern for the special needs of our ailing, idle and disoriented aging has been admirable. But we need to refocus our attention on how to employ the special talents and resources of our most experienced citizens. (Boorstin, 1989)

Out of a desire to rectify this situation, and animated by the rationale for involving seniors in volunteer service of essential value to communities, a small but growing number of observers have issued calls for one such new institution: a national service program engaging older Americans.

Twenty-five years ago physician and gerontologist Robert Butler called for creation of a National Senior Service Corps in *Why Survive? Growing Old in America*, his Pulitzer Prize-winning book on aging in America. More recently, Undersecretary of the Navy Richard Danzig and policy analyst Peter Szanton conclude in their book, *National Service: What Would It Mean*, that "persons at or beyond retirement age may have more to give and more reason to benefit from national service than any other age group." Gerontologist Ken Dychtwald envisions creation of an "Elder

Corps" that would function as the domestic equivalent of a Peace Corps composed of seniors, while former HEW Secretary and Common Cause founder John Gardner has argued for the establishment of a national "Experience Corps" designed to place the "talent, experience and commitment" of older adults "at the disposal of our fellow Americans" (Butler, 1975; Danzig & Szanton, 1987; Dychtwald & Flower, 1990; Gardner, 1988).

Although the talents of seniors might be applied to address a wide variety of problems afflicting society, a number of experts have urged focusing particularly on helping children. Economist Sylvia Ann Hewlett argues in *When the Bough Breaks* that "tapping the energy and compassion of seniors might go some distance toward filling the enormous parenting deficit in our society," while Richard Louv, author of *Childhood's Future,* calls for the creation of "a national army of winter soldiers," placing the goodwill and efforts of older Americans in the service of our children (Louv, 1994). Brookings Institution economist Laurel McFarland has proposed creating a service corps consisting entirely of older Americans and focusing exclusively on child care (naming it the "Pepper Corps," in honor of the late Congressman and advocate for the elderly, Claude Pepper) (Hewlett, 1991; Louv, 1994; McFarland, 1993).

However, as intuitively appealing as the prospect of engaging seniors in service seems, particularly at this time of tight budgets and expanding needs, many questions about the feasibility of this strategy remain. Can this ideal be made real, or is it yet another appealing but impractical notion? Indeed, the history of American social policy is littered with similarly tantalizing proposals that never went anywhere.

Fortunately, in searching for answers to these questions, policymakers are not confined to the abstract. In fact, there are a number of encouraging realities suggesting that engaging seniors as community builders may, in fact, be quite practical, and that social policy can play an important part in creating these roles.

First, there are a set of small, but compelling pilot programs offering insights about the wide variety of contributions seniors might make. Outside Boston, retired teamsters, electrical workers, policemen and others are part of a labor union-sponsored initiative helping nonviolent juvenile offenders find and keep blue-collar jobs. In Hilton Head, South Carolina, a group of retired physicians and nurses have formed a free health clinic that provides, among other things, preventive care for low-income families. In Virginia and Montana, the Senior Environmental Corps is dedicated to alerting doctors, the elderly, and the public to the special environmental hazards faced by the older population. In other locations around the country, seniors are actively involved in useful and innovative volunteer activities through a variety of community-based organizations.

Alongside these local models exist national programs, the most significant of which is the National Senior Service Corps, consisting of half a million elders in the RSVP, Senior Companion, and Foster Grandparent programs. Over 60,000 of these seniors serve 20 hours a week or more, making this effort more than three times as large as the higher profile and youth focused AmeriCorps initiative. In addition, the Senior Community Service Employment Program, Title V of the Older Americans Act places another 60,000 older adults in service assignments across the country (Freedman, 1994).

Much of the evidence coming from these programs is heartening. Overall, they suggest that this undertaking is practical, that it is possible to translate abstract appeal into effective programming. The local models, in particular, show the wide variety of ways in which seniors can contribute to the community and benefit themselves in the process. They also underscore the critical role that social entrepreneurs, responding to local needs, can play in creating opportunities for older adults to become engaged. The national efforts convey some of these same lessons and add an additional layer. For one, they are national: they reveal how promising projects can be carried out across a large and diverse country like the United States while maintaining quality controls and faithfulness to core principles. They also demonstrate that such structures can be sustained. The National Senior Service Corps programs have lasted a quarter century or longer, spanning a wide array of Democratic and Republican administrations and congresses. They reveal government at its best, in an enabling role with respect to voluntarism that promotes stability without suffocating local control.

For all these virtues, there are limitations–profound ones–present. The local models, while richly suggestive, remain small and scattered. In fact, without a sustaining infrastructure, they tend to come in and out of existence, rarely managing to move very far along the learning curve. At the same time, the federally sponsored initiatives themselves, while large in absolute numbers, remain far too small and diffused at the ground level. It is difficult to find a single location where there is a strong, visible presence at the community level, or within the institutions being served.

There are other issues as well. When we look at the numbers of seniors volunteering, the message is mixed. On the one hand, more than three times the number of seniors are serving today than prior to the creation of the first of the National Senior Service Corps initiatives in 1965. On the other hand, older Americans volunteer less than any other population group, and surveys reveal again and again that many more elders would volunteer if better opportunities existed. At the same time, the current population of elder volunteers is overwhelmingly women, well beyond what the demographics would predict. And when we look at national service slots–those enabling people to serve half-to-full time (to make a major life commitment to service for a defined period of time)–these participants are primarily low-income individuals, likely a function both of the income-support supplied by these programs and legal restrictions discouraging those living above the poverty line.

Alongside recruitment issues are ones of quality. The Title V program illustrates. Although this initiative has historically received three times the funding of the National Senior Service Corps efforts, over time the program's service capacity was weakened considerably by joint emphasis on employment transition goals. The result is that host agencies are reluctant to provide substantial service roles to older adults who will likely only be around for a short period, while Title V sponsoring agencies commonly rotate participants out of host agencies for fear that they will become too comfortable in service roles and as a result lose interest in locating "unsubsidized" employment. The lesson is clear: service must be the focus of service programs. They cannot attempt to take on a multiplicity of objectives without falling into the trap that has attended most public service employment efforts over the past thirty years.

In short, a considerable gap continues to exist between promise and practice not only in the national programs, and in intergenerational efforts on behalf of children, but in the overall realm of senior service. While we do possess the rudiments of new institutional arrangements in this area, much work remains to be done before we can begin to rectify the continuing mismatch that Riley, Boorstin, and others identify. We must do so not only out of a desire to meet current needs and fill the void existing in the wake of the gender revolution, but to produce what Cambridge University historian Peter Laslett calls the "institutional inheritance" for coming waves of older Americans (Laslett, 1996).

To start, any national service program for seniors should build off the achievements and credibility of the National Senior Service Corps. These efforts, specifically the Foster Grandparent and Senior Companion programs, are superb illustrations of older adults carrying out caring functions women long assumed, particularly women in the middle generation. These seniors nurture the young and provide connections for frail elders aimed at promoting independent living. In these ways, they also pick up functions long carried out informally (by family and friends) but that have fallen victim to the time squeeze and mobility issues weakening our communities.

In determining the focus of a revamped national service effort for seniors, three obvious areas emerge. The first, promoting independent living by the elderly, emphasizes self-help and the responsibility of older adults for each other; the other two, preserving the environment and helping children, concentrate on elders' responsibilities for future generations.

- *Promoting Independent Living Among the Elderly:* This is an area where, as already mentioned, we already possess considerable experience and a track record of success not only through Senior Companions, but through AARP's independent living initiative, the Interfaith Caregivers project, and other efforts. Not only does an independent living focus address an important and growing need in a society where the "oldest old" are the fastest growing segment of the population, and accord with the highly-ranked preference of elders in surveys to do volunteer work that assists peers, but it sends the powerful message of self-help: that older adults are taking responsibility for each other and working to alleviate the burden of care that must also be born, in part, by younger generations.
- *Preserving and Sustaining the Environment:* Conservation projects have long been a focus of national service efforts involving youth. The Civilian Conservation Corps helped build many of our national parks. Urban youth corps work in crews to develop city parks, gardens, and recreation areas. Peace Corps volunteers are involved in a wide array of ecological efforts in the developing world. Although youth service programs are more identified with work in this area, there is reason to think that elders may have a great deal to offer, and a great deal of interest in, environmentally-based service. For one, seniors are among the heaviest users of the national park system, and form a substantial proportion of membership in groups such as the Sierra Club. There is some experience in this area, too: for example, the Green Thumb program began initially as a highway beautification project, and evolved over part of its history into an effort dedicated to testing and implementing new conservation strategies. The Environmental Alliance for Senior Involvement, launched in 1992 by AARP and the EPA, is aimed at expanding senior volunteer opportunities, developing leadership by elders in the environmental field, and conducting environmental education.
- *Fostering the Well-Being of Children:* This area offers both the most urgent and promising opportunity for moving forward. Young people in this country are in desperate need of help. One in four children, two of three African-American children are born into single parent households. Poverty rates among children are the highest of

any group in the nation. Our public education system is in a shambles. A great many young people succumb to violence, drugs, school failure, and other pitfalls along the way to adulthood. Some argue that older adults contribute to this problem, through depriving the younger generation of their fair share of society's resources. In fact, older adults are natural allies of youth, and a wide range of intergenerational initiatives show how seniors can make an important contribution to the well-being of youth. This area should be a top priority for senior service: in part, in response to the urgent needs of young people; in part, because seniors polled consistently select intergenerational work as their number one choice for volunteer assignments; and, in equal measure, because of its symbolic significance in reminding the broader society that older persons care about youth and are willing to act on that conviction.

In thinking about what a national service program for the future should look like, it is necessary to identify not just the chief areas of endeavor, but the type of contribution seniors might make in these realms. In other words, what is the distinct role or contribution of national service with respect to other forms of voluntarism, which tend to involve individuals a few hours a week as opposed to half-to-full time?

The particular advantage from national service derives from the high level of commitment required–significant hours, week in and week out, for a defined period of time, usually at least one year. This enterprise must be a central focus, if not the central focus, of the older person's life during the period of service. It is not a sideline undertaken along with an array of other hobbies. In this respect, it is not only promising as a vehicle for accomplishing significant amounts of work, but for wielding a substantial impact on the volunteer's life.

National service participants are uniquely placed to perform two types of work. One is to fulfill assignments that require consistent and intensive effort that can't be accomplished nearly as well by someone who shows up for a few hours a week or every other week. The other type of work best suited to national service, less well developed than direct service, is in building an infrastructure for service.

A cardinal lesson of volunteer management is that individuals won't volunteer unless asked. Another lesson is that people won't be happy volunteering unless adequate preparation, job development, support, and follow-through are present. Despite these clear imperatives, and a burgeoning need for volunteers, sufficient funding is often lacking to hire professional volunteer managers to do this important work.

National service participants, who combine consistent effort with relatively low cost, might well be deputized to assist professional volunteer managers in the development of adequate infrastructure to support senior volunteers who might serve in a variety of capacities, such as episodically or for a few hours each week. In the final analysis, national service for seniors should be designed with the objectives of accomplishing important work directly, liberating salaried professional staff to do their jobs better and more efficiently, and leveraging the efforts of new ranks of volunteers.

On the issue of cost it is important to note that, in general, senior service participants cost far less than youth service participants not only due to efficiencies gained through this population's comparatively greater work experience but because these efforts, stipended or not, build off of entitlements, pensions, and other allowances providing a basic standard of living for many elders. In the case of youth, it is often necessary to provide enough money to cover food, clothing, shelter, and transportation directly through the service program.

Before turning to the broader question of what this all might mean for the future of our society and for the redefinition of what it means to grow old in this country, three additional points need to be registered.

The impetus for a full-fledged national service effort engaging older Americans must come from older Americans. Alongside the important reason of credibility, older Americans possess the institution-building capacity needed to accomplish this work. Without devaluing the kinds of direct service contributions elders can make, James Birren, Director of the Borun Center for Gerontological Research at UCLA, points out that we often underestimate another set of skills residing in the older population. To illustrate this institution-building strength, he describes the experience of a retirement community in California: "The residents realized that as the community grew older it would need a hospital. They organized a committee, and through their own initiative and skills, they built the hospital. These retirees possessed valuable planning, management, and fundraising skills" (Birren, 1991). The University of the Third Age is a more sweeping example from abroad of this same process. Programs like SCORE and the National Executive Service Corps provide examples of the management and leadership talents of elders. These talents will be essential to constructing the new institutions we will need in the coming century.

At the same time that senior leadership, particularly in the institution-building role, is required, an organizational partnership including the federal government, major aging organizations, and the philanthropic sector will also be necessary to move this enterprise forward. As already argued, there is considerable evidence to suggest that the federal government can play an important enabling, sustaining, and stabilizing role through the financing of senior service efforts. Major aging organizations, such as AARP, can bring experience with volunteer management, a membership base and considerable policy influence to the table. National foundations can supply the flexible funding required for experimentation, research, and demonstration activities that will be required to move past current arrangements. As yet, no tripartite collaboration of this kind has been attempted on a scale commensurate with the vast potential of senior service and voluntarism.

Whatever partnerships are forged nationally, success in this arena will require new arrangements locally. At present no highly visible, easily accessible, one-stop entity exists in most locales to attract and deploy older adults interested in serving. A full-service incarnation would combine recruitment, marketing, training, project development, and other key functions, perhaps concentrating on the three areas of service set out above, or integrating others of particular local importance.

THE GENERATIVE SOCIETY

As the battle over Medicare rages in Congress, the image of the "greedy geezer" is once again in public consciousness. One magazine headline blares, "Senior Power Rides Again," while another describes entitlements for the elderly as "the third rail in American politics." They contribute to the image of older Americans as a self-centered, disengaged, interest group out to produce American communities where, as Daniel Callahan complains, all the hospitals are new and shiny, and the schools deteriorated from neglect.

This paper offers a different perspective. It argues that older Americans and the aging of our society offer our best hope for social renewal, and intergenerational programming the best opportunity. Specifically, the case is made for elders assuming the mantle of community-keepers, a role that women in our society have long fulfilled, but that has fallen into neglect as a result of the mass entrance of mothers into the workforce. At present, the distribution of time in our society is extremely skewed: at the same juncture that middle-aged Americans confront a time famine, many older persons are drowning in a surplus of unstructured time. There is evidence to suggest that redressing this imbalance makes good sense for both generations.

It also constitutes an exciting opportunity for social change. As British sociologist Michael Young (himself in his 80s) points out, older adults are potential pioneers in the sphere of time, in the unprecedented position in the history of our society to redefine how an abundance of time can best be used. As Young's countryman (and age mate) Peter Laslett notes, the 20th century has witnessed the democratization of free time through retirement. Leisure is no longer the monopoly of a small group of elites numbering in the hundreds or thousands. It has become, in Laslett's words, "a commodity of millions of our citizens, our elderly citizens, those in the Third Age."

At a juncture when social connections are shriveling in American communities, older adults have the time to care. However, it would be a mistake to view the rationale for engaging seniors as simply a matter of available hours. Another aspect of time is equally important: experience. Experience is a function of time lived, of what one has learned from participating in life. (Betty Friedan recalls interviewing a 70-year-old woman in Florida who proudly announces that she feels like she's seventeen. Friedan remembers thinking, "you mean you haven't learned anything in 53 years!") Older adults bring the experience–and the social capital–that derives from decades as workers, citizens, and family members. In some elders, this experience produces a wisdom that is a function of age, a perspective Cicero saw characterized by "thought, reason, and deliberation."

These observations on age and time lead to a third, concerning the relationship of time and human development. The awareness in age that death is closer than birth, that one most likely has more years behind than ahead, drives questions about the meaning and purpose of one's life, about one's legacy, about what it means, to return to Erikson's terminology, to be generative. Although the generative impulse is most vividly displayed in parenting, Erikson situates this impulse more broadly in any caring activity that contributes to the nurturance and spirit of future generations. According to John Snarey, a developmental psychologist at Emory University, and expert on Erikson's formulation: "While biological generativity focuses on continuing one's personal genetic inheritance, and parental generativity focuses on parenting one's present children, societal generativity can encompass the future of *all* children-becoming-adults and promote an ethically inclusive cycle of generations" (Snarey, 1993).

For Erikson, the alternative to being generative in this way is stagnation, a failure with both personal and societal implications, because generativity constitutes the link between "the life cycle and the generational cycle." In *Identity, Youth, and Crisis*, he explains that the qualities that go into generativity are essential for the ongoing vitality of society. "Without them," Erikson writes, "institutions wilt" (Erikson, 1968b).

In the last years of his life, Erikson grew increasingly concerned that the generative impulse in America was wilting, and that we face a self-centered stagnation that threatens to undermine the health of our society. In 1988, at the age of 86, he told Daniel Goleman of *The New York Times*:

> The only thing that can save us as a species is seeing how we're not thinking about future generations in the way we live. What's lacking is a generativity, a generativity that will promote positive values in the lives of the next generation. Unfortunately, we set the example of greed . . . with no thought of what will make it a better world for our great-grandchildren. That's why we go on depleting the earth: we're not thinking of the next generation. (Goleman, 1988)

As we prepare to enter a period of dramatic demographic change, an era that will almost certainly force a redefinition of what it means to grow old in this country, Erikson's notion of generativity at the individual and societal levels might well serve as a framework for our deliberations. Who better to revitalize the sense of generativity in society, to cultivate and nurture the sense of connection, interdependence, and care for the future, than older adults? Elders have the time to care. In developmental terms, they need *to care*. Society desperately needs new sources of caring–for the young, the frail old, the natural environment, the future of this country. If elders do not step in and fill this vacuum, who will?

One reads much about productive aging these days, as the field of gerontology and social policy for older Americans moves happily toward greater balance between the needs and the contributions of our older citizens. Unfortunately, however, reflection on the contribution of elders is dominated by the view of seniors as potential employees. For every article about elder volunteers there are two dozen about older workers. Policy interest centers far more on a issues of paid employment, than on how elders can help replenish our badly depleted social capital.

As Jeremy Rifkin argues in *The End of Work,* it is far from clear whether jobs will be available in the future for many older adults to occupy, even in the context of a "baby bust." There is also the issue of the kind of jobs available (Rifkin, 1995). Consider a visit to a Minneapolis Burger King for lunch with a Senior Companion and his client (a blind retired postal worker in his 70s). Behind the counter of the fast food restaurant stands another older man, dressed in an orange and blue polyester uniform, wearing an ill-fitting Burger King beanie, punching in icons of hamburgers and cokes on the cash register. With this scenario in mind, it is not difficult to understand why an older person, even a low-income individual like the Senior Companion, would happily forego higher compensation to take on a role that provided dignity and a sense of helping the community.

This example, while admittedly extreme, simultaneously begs the question of how we best engage, as a society, our "only increasing natural resource." While there is no question that employment options should be made free of discrimination for older adults, as a country we need to think very carefully about how we might encourage a more elevated role for elders, one that takes into account what older persons have learned from life, the developmental imperatives of the third age, and an assessment of the most pressing needs of American society today and in the foreseeable future. Perhaps we should place "civic aging" above "productive aging" in our policy decisions regarding older adults.

Reflecting on precisely this issue, Peter Laslett argues that older persons should become the trustees of the "social future." UCLA's James Birren offers that we should be encouraging "the grandparenting of society" by our elders. Rabbi Zalman Schachter talks about how elders can become society's "healers," while Northwestern University anthropologist David Gutmann proposes that we reserve for older persons that status of "emeritus parents," providing roles "necessary for the well-being of all age groups, particularly the young."

Within these conceptions reside a vision for aging in America centered on generativity, forcing us to think about how we can move this impulse from a force of individual development to one of broad social renewal. For all its appeal, such a shift won't happen easily, or automatically, as a result of having more older people. It will take institutions, new and ingenious structures, built off of our current successes, and capable of making generative opportunities available to a great many more of our elder citizens (Schacter-Shalomi, 1995; Guttmann, 1994).

As William James (the man who first raised the idea of national service in his 1906 essay "The Moral Equivalent of War") observed in his final years, "The great use of life is to spend it for something that will outlast us." There could be no clearer articulation of the generative impulse, or reminder about why we must move forward in this enterprise with all the resolve and ingenuity we can muster.

AUTHOR NOTE

Marc Freedman's latest book, *The Kindness of Strangers* was about intergenerational mentoring. A delegate to the 1995 White House Conference on Aging, he is currently directing the Experience Corps, which focuses on engaging older adults to strengthen urban elementary schools in five cities.

REFERENCES

Birren, James (1991). "Abilities, Opportunities, and Responsibilities in the Third Quarter of Life." In *Resourceful Aging: Today and Tomorrow.* Washington, DC: AARP, 1991, Vol I, pp. 15-21.

Boorstin, Daniel (1989). "Speech to Herbert Hoover Library," West Branch, Iowa.

Butler, Robert (1975). *Why Survive? Growing Old in America.* New York: Harper and Row, p. 102;

Bradley, Bill (1996). *Time Present, Time Past: A Memoir.* New York: Knopf, 412-414.

Danzig, R. and P. Szanton (1987). *National Service: What Would It Mean?* Lexington, MA: Lexington Books.

Dychtwald, Ken and Joe Flower (1990). *Age Wave: How the Most Important Trend of Our Time Will Change Your Future.* New York: Bantam Books, p. 160.

Erikson, Erik (1968a). *Identity: Youth and Crisis.* New York: W.W. Norton, p. 141.

Erikson, Erik (1968b). *Identity:Youth.and Crisis.* New York: W.W. Norton, p. 141.

Freedman, Marc (1993). *The Kindness of Strangers.* San Francisco: Jossey-Bass.

Freedman, Marc (1994). "Seniors in National and Community Service." Philadelphia: Public/Private Ventures.

Friedan, Betty (1995). *The Fountain of Age.* New York: Simon and Schuster, 80-103.

Gardner, John (1991). *Building Community.* Washington, D.C.: Independent Sector, p. 5.

Gardner, John (1988). "The Experience Corps," concept paper, 1988.

Goleman, Daniel (1988). "Erikson, In His Own Old Age, Expands His View of Life," *The New York Times,* June 14, 1988.

Gutmann, David (1994). *Reclaimed Powers.* Evanston: Northwestern University Press.

Hewlett, Sylvia Ann (1991). *When the Bough Breaks: The Cost of Neglecting Our Children.* New York: Basic Books p. 259.

Hochschild, Arlie (1989). *The Second Shift.* New York: Avon, pp. 2-5.

Independent Sector (1996). *Giving and Volunteering in the United States.* Washington, D.C., Independent Sector, 1-15.

Kotre, John (1969). *Outliving the Self.* New York: Norton.

Laslett, Peter (1996). *A Fresh Map of Life.* London: Weidenfeld and Nicolson, Ltd., pp. 256-260.

Louv, Richard (1994a). *101 Things You Can Do for Our Children's Future.* New York: Anchor Books, pp. 155-56.

Louv, Richard (1994b). *101 Things You Can Do for Our Children's Future,* p. 334.

McFarland, Laurel. (1993). "A Golden National Service," *The Brookings Review,* Summer 1993, p. 48.

Mead, Margaret (1970). *Culture and Commitment.* Garden City, NY: Natural History Press, p. 2.

Marriott Senior Living Services (April 1991). *Marriott Senior Volunteerism Study,* Tables 1-6.

Moen, Phyllis (1994). "Women, Work, and Family: A Sociological Perspective on Changing Roles." In Riley, Kahn, and Foner, *Age and Structural Lag.* New York: John Wiley and Sons, 151-155.

Newsweek (October 20, 1986), p. 37.

Putnam, Robert (1995). "Bowling Alone." *Journal of Democracy,* January 1995, 65-77.

Putnam, Robert (1996). "The Strange Disappearance of Civic America." *The American Prospect,* Winter, 1996, 34-49

Rifkin, Jeremy. *The End of Work.* New York: Tarcher/Putnam.

Riley, Matilda White, Robert L. Kahn and Anne Foner, eds. (1994). *Age and Structural Lag: Society's Failure to Provide Meaningful Opportunities in Work, Family and Leisure.* New York: J. Wiley, pp. 1-11.

Robinson, John (May 1991). "Quitting Time," *American Demographics.* p. 34.

Schachter-Shalomi, Zalman (1995). *From Ageing to Sageing.* New York: Warner Books.

Juliet Schor (1991) *The Overworked American.* New York: Basic Books.

Sirianni, Carmen and Andrea Walsh (1991). Through the Prism of Time."In Alan Wolfe, *America at Century's End.* Berkeley: University of California Press, 421.

Snarey, John (1993). *How Fathers Care for the Next Generation.* Cambridge: Harvard University Press.

Tocqueville, Alexis de (1863). *Democracy in America.* Cambridge: Sever and Francis, II, p. 123.

U.S. Bureau of the Census (1966). "65+ in the United States." Washington, D.C.

Index

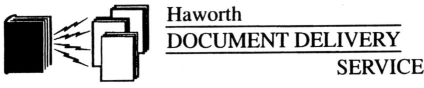

Haworth
DOCUMENT DELIVERY
SERVICE

This valuable service provides a single-article order form for any article from a Haworth journal.

- *Time Saving:* No running around from library to library to find a specific article.
- *Cost Effective:* All costs are kept down to a minimum.
- *Fast Delivery:* Choose from several options, including same-day FAX.
- *No Copyright Hassles:* You will be supplied by the original publisher.
- *Easy Payment:* Choose from several easy payment methods.

Open Accounts Welcome for ...
- Library Interlibrary Loan Departments
- Library Network/Consortia Wishing to Provide Single-Article Services
- Indexing/Abstracting Services with Single Article Provision Services
- Document Provision Brokers and Freelance Information Service Providers

MAIL or *FAX* THIS ENTIRE ORDER FORM TO:

Haworth Document Delivery Service
The Haworth Press, Inc.
10 Alice Street
Binghamton, NY 13904-1580

or FAX: 1-800-895-0582
or CALL: 1-800-342-9678
9am-5pm EST

PLEASE SEND ME PHOTOCOPIES OF THE FOLLOWING SINGLE ARTICLES:

1) Journal Title: _____
   Vol/Issue/Year: _____ Starting & Ending Pages: _____
Article Title: _____
_____

2) Journal Title: _____
   Vol/Issue/Year: _____ Starting & Ending Pages: _____
Article Title: _____
_____

3) Journal Title: _____
   Vol/Issue/Year: _____ Starting & Ending Pages: _____
Article Title: _____
_____

4) Journal Title: _____
   Vol/Issue/Year: _____ Starting & Ending Pages: _____
Article Title: _____
_____

(See other side for Costs and Payment Information)

COSTS: Please figure your cost to order quality copies of an article.

1. Set-up charge per article: $8.00
   ($8.00 × number of separate articles) _____

2. Photocopying charge for each article:

   1-10 pages: $1.00 _____

   11-19 pages: $3.00 _____

   20-29 pages: $5.00 _____

   30+ pages: $2.00/10 pages _____

3. Flexicover (optional): $2.00/article _____

4. Postage & Handling: US: $1.00 for the first article/
   $.50 each additional article _____

   Federal Express: $25.00 _____

   Outside US: $2.00 for first article/
   $.50 each additional article_____

5. Same-day FAX service: $.35 per page _____

GRAND TOTAL: _____

METHOD OF PAYMENT: (please check one)

❑ Check enclosed   ❑ Please ship and bill. PO # _____
(sorry we can ship and bill to bookstores only! All others must pre-pay)

❑ Charge to my credit card: ❑ Visa;   ❑ MasterCard;   ❑ Discover;
❑ American Express;

Account Number:_____ Expiration date:_____

Signature: *X*_____

Name: _____ Institution: _____

Address: _____

_____

City: _____ State:_____ Zip:_____

Phone Number: _____ FAX Number: _____

MAIL or *FAX* THIS ENTIRE ORDER FORM TO:

Haworth Document Delivery Service
The Haworth Press, Inc.
10 Alice Street
Binghamton, NY 13904-1580

or FAX: 1-800-895-0582
or CALL: 1-800-342-9678
9am-5pm EST)